PLUMBER'S
AND PIPEFITTER'S
HANDBOOK

PLUMBER'S AND PIPEFITTER'S HANDBOOK

WILLIAM J. HORNUNG

*California State Polytechnic University
Pomona, California*

PRENTICE-HALL, INC., Upper Saddle River, New Jersey 07458

Library of Congress Cataloging in Publication Data

Hornung, William J.
   Plumber's and pipefitter's handbook.

   Includes index.
   1. Plumbing—Handbooks, manuals, etc. 2. Pipe-fitting
—Handbooks, manuals, etc. I. Title.
TH6125.H67 1984   696'.1   83-19176
ISBN 0-13-683912-6

Editorial/production supervision and
   interior design: Virginia Huebner
Cover design: Edsal Enterprises
Manufacturing buyer: Anthony Caruso

Printed in the United States of America

10 9 8 7 6 5

ISBN 0-13-683912-6

Prentice-Hall International, Inc., *London*
Prentice-Hall of Australia Pty. Limited, *Sydney*
Editora Prentice-Hall do Brasil, Ltda., *Rio de Janeiro*
Prentice-Hall Canada Inc., *Toronto*
Prentice-Hall of India Private Limited, *New Delhi*
Prentice-Hall of Japan, Inc., *Tokyo*
Prentice-Hall of Southeast Asia Pte. Ltd., *Singapore*
Whitehall Books Limited, *Wellington, New Zealand*

CONTENTS

3 VALVES; SPECIFIC GRAVITY   27

4 PLASTIC PIPING   38

5 THE DRAINAGE SYSTEM   60

6 INSTALLING THE DRAINAGE SYSTEM   76

15 SHEET METAL STANDARDS AND CONVENTIONS   176

16 TOOLS FOR PLUMBING   191

APPENDIX   206

INDEX   223

PREFACE

Here is a ready source of information essential to the pipefitter, plumber, and to the student of plumbing, heating, and ventilating.

The book, a new approach, begins with a short, but noteworthy, treatise on metals for the piping industry, including American Standard pipe, fittings, and valves, and their characteristics, available sizes, dimensions, and weights.

Important information on plastic pipe, fittings, and valves and their many modern uses is discussed in Chapter 4.

The complete drainage system, Chapter 5, begins with the public sewer or septic tank and leaching field, then follows with discussions of the house sewer, house drain, soil, waste, and vent stack, branch lines and branch vents, fixtures, and fixture units. Data on sizing such piping are included.

Chapters 6 and 7 provide information on how to install the entire drainage system, together with the installation of fixtures, such as the water closet, the dishwasher, and a single-lever mixing unit, and the many repairs that are often required on faucets, stem washers, and the flush tank for the water closet.

The entire pressurized water supply system to fixtures and the hot water tank, including the problem of water hammer, is discussed in Chapters 9 and 10, and clarified with numerous line drawings.

The typical storm water drainage system is developed by sizing its vertical and horizontal rainwater piping, including solutions to underground water problems.

In Chapters 12 and 13, various types of heating systems in common use, and some that are not used as often, are illustrated and described. Fuels for heating systems are included and their Btu values per unit are compared.

A comprehensive method of calculating heat loss for a building, together with insulation R-values of construction elements, is provided, in Chapter 14. The sizing of a warm air heating duct system, the furnace heating capacity, and data on standard air velocities rounds out the chapter.

The final chapters, 15 and 16, deal with sheet metal duct standards, conventions, and symbols, as well as the most essential tools for the pipefitter and plumber.

The author is indebted to many manufacturers for the use of their plumbing and piping products, and particularly to the following companies and organizations for their permission in the use of tables and illustrations: International Association of Plumbing and Mechanical Officials (IAPMO); Celanse Piping System, Inc.; *National Plumber's Code*; *Uniform Plumbing Code*; Rockwell Manufacturing Co.; and the American Society for Heating, Refrigeration and Air-Conditioning Engineers.

WILLIAM J. HORNUNG

Mission Viejo, California

PLUMBER'S
AND PIPEFITTER'S
HANDBOOK

1

METALS FOR THE PIPING INDUSTRY

TYPES OF METALS

Metals that are extensively used in the piping industry are: iron, steel, stainless steel, aluminum, lead, brass, and copper. These metals are divided into two major groups, ferrous and nonferrous.

Ferrous, the Latin word for iron, includes iron and iron-based metals such as various steels and stainless steels. Aluminum, brass, and copper are *nonferrous* metals.

As a group, metals are substances that have a hardness, can conduct heat and electricity, and possess certain mechanical properties. The most important characteristic is their power to resist change in shape. Almost all metals used in the piping industry are alloys and not the pure metals. Pure iron, for example, is as soft and bendable as copper.

Most metals deteriorate as a result of substances in the air, soil, and water, or of chemical agents to which they are exposed. This is called *corrosion*.

STEEL

Steel is a strong, hard material which can be rolled, drawn, bent, and cast. It can be welded by any of the generally used methods and formed into pipe of many diameters and can be threaded.

TABLE 1-1 Minimum Bend Radii of Iron and Steel Pipe[a]

Diameter of Pipe	Minimum Radii	Diameter of Pipe	Minimum Radii
$\frac{1}{8}$	$1\frac{1}{4}$	3	15
$\frac{1}{4}$	$1\frac{1}{4}$	$3\frac{1}{2}$	$17\frac{1}{2}$
$\frac{1}{2}$	$2\frac{1}{2}$	4	20
$\frac{3}{4}$	$3\frac{3}{4}$	5	30
1	5	6	42
$1\frac{1}{2}$	$7\frac{1}{2}$	8	45
2	10	10	50
$2\frac{1}{2}$	$12\frac{1}{2}$	12	60

[a]All dimensions in inches.

Smaller-size pipes are often bent to create changes in direction without heating them first. However, minimum allowable bend radii should be employed when bending iron or steel pipe of various diameters. Table 1-1 lists the minimum bend radii of iron and steel pipe diameters.

STAINLESS STEEL

Stainless steel is a corrosion-resistant material, due to the amount of chromium present as an alloy with iron or with iron and nickel. Steels with quantities of chromium over 5% are known as stainless steels. These can be machined, cast, bent, drawn, rolled, formed, welded, and soldered. Stainless steel is manufactured in plate, bar, pipe, tubing, castings, and many structural shapes used in the building and piping industry.

ALUMINUM

Aluminums are alloys and vary from soft to almost as strong as steel; all are very corrosion resistant. Since aluminum is a lightweight metal, it has many advantages over other metals, such as copper, brass, and steel. This light weight reduces handling, installing, and shipping costs.

Aluminum alloys are divided into two main categories: those for *casting* and those for *wrought* aluminum products. Wrought aluminum can be extruded, formed, bent, rolled, spun, machined, welded, and soldered by special methods. It is manufactured in strip, sheet, pipe, tube, wire, and many other extruded shapes, both standard and specially designed.

Aluminum has a melting point of about 1218° F. It is nonmagnetic and has good electrical and thermal conductivity, about 60% that of copper.

COPPER

Copper is a soft, corrosion-resistant, reddish metal used extensively for piping. It is lightweight, very durable, and easy to work with. It has a smooth inner surface which offers little frictional resistance to the flow of liquids. Rigid copper pipe is available in the following types and weights:

Type K: heaviest—used for underground work
Type L: medium weight—used for interior plumbing work
Type M: lightweight—where permitted also used for interior work
Type DWV: thinner than type M—used only for vent, waste, and drainage pipe; forbidden in some areas

Type M pipe is used for carrying water under pressure. The thinner DWV pipe is used only for vent, waste, and drainage pipes which do not run under pressure. As a rule, standard copper pipe lengths are available in 20-ft lengths, but 10-ft lengths can also be gotten.

Copper and its alloys can be classified into four general categories: (1) those classified as copper; (2) the brasses, in which zinc is the principal alloy; (3) the bronzes, in which tin is the principal alloy; and (4) the nickel alloy.

LEAD

Lead has a low melting point, low strength, and is a dense and heavy material. However, it has high corrosion resistance and poor electrical conductivity, although its lubricating qualities make it useful in pipe joint compounds.

By being alloyed with antimony and tin, the strength of lead can be increased. Tin as an alloy makes it possible to bond lead with metals such as copper and steel.

DESIGNATIONS FOR METAL PRODUCTS

Wire is designated by gauge number for ferrous and nonferrous metals. It is also designated by diameter in decimals of an inch, as shown in Table 1-2. The smaller the gauge number, the larger the diameter.

TABLE 1-2 Wire Gauges[a]

Gauge No.	Ferrous American Wire	Nonferrous American Wire
00	0.3310	0.3648
0	0.3065	0.3249
1	0.2830	0.2893
2	0.2625	0.2576
3	0.2437	0.2294
4	0.2253	0.2048
5	0.2070	0.1819
6	0.1920	0.1620
7	0.1770	0.1443
8	0.1620	0.1285
9	0.1483	0.1144
10	0.1350	0.1019
11	0.1205	0.0907
12	0.1055	0.0808
13	0.0915	0.0720
14	0.0800	0.0641
15	0.0720	0.0571
16	0.0625	0.0508
17	0.0540	0.0453
18	0.0475	0.0403
19	0.0410	0.0359
20	0.0348	0.0320

[a]All dimensions in inches.

There are different methods of designating sheet and strip metals. For instance, steel sheets are designated by gauge numbers and their thickness in inches; aluminum is designated by its alloy number and its various thicknesses; zinc is designated by the gauge and its thickness in inches; and copper is designated by its weight per square foot in ounces in the various available thicknesses (see Table 1-3).

COLOR VARIATIONS IN BRASS

When copper and zinc are combined, the result is an alloy called *brass*. This material can vary in color, strength, and corrosion resistance depending on the percentage of copper and zinc (Table 1-4).

IRON-CARBON PERCENTAGES

Iron, an element, is used to make wrought iron, cast iron, steel, and stainless steel. The characteristics of these irons and steels depend on

TABLE 1-3 Methods of Designating Sheet and Strip Metal[a]

(a) Steel and Stainless Steel

Gauge No.	Steel Thickness	Stainless Steel Thickness
8	0.1644	0.1719
9	0.1495	0.1563
10	0.1345	0.1406

(b) Aluminum

Alloy	Available Thickness
1100-0	0.02, 0.028, 0.032
1100-H14	0.04, 0.051, 0.064
3003-H14	0.02, 0.028, 0.032

(c) Zinc

Gauge No.	Thickness
9	0.018
10	0.020
11	0.024
12	0.028

(d) Copper

Weight per Square Foot (oz)	Thickness
16	0.0190
20	0.0245
24	0.0300
32	0.0405

[a]All dimensions in inches except as noted.

TABLE 1-4 How Alloys Affect Color

Copper (%)	Zinc (%)	Resulting Color
90	10	Bronze color
85	15	Golden color
80	20	Yellow color
55	45	Silvery white

TABLE 1-5 Percentages of Carbon Added to Iron to Make
Various Metals

Wrought Iron	Cast Iron	Carbon Steel	Stainless Steel
Less than 0.1	More than 2.0	Less than 2.0	Less than 0.2

the iron–carbon percentages and the addition of small quantities of
other elements, such as nickel, chromium, manganese, boron, aluminum, copper, and silicon (Table 1-5).

GALVANIC ACTION

When different metals or alloys are joined or brought into contact with
each other and moisture is present, an electric current starts to flow
from one metal to the other and in time one of the metals is eaten away
while the other remains intact. This process is known as *galvanic action.*
The length of time this takes depends on the amount of moisture present, even if it is only the humidity in the air. Near salt water, or coastal
areas, galvanic action can become much more intense.

If, for example, aluminum siding is applied with steel nails, the
aluminum around the steel will gradually be eaten away and the siding
will eventually fall off. To overcome galvanic action, metal must be
isolated or applied with metals that are compatible and will not start
this electric action. Table 1-6 shows the metals listed in sequence in
which each is attacked through galvanic action by all the metals that
follow in the table. Aluminum is attacked by all metals, whereas gold
is not attacked by any of the metals. Steel nails cannot be used to
secure stainless steel; the stainless steel will, through galvanic action,
disintegrate the steel nail.

TABLE 1-6 Galvanic Table

Aluminum
Zinc
Iron and steel
Stainless steel
Lead
Brasses
Copper
Bronze
Gold

SELF-TESTING REVIEW QUESTIONS

1. Name four metals that are used extensively in the piping industry.
2. Name a ferrous and a nonferrous metal.
3. What is the smallest bend radius to which a $\frac{3}{4}$-in.-diameter pipe can be bent?
4. All aluminums are alloys. What are some of the alloying metals?
5. Name the four types of rigid copper.
6. When copper and zinc are combined, what is the resulting alloy?
7. An iron nail is driven into a stainless piece of sheet steel. In time, which of the two will corrode, the nail or the stainless steel sheet surrounding the nail?

2

AMERICAN STANDARD PIPE AND FITTINGS

WEIGHTS OF PIPE

American Standard pipe is usually specified by its inside nominal diameter. There are three different weights of pipe—*standard*, *extra strong*, and *double extra strong* (Fig. 2-1)—used for various pressures of water or steam. Although the three pipes represent a nominal inside diameter, say 1 in., their actual inside diameters are 1.049, 0.957, and 0.599 in., while the actual outside diameter of all three is 1.315 in.

Pipe of this type is generally specified by its nominal size, but on diameters of 12 in. and over, the outside diameter of the pipe is given, with the thickness of the wall.

THREADS ON PIPE

Pipe threads are similar to the American Standard Machine thread in that the angle of the thread is 60°. The root and the crest are somewhat flattened, so that the depth of the thread is 0.866 of the pitch. The threads are cut to a slight taper to make tight joints. Figure 2-2 shows a detail of the American Standard Pipe thread and its proportions. Table 2-1 shows diameters of American Standard Pipe thread and their number of threads per inch.

STANDARD
EXTERNAL DIA. 1.315
INTERNAL DIA. 1.049

EXTRA STRONG
EXTERNAL DIA. 1.315
INTERNAL DIA. 0.957

DOUBLE EXTRA STRONG
EXTERNAL DIA. 1.315
INTERNAL DIA. 0.599

Figure 2-1 Three Different Weights of Pipe

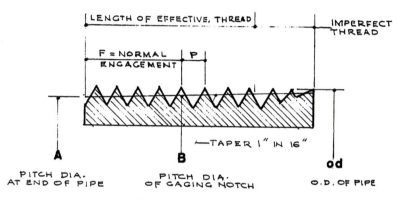

Figure 2-2 Pipe Thread

Nominal-size pipe diameters with their inside and external diameters, nominal pipe thickness, and threads per inch are shown in Table 2-2. Extra strong and double extra strong pipe diameters, and their external and interior diameters, are shown in Table 2-3.

TABLE 2-1 American Standard Pipe Thread

Nominal Size (in.)	Number of Threads per Inch	Nominal Size (in.)	Number of Threads per Inch
$\frac{1}{8}$	27	2	$11\frac{1}{2}$
$\frac{1}{4}$	18	$2\frac{1}{2}$	8
$\frac{3}{8}$	18	3	8
$\frac{1}{2}$	14	$3\frac{1}{2}$	8
$\frac{3}{4}$	14	4	8
1	$11\frac{1}{2}$	$4\frac{1}{2}$	8
$1\frac{1}{4}$	$11\frac{1}{2}$	5	8
$1\frac{1}{2}$	$11\frac{1}{2}$	6	8

TABLE 2-2 American Standard Pipe[a]

Nominal Size	Inside Diameter	External Diameter	Nominal Thickness	Number of Threads
$\frac{1}{8}$	0.269	0.405	0.068	27
$\frac{1}{4}$	0.364	0.540	0.088	18
$\frac{3}{8}$	0.493	0.675	0.091	18
$\frac{1}{2}$	0.622	0.840	0.109	14
$\frac{3}{4}$	0.824	1.050	0.113	14
1	1.049	1.315	0.133	$11\frac{1}{2}$
$1\frac{1}{4}$	1.380	1.660	0.140	$11\frac{1}{2}$
$1\frac{1}{2}$	1.610	1.900	0.145	$11\frac{1}{2}$
2	2.067	2.375	0.154	$11\frac{1}{2}$
$2\frac{1}{2}$	2.469	2.875	0.203	8
3	3.068	3.500	0.216	8
$3\frac{1}{2}$	3.548	4.000	0.226	8
4	4.026	4.500	0.237	8
$4\frac{1}{2}$	4.508	5.000	0.247	8
5	5.047	5.563	0.258	8
6	6.065	6.625	0.280	8
7	7.023	7.265	0.301	8
8	8.071	8.625	0.277	8
9	8.941	9.625	0.342	8
10	10.192	10.750	0.270	8
10	10.136	10.750	0.307	8
10	10.020	10.750	0.365	8
11	11.000	11.750	0.375	8
12	12.090	12.750	0.320	8
12	12.000	12.750	0.375	8

[a] All dimensions in inches.

HOW TO MEASURE THREADED PIPE

There are four different methods of pipe measurement: (1) end to end, (2) end to center, (3) end to face, and (4) face to face. A fifth method is center to center, but it is used in the same situation as the face-to-face measure.

1. *End-to-end* measure is the total length of the pipe, including the ends that go inside the fittings (Fig. 2-3a).
2. *End-to-center* measure is used for a length of pipe which has one fitting at one end (Fig. 2-3b).

TABLE 2-3 Extra Strong and Double Extra Strong Pipe[a]

Nominal Size	External Diameter	Internal Diameter	
		Extra Strong	Double Extra Strong
$\frac{1}{8}$	0.405	0.215	—
$\frac{1}{4}$	0.540	0.302	—
$\frac{3}{8}$	0.675	0.423	—
$\frac{1}{2}$	0.840	0.546	0.252
$\frac{3}{4}$	1.050	0.742	0.434
1	1.315	0.957	0.599
$1\frac{1}{4}$	1.660	1.278	0.896
$1\frac{1}{2}$	1.900	1.500	1.100
2	2.375	1.939	1.503
$2\frac{1}{2}$	2.875	2.323	1.771
3	3.500	2.900	2.300
$3\frac{1}{2}$	4.000	3.364	2.728
4	4.500	3.826	3.152

[a]All dimensions in inches.

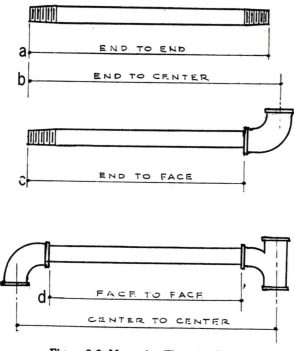

Figure 2-3 Measuring Threaded Pipe

3. *End-to-face* measure is also used for a pipe length with a fitting at one end only. The pipe length is equal to the measure from one end to the fitting, plus the length of overlap, or the engagement into the fitting (Fig. 2-3c).

4. *Face-to-face* measure is used for a length of pipe having fittings at both ends. The pipe length is equal to the distance from one fitting to the other, plus twice the length of the overlap (Fig. 2-3d).

PIPE FITTINGS FOR LINES CONVEYING LIQUIDS OR GASES

Pipe fittings used on lines conveying liquids or gases can be classified by the method of making up a joint, such as (1) flanged cast steel fittings, (2) flanged cast iron fittings, (3) welded forged steel fittings, (4) screwed fittings, and (5) brazed fittings.

Flanged Cast Steel Fittings

Flanged cast steel fittings of the 150- and 300-lb classes have a $\frac{1}{16}$ -in. raised surface included on the flange thickness and center-to-center face dimensions. Above these pressure ratings they have a $\frac{1}{4}$-in. raised surface which is not included in the flange thickness but is included in the center-to-center surface dimension.

Sizes of flanged cast steel fittings for various pressures are as follows:

150 lb: from 1 to 24 in.
300 lb: from 1 to 24 in.
400 lb: from 4 to 24 in.
600 lb: from $\frac{1}{2}$ to 24 in.
800 lb: from 4 to 24 in.
1500 lb: from 1 to 12 in.

Flanged Cast Iron Fittings

Cast iron flanges (Fig. 2-4), of the 125-lb class have plain faces. Bolt lengths are for flanges of thickness shown in Table 2-4. When flanges are integral with valves or fittings, the bolt holes, which are in multiples of four, are drilled to straddle the center lines unless otherwise desired.

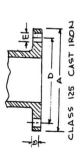

LENGTH OF MACHINE BOLT

CLASS 125 CAST IRON

Figure 2-4 Flanged Cast Iron Fittings

TABLE 2-4 Class 125 Cast Iron Flanges[a]

Nominal Pipe Size	Flanges		Drilling		Bolting		
	Flange Diameter (A)	Flange Thickness (B)	Diameter of Bolt Circle (D)	Diameter of Bolt Holes (E)	Number of Bolts	Diameter of Bolts	Length of Machine Bolts (F)
1	$4\frac{1}{4}$	$\frac{7}{16}$	$3\frac{1}{8}$	$\frac{5}{8}$	4	$\frac{1}{2}$	$1\frac{3}{4}$
$1\frac{1}{4}$	$4\frac{5}{8}$	$\frac{1}{2}$	$3\frac{1}{2}$	$\frac{5}{8}$	4	$\frac{1}{2}$	2
$1\frac{1}{2}$	5	$\frac{9}{16}$	$3\frac{7}{8}$	$\frac{5}{8}$	4	$\frac{1}{2}$	2
2	6	$\frac{5}{8}$	$4\frac{3}{4}$	$\frac{3}{4}$	4	$\frac{5}{8}$	$2\frac{1}{4}$
$2\frac{1}{2}$	7	$\frac{11}{16}$	$5\frac{1}{2}$	$\frac{3}{4}$	4	$\frac{5}{8}$	$2\frac{1}{2}$
3	$7\frac{1}{2}$	$\frac{3}{4}$	6	$\frac{3}{4}$	4	$\frac{5}{8}$	$2\frac{1}{2}$
4	9	$\frac{15}{16}$	$7\frac{1}{2}$	$\frac{3}{4}$	8	$\frac{5}{8}$	3
5	10	$\frac{15}{16}$	$8\frac{1}{2}$	$\frac{7}{8}$	8	$\frac{3}{4}$	3
6	11	1	$9\frac{1}{2}$	$\frac{7}{8}$	8	$\frac{3}{4}$	3
8	$13\frac{1}{2}$	$1\frac{1}{8}$	$11\frac{3}{4}$	$\frac{7}{8}$	8	$\frac{3}{4}$	$3\frac{3}{4}$
10	16	$1\frac{3}{16}$	$14\frac{1}{4}$	1	12	$\frac{7}{8}$	$3\frac{1}{2}$
12	19	$1\frac{1}{4}$	17	1	12	$\frac{7}{8}$	$3\frac{3}{4}$
14	21	$1\frac{3}{8}$	$18\frac{3}{4}$	$1\frac{1}{8}$	12	1	$4\frac{1}{4}$
16	$23\frac{1}{2}$	$1\frac{7}{16}$	$21\frac{1}{4}$	$1\frac{1}{8}$	16	1	$4\frac{1}{2}$
18	25	$1\frac{9}{16}$	$22\frac{3}{4}$	$1\frac{1}{4}$	16	$1\frac{1}{8}$	$4\frac{3}{4}$
20	$27\frac{1}{2}$	$1\frac{11}{16}$	25	$1\frac{1}{4}$	20	$1\frac{1}{8}$	5
24	32	$1\frac{7}{8}$	$29\frac{1}{2}$	$1\frac{3}{8}$	20	$1\frac{1}{4}$	$5\frac{1}{2}$
30	$38\frac{3}{4}$	$2\frac{1}{8}$	36	$1\frac{3}{8}$	28	$1\frac{1}{4}$	$6\frac{1}{4}$
36	46	$2\frac{3}{8}$	$42\frac{3}{4}$	$1\frac{5}{8}$	32	$1\frac{1}{2}$	7

[a] All dimensions in inches.   *Source:* The Walworth Company.

Welded Forged Steel Fittings

Welded forged steel fittings are mostly used in steam and hot process lines of pressures 150 lb and over. They have a low maintainance cost due to the elimination of worn gaskets. Welded pipe and fittings cuts down on weight by the elimination of flanges and bolts. Forged steel fittings may be of the butt or socket-type weld.

Screwed Fittings

Screwed fittings made of malleable iron are used for conveying water, steam, air, and process materials. Malleable iron is capable of withstanding considerably more shock than ordinary black iron castings. Screwed fittings of malleable iron are rated at 150 lb of steam pressure at 450°F, or 300 lb of nonshock water, oil, or gas at 150°F.

Brazed Fittings

Brazed fittings of malleable iron is used on pipe that does not warrant the cost of the welded joint. They are threadless fittings which if properly installed ensure a satisfactory leakproof connection.

Brazed fittings are lighter in weight than the same size and kind of screwed fittings due to the elimination of the heavier wall required for threading. To install this type of fitting, the pipe is cut off so that the end is square and free of burrs, full-sized, and not out of round if a tight connection is to be gotten. After applying flux to both pipe and fitting, the pipe is inserted against the bottom of the cup when the assembly is properly supported. The flame is applied until the flux bubbles and the brazing alloy is then added which flows by capillary attraction into the clearance between pipe and cup. Enough alloy is added to fill the space and form a small fillet around the pipe.

MEASURING PIPE LENGTH BETWEEN VARIOUS TYPES OF FITTINGS

Length of Pipe Between Flanged Fittings

Suppose that we want to find the length of a 3-in. pipe between two 90° flanged elbows when the center-to-center distance of 3 ft 6¼ in. is given. Refer to Fig. 2-5. First, find the center-to-face distance from Table 2-5 under A and opposite a 3-in.-diameter flanged fitting. This distance is 5½ in. Subtract two times 5½ in. from 3 ft 6¼ in. and then subtract two times 1/16 in. for the gasket space at both ends. The actual

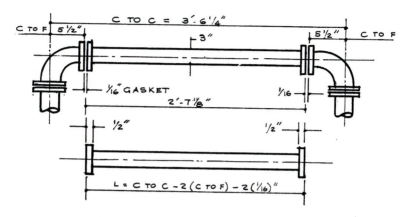

Figure 2-5 Pipe Between Flanged Elbows

flange thickness is $\frac{1}{2}$ in. (see Table 2-6, dimension T). Subtract twice the flange thickness from 2 ft $7\frac{1}{8}$ in. to arrive at the actual length of pipe.

Length of Pipe Welded Between 90° Elbows

When the center-to-center distance of 3 ft $6\frac{1}{4}$ in. is given (Fig. 2-8), to find the length of pipe, proceed as follows. Find the center-to-end distance for the 2-in.-diameter welded 90° elbow fitting shown in Table 2-7. Subtract two times the center-to-end distance to arrive at the 3 ft $0\frac{1}{4}$ in. pipe length.

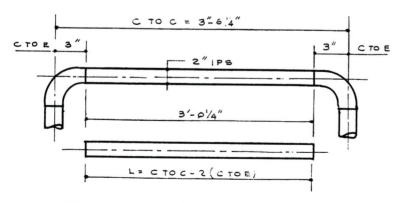

Figure 2-6 Length of Pipe between Welded Fittings

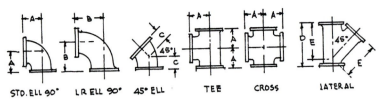

Figure 2-7 Fittings for Table 2-5

TABLE 2-5 Stainless Steel Flanged Fitting Dimensions In Inches

	Flange			Center-to-Face Surface				
Size	Diameter	Minimum Thickness	Raised Face	A	B	C	D	E
1	$4\frac{1}{4}$	$\frac{3}{8}$	2	$3\frac{1}{2}$	5	$1\frac{3}{4}$	$7\frac{1}{2}$	$5\frac{3}{4}$
$1\frac{1}{4}$	$4\frac{5}{8}$	$\frac{13}{32}$	$2\frac{1}{2}$	$3\frac{3}{4}$	$5\frac{1}{2}$	2	8	$6\frac{1}{4}$
$1\frac{1}{2}$	5	$\frac{7}{16}$	$2\frac{7}{8}$	4	6	$2\frac{1}{4}$	9	7
2	6	$\frac{1}{2}$	$3\frac{3}{8}$	$4\frac{1}{2}$	$6\frac{1}{2}$	$2\frac{1}{2}$	$10\frac{1}{2}$	8
$2\frac{1}{2}$	7	$\frac{9}{16}$	$4\frac{1}{8}$	5	7	3	12	$9\frac{1}{2}$
3	$7\frac{1}{2}$	$\frac{5}{8}$	5	$5\frac{1}{2}$	$7\frac{3}{4}$	3	13	10
4	9	$\frac{11}{16}$	$6\frac{3}{16}$	$6\frac{1}{2}$	9	4	15	12
6	11	$\frac{13}{16}$	$8\frac{1}{2}$	8	$11\frac{1}{2}$	5	18	$14\frac{1}{2}$
8	$13\frac{1}{2}$	$\frac{15}{16}$	$10\frac{5}{8}$	9	14	$5\frac{1}{2}$	22	$17\frac{1}{2}$
10	16	1	$12\frac{3}{4}$	11	$16\frac{1}{2}$	$5\frac{1}{2}$	$25\frac{1}{2}$	$20\frac{1}{2}$

Figure 2-8 125 lb Forged Steel Lightweight Flanges

TABLE 2-6 Lightweight Flanges: 125-lb Forged Steel[a]

Pipe Size	O.D. A	Thickness T	I.D. B	Length of Hub L	O.D. E	Number of Bolts
3	$7\frac{1}{2}$	$\frac{1}{2}$	$3\frac{3}{4}$	$\frac{7}{8}$	$4\frac{1}{4}$	4
4	9	$\frac{1}{2}$	$4\frac{1}{2}$	$\frac{7}{8}$	$5\frac{5}{16}$	8
5	10	$\frac{9}{16}$	$5\frac{1}{4}$	$\frac{7}{8}$	$6\frac{7}{16}$	8
6	11	$\frac{9}{16}$	$6\frac{1}{4}$	$1\frac{1}{8}$	$7\frac{9}{16}$	8
8	$13\frac{1}{2}$	$\frac{9}{16}$	$8\frac{1}{4}$	$1\frac{1}{8}$	$9\frac{11}{16}$	8
10	16	$\frac{11}{16}$	$10\frac{5}{16}$	$1\frac{3}{16}$	12	12
12	19	$\frac{11}{16}$	$12\frac{5}{16}$	$1\frac{7}{16}$	$14\frac{3}{8}$	12
14	21	$\frac{3}{4}$	$14\frac{5}{16}$	$1\frac{7}{16}$	$15\frac{3}{4}$	12
16	$23\frac{1}{2}$	$\frac{3}{4}$	$16\frac{5}{16}$	$1\frac{1}{2}$	18	16
18	25	$\frac{3}{4}$	$18\frac{3}{8}$	$1\frac{1}{2}$	$19\frac{3}{8}$	16
20	$27\frac{1}{2}$	$\frac{3}{4}$	$20\frac{3}{8}$	$1\frac{1}{2}$	22	20
22	$29\frac{1}{2}$	1	$22\frac{7}{16}$	$1\frac{1}{2}$	$24\frac{1}{8}$	20
24	32	1	$24\frac{7}{16}$	$1\frac{1}{8}$	$26\frac{1}{8}$	20
26	$34\frac{1}{4}$	1	$26\frac{9}{16}$	$1\frac{7}{8}$	$28\frac{1}{2}$	24
28	$36\frac{1}{2}$	1	$28\frac{9}{16}$	$1\frac{7}{8}$	$30\frac{1}{2}$	28

[a] All dimensions in inches. O.D., outside diameter; I.D., inside diameter.

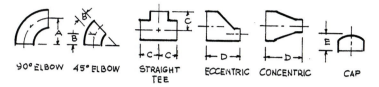

Figure 2-9 Welding Fittings

TABLE 2-7 Welding Fittings: Schedule 10[a,b]

Pipe Size	O.D.	Thickness	A	B	C	D	E
$\frac{3}{4}$	1.050	0.083	$1\frac{1}{8}$	$\frac{7}{16}$	$1\frac{1}{4}$	—	—
1	1.315	0.109	$1\frac{1}{2}$	$\frac{7}{8}$	$1\frac{1}{2}$	2	$1\frac{1}{2}$
$1\frac{1}{4}$	1.660	0.109	$1\frac{7}{8}$	1	$1\frac{7}{8}$	2	$1\frac{1}{2}$
$1\frac{1}{2}$	1.900	0.109	$2\frac{1}{4}$	$1\frac{1}{8}$	$2\frac{1}{4}$	$2\frac{1}{2}$	$1\frac{1}{2}$
2	2.375	0.109	3	$1\frac{3}{8}$	$2\frac{1}{2}$	3	$1\frac{1}{2}$
$2\frac{1}{2}$	2.875	0.120	$3\frac{3}{4}$	$1\frac{3}{4}$	3	$3\frac{1}{2}$	$1\frac{1}{2}$
3	3.500	0.120	$4\frac{1}{2}$	2	$3\frac{3}{8}$	$3\frac{1}{2}$	2
$3\frac{1}{2}$	4.000	0.120	$5\frac{1}{4}$	$2\frac{1}{4}$	$3\frac{3}{4}$	4	$2\frac{1}{2}$
4	4.500	0.120	6	$2\frac{1}{2}$	$4\frac{1}{8}$	4	$2\frac{1}{2}$
6	6.625	0.134	9	$3\frac{3}{4}$	$5\frac{5}{8}$	$5\frac{1}{2}$	$3\frac{1}{2}$
8	8.625	0.148	12	5	7	6	4
10	10.750	0.165	15	$6\frac{1}{4}$	$8\frac{1}{2}$	7	5
12	12.750	0.180	18	$7\frac{1}{2}$	10	8	6

[a] Schedule number = $1000 \times \dfrac{P(\text{internal pressure}), \text{psi}}{S(\text{allowable fiber stress}), \text{psi}}$.

[b] All dimensions in inches.

Length of Pipe Between Screwed Fittings

When the center-to-center distance between elbows 1 and 2 is 28 in. (Fig. 2-10), find the length of the $1\frac{1}{2}$-in.-diameter threaded pipe A. First, subtract twice the distance from the center of the elbow to the face of the elbow. This distance can be found in Table 2-9.

For a $1\frac{1}{4}$-in.-diameter threaded elbow, the center-to-face measure is $1\frac{15}{16}$ in., which is $3\frac{7}{8}$ in. for both ends. Subtract $3\frac{7}{8}$ from 28 to get the distance from face-to-face of fitting, which becomes $24\frac{1}{8}$ in. Now add the thread engagement for both ends, also found in Table 2-9. In this case the thread engagement L is $\frac{3}{4}$ in. for each end. The total length of the threaded pipe A is therefore $24\frac{1}{8} + 1\frac{1}{2} = 25\frac{5}{8}$ in.

The length of the $1\frac{1}{2}$-in.-diameter threaded pipe B between 2 and 3 is found similarly, such as

$$33 \text{ in.} - 3\frac{7}{8} \text{ in.} = 29\frac{1}{8} \text{ in.} + 1\frac{1}{2} \text{ in.} = 30\frac{5}{8} \text{ in.}$$

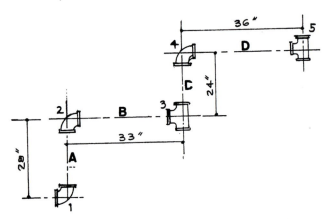

Figure 2-10 Length of Pipe Between Screwed Fittings

TABLE 2-8 Steel-Welding Fitting Dimensions[a]. Refer to Figure 2-11

Nominal Pipe Size	A	B	C	D	E	F	G	H[b]	J	K
1	$1\frac{1}{2}$		$2\frac{1}{16}$	$1\frac{5}{8}$	$\frac{7}{8}$	2	$1\frac{1}{2}$	$1\frac{1}{2}$	2	4
$1\frac{1}{2}$	$2\frac{1}{4}$		$3\frac{1}{4}$	$2\frac{7}{16}$	$1\frac{1}{8}$	$2\frac{1}{2}$	$2\frac{1}{4}$	$1\frac{1}{2}$	$2\frac{7}{8}$	4
2	3		$4\frac{3}{16}$	$3\frac{5}{16}$	$1\frac{3}{8}$	3	$2\frac{1}{2}$	$1\frac{1}{2}$	$3\frac{5}{8}$	6
3	$4\frac{1}{2}$	Same as nominal pipe size	$6\frac{1}{4}$	$4\frac{3}{4}$	2	$3\frac{1}{2}$	$3\frac{3}{8}$	2	5	6
4	6		$8\frac{1}{4}$	$6\frac{1}{4}$	$2\frac{1}{2}$	4	$4\frac{1}{8}$	$2\frac{1}{2}$	$6\frac{3}{16}$	6
6	9		$12\frac{3}{4}$	$9\frac{5}{16}$	$3\frac{3}{4}$	$5\frac{1}{2}$	$5\frac{5}{8}$	$3\frac{1}{2}$	$8\frac{1}{2}$	8
8	12		$16\frac{5}{16}$	$12\frac{5}{16}$	5	6	7	4	$10\frac{5}{8}$	8
10	15		$20\frac{3}{8}$	$15\frac{3}{8}$	$6\frac{1}{4}$	7	$8\frac{1}{2}$	5	$12\frac{3}{4}$	10
12	18		$24\frac{3}{8}$	$18\frac{3}{8}$	$7\frac{1}{2}$	8	10	6	15	10
14	21		28	21	$8\frac{3}{4}$	13	11^c	$6\frac{1}{2}$	$16\frac{1}{4}$	12
16	24		32	23	10	14	12^c	7	$18\frac{1}{2}$	12
18	27		36	$25\frac{1}{2}$	$11\frac{1}{4}$	15	$13\frac{1}{2}^c$	8	21	12
20	30		40	$30\frac{1}{2}$	$12\frac{1}{2}$	20	15^c	9	23	12
24	36		48	34	15	20	17^c	$10\frac{1}{2}$	$27\frac{1}{4}$	12

[a] All dimensions in inches.

[b] For standard weight and extra strong, see ASA B16.9 for dimensions of other thicknesses.

[c] Center-to-center dimensions for outlet are not standardized in 14 in. and larger. Dimensions given are in common use.

The length of the $1\frac{1}{2}$-in.-diameter threaded pipe C between 3 and 4 is found similarly, such as

$$24 \text{ in.} - 3\frac{7}{8} \text{ in.} = 20\frac{1}{8} \text{ in.} + 1\frac{1}{2} \text{ in.} = 21\frac{5}{8} \text{ in.}$$

The length of the $1\frac{1}{2}$-in.-diameter threaded pipe D between 4 and 5 is found similarly, such as

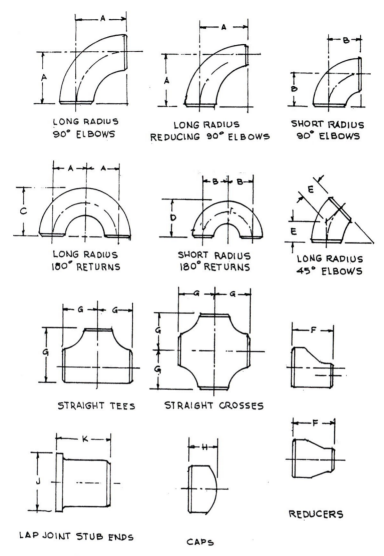

Figure 2-11 Steel-Welding Fitting Dimensions.
Refer to Table 2-8.

$$36 \text{ in.} - 3\tfrac{7}{8} \text{ in.} = 33\tfrac{1}{8} \text{ in.} + 1\tfrac{1}{2} \text{ in.} = 34\tfrac{5}{8} \text{ in.}$$

The combined or total length of pipe required for lengths A, B, C, and D is

$$25\tfrac{5}{8} \text{ in.} + 30\tfrac{5}{8} \text{ in.} + 21\tfrac{5}{8} \text{ in.} + 34\tfrac{5}{8} \text{ in.} = 112\tfrac{1}{2} \text{ in.}$$

or 9.375 ft. Allow a little extra for possible waste, say a total of 9 ft 6 in.

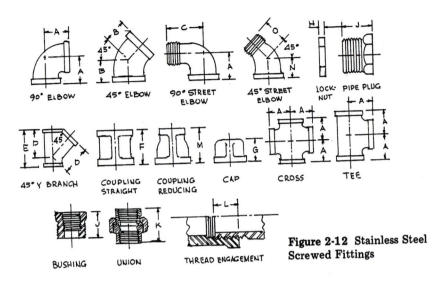

90° ELBOW   45° ELBOW   90° STREET   45° STREET   LOCK-   PIPE PLUG
                                  ELBOW   ELBOW   NUT

45° Y BRANCH   COUPLING   COUPLING   CAP   CROSS   TEE
                 STRAIGHT   REDUCING

BUSHING   UNION   THREAD ENGAGEMENT

Figure 2-12 Stainless Steel
Screwed Fittings

HUB AND SPIGOT PIPE

Cast Iron Hub and Spigot Soil Pipe Fittings

There are two available weights of cast iron hub and spigot soil pipe: *extra heavy* pipe and *service weight* pipe. The pipe may be either *single hub* with a hub at one end and a spigot on the other, or *double hub* with a hub at each end.

The length of a single-hub pipe is such as to lay 5 ft. Double-hub pipe is of the same overall length as a single-hub pipe; therefore, its laying length is 5 ft minus the telescoping length (see Fig. 2-13).

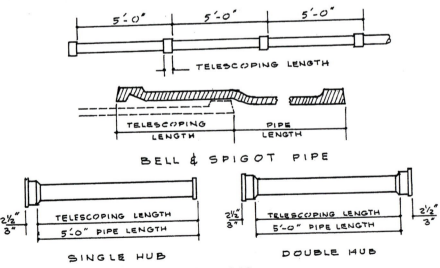

Figure 2-13

TABLE 2-9 Stainless Steel Screwed Fitting Dimensions[a]. Refer to Figure 2-12.

Diameter	A	B	C	D	E	F	G	H	J	K	L	M	N	O
$\frac{1}{8}$	$\frac{11}{16}$	$\frac{11}{16}$	1	1	$1\frac{5}{16}$	$\frac{7}{8}$	$\frac{5}{8}$	$\frac{3}{16}$	$\frac{5}{8}$	$1\frac{3}{16}$	$\frac{1}{4}$	—	—	—
$\frac{1}{4}$	$\frac{13}{16}$	$\frac{3}{4}$	$1\frac{3}{16}$	$1\frac{3}{16}$	$1\frac{5}{8}$	$1\frac{1}{16}$	$\frac{11}{16}$	1	$\frac{11}{16}$	$1\frac{1}{2}$	$\frac{3}{8}$	1	$\frac{3}{4}$	$\frac{15}{16}$
$\frac{3}{8}$	$\frac{15}{16}$	$\frac{13}{16}$	$1\frac{7}{16}$	$1\frac{7}{16}$	$1\frac{15}{16}$	$1\frac{3}{16}$	$\frac{11}{16}$	$\frac{1}{4}$	$\frac{3}{4}$	$1\frac{5}{8}$	$\frac{3}{8}$	$1\frac{1}{8}$	$\frac{13}{16}$	$1\frac{1}{32}$
$\frac{1}{2}$	$1\frac{1}{8}$	$\frac{7}{8}$	$1\frac{5}{8}$	$1\frac{11}{16}$	$2\frac{5}{16}$	$1\frac{5}{16}$	$\frac{7}{8}$	$\frac{9}{32}$	$\frac{15}{16}$	$1\frac{11}{16}$	$\frac{7}{16}$	$1\frac{1}{4}$	$\frac{7}{8}$	$1\frac{5}{32}$
$\frac{3}{4}$	$1\frac{5}{16}$	1	$1\frac{7}{8}$	$2\frac{1}{16}$	$2\frac{3}{4}$	$1\frac{1}{2}$	1	$\frac{11}{32}$	1	$1\frac{15}{16}$	$\frac{1}{2}$	$1\frac{7}{16}$	1	$1\frac{5}{16}$
1	$1\frac{1}{2}$	$1\frac{1}{8}$	$2\frac{1}{8}$	$2\frac{7}{16}$	$3\frac{5}{16}$	$1\frac{11}{16}$	$1\frac{3}{16}$	$\frac{3}{8}$	$1\frac{1}{8}$	$2\frac{1}{2}$	$\frac{9}{16}$	$1\frac{11}{16}$	$1\frac{1}{8}$	$1\frac{1}{2}$
$1\frac{1}{4}$	$1\frac{3}{4}$	$1\frac{5}{16}$	$2\frac{7}{16}$	$2\frac{11}{16}$	$3\frac{15}{16}$	$1\frac{15}{16}$	$1\frac{5}{32}$	$\frac{7}{16}$	$1\frac{1}{8}$	3	$\frac{11}{16}$	$2\frac{1}{16}$	$1\frac{5}{16}$	$1\frac{23}{32}$
$1\frac{1}{2}$	$1\frac{15}{16}$	$1\frac{7}{16}$	$2\frac{11}{16}$	$3\frac{5}{16}$	$4\frac{3}{8}$	$2\frac{1}{8}$	$1\frac{5}{16}$	$\frac{15}{32}$	$1\frac{1}{8}$	3	$\frac{3}{4}$	$2\frac{5}{16}$	$1\frac{7}{16}$	$1\frac{7}{8}$
2	$2\frac{1}{4}$	$1\frac{11}{16}$	$3\frac{1}{4}$	$3\frac{15}{16}$	$5\frac{3}{16}$	$2\frac{1}{2}$	$1\frac{7}{16}$	$\frac{17}{32}$	$1\frac{1}{4}$	$3\frac{3}{8}$	$\frac{3}{4}$	$2\frac{13}{16}$	$1\frac{11}{16}$	$2\frac{5}{32}$
$2\frac{1}{2}$	$2\frac{11}{16}$	$1\frac{15}{16}$	$3\frac{7}{8}$	$4\frac{3}{4}$	$6\frac{1}{4}$	$2\frac{7}{8}$	$1\frac{11}{16}$	$\frac{17}{32}$	$1\frac{7}{16}$	$3\frac{1}{2}$	$\frac{7}{8}$	$3\frac{1}{4}$	$1\frac{15}{16}$	$2\frac{9}{16}$
3	$3\frac{7}{16}$	$2\frac{3}{16}$	$4\frac{1}{2}$	$5\frac{9}{16}$	$7\frac{1}{4}$	$3\frac{3}{16}$	$1\frac{13}{16}$	$\frac{11}{16}$	$1\frac{1}{2}$	$4\frac{1}{8}$	1	$3\frac{11}{16}$	$2\frac{3}{16}$	3
4	$3\frac{13}{16}$	$2\frac{5}{8}$	$5\frac{11}{16}$	7	9	$3\frac{11}{16}$	$2\frac{1}{16}$	$\frac{13}{16}$	$1\frac{3}{4}$	$4\frac{3}{8}$	$1\frac{1}{16}$	$4\frac{3}{8}$	$2\frac{5}{8}$	$3\frac{11}{16}$

[a] All dimensions in inches.

Figure 2-14 and Table 2-10 give the dimensions for cast iron hub and spigot soil pipe fittings.

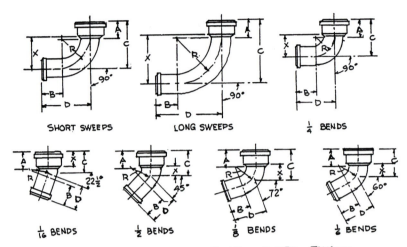

Figure 2-14 Hub and Spigot Cast Iron Soil-Pipe Fittings

TABLE 2-10 Cast Iron Hub and Spigot Soil Pipe Fittings[a]

Diameter	A	B	Telescoping Length T	C	D	R	X
			Short-Sweep Elbows				
2	$2\frac{3}{4}$	3	2.50	$7\frac{3}{4}$	8	5	$5\frac{1}{4}$
3	$3\frac{1}{4}$	$3\frac{1}{2}$	2.75	$8\frac{3}{4}$	9	$5\frac{1}{2}$	6
4	$3\frac{1}{2}$	4	3.00	$9\frac{1}{8}$	10	6	$6\frac{1}{2}$
5	$3\frac{1}{2}$	4	3.00	10	$10\frac{1}{2}$	$6\frac{1}{2}$	7
6	$3\frac{1}{2}$	4	3.00	$10\frac{1}{2}$	11	7	$7\frac{1}{2}$
8	$4\frac{1}{8}$	$5\frac{1}{2}$	3.50	$12\frac{1}{8}$	$13\frac{1}{2}$	8	$9\frac{5}{8}$
10	$4\frac{1}{8}$	$5\frac{1}{2}$	3.50	$13\frac{1}{8}$	$14\frac{1}{2}$	9	$9\frac{5}{8}$
12	5	7	4.25	15	17	10	$10\frac{3}{4}$
15	5	7	4.25	$16\frac{1}{2}$	$18\frac{1}{2}$	$11\frac{1}{2}$	$12\frac{1}{4}$
			Long-Sweep Elbows				
2	$2\frac{3}{4}$	3	2.50	$10\frac{3}{4}$	11	8	$8\frac{1}{4}$
3	$3\frac{1}{4}$	$3\frac{1}{2}$	2.75	$11\frac{3}{4}$	12	$8\frac{1}{2}$	9
4	$3\frac{1}{2}$	4	3.00	$12\frac{1}{2}$	13	9	$9\frac{1}{2}$
5	$3\frac{1}{2}$	4	3.00	13	$13\frac{1}{2}$	$9\frac{1}{2}$	10
6	$3\frac{1}{2}$	4	3.00	$13\frac{1}{2}$	14	10	$10\frac{1}{2}$
8	$4\frac{1}{8}$	$5\frac{1}{2}$	3.50	$15\frac{1}{8}$	$16\frac{1}{2}$	11	$11\frac{5}{8}$

TABLE 2-10 (Continued)

Diameter	A	B	Telescoping Length T	C	D	R	X
			Long-Sweep Elbows				
10	$4\frac{1}{8}$	$5\frac{1}{2}$	3.50	$16\frac{1}{8}$	$17\frac{1}{2}$	12	$12\frac{5}{8}$
12	5	7	4.25	18	20	13	$13\frac{3}{4}$
15	5	7	4.25	$19\frac{1}{2}$	$21\frac{1}{2}$	$14\frac{1}{2}$	$15\frac{1}{4}$
			$\frac{1}{4}$-Bend Elbows				
2	$2\frac{3}{4}$	3	2.50	$5\frac{3}{4}$	6	3	$3\frac{1}{4}$
3	$3\frac{1}{4}$	$3\frac{1}{2}$	2.75	$6\frac{3}{4}$	7	$3\frac{1}{2}$	4
4	$3\frac{1}{2}$	4	3.00	$7\frac{1}{2}$	8	4	$4\frac{1}{2}$
5	$3\frac{1}{2}$	4	3.00	8	$8\frac{1}{2}$	$4\frac{1}{2}$	5
6	$3\frac{1}{2}$	4	3.00	$8\frac{1}{2}$	9	5	$5\frac{1}{2}$
8	$4\frac{1}{8}$	$5\frac{1}{2}$	3.50	$10\frac{1}{8}$	$11\frac{1}{2}$·	6	$6\frac{5}{8}$
10	$4\frac{1}{8}$	$5\frac{1}{2}$	3.50	$11\frac{1}{8}$	$12\frac{1}{2}$	7	$7\frac{5}{8}$
12	5	7	4.25	13	15	8	$8\frac{3}{4}$
15	5	7	4.25	$14\frac{1}{2}$	$16\frac{1}{2}$	$9\frac{1}{2}$	$10\frac{1}{4}$
			$\frac{1}{8}$-Bend Elbows				
2	$2\frac{3}{4}$	3	2.50	4	$4\frac{1}{4}$	3	$1\frac{1}{2}$
3	$3\frac{1}{4}$	$3\frac{1}{2}$	2.75	$4\frac{11}{16}$	$4\frac{15}{16}$	$3\frac{1}{2}$	$1\frac{15}{16}$
4	$3\frac{1}{2}$	4	3.00	$5\frac{3}{16}$	$5\frac{11}{16}$	4	$2\frac{3}{16}$
5	$3\frac{1}{2}$	4	3.00	$5\frac{3}{8}$	$5\frac{7}{8}$	$4\frac{1}{2}$	$2\frac{3}{8}$
6	$3\frac{1}{2}$	4	3.00	$5\frac{9}{16}$	$6\frac{1}{16}$	5	$2\frac{9}{16}$
8	$4\frac{1}{8}$	$5\frac{1}{2}$	3.50	$6\frac{5}{8}$	8	6	$3\frac{1}{8}$
10	$4\frac{1}{8}$	$5\frac{1}{2}$	3.50	7	$8\frac{3}{8}$	7	$3\frac{1}{2}$
12	5	7	4.25	$8\frac{5}{16}$	$10\frac{5}{16}$	8	$4\frac{1}{4}$
15	5	7	4.25	$8\frac{15}{16}$	$10\frac{15}{16}$	$9\frac{1}{2}$	$4\frac{11}{16}$
			$\frac{1}{16}$-Bend Elbows				
2	$2\frac{1}{8}$	3	2.50	$3\frac{3}{8}$	$3\frac{5}{8}$	3	$\frac{7}{8}$
3	$3\frac{1}{4}$	$3\frac{1}{2}$	2.75	$3\frac{15}{16}$	$4\frac{3}{16}$	$3\frac{1}{2}$	$1\frac{3}{16}$
4	$3\frac{1}{2}$	4	3.00	$4\frac{5}{16}$	$4\frac{13}{16}$	4	$1\frac{5}{16}$
5	$3\frac{1}{2}$	4	3.00	$4\frac{3}{8}$	$4\frac{7}{8}$	$4\frac{1}{2}$	$1\frac{3}{8}$
6	$3\frac{1}{2}$	4	3.00	$4\frac{1}{2}$	5	5	$1\frac{1}{2}$
8	$4\frac{1}{8}$	$5\frac{1}{2}$	3.50	$5\frac{5}{16}$	$6\frac{11}{16}$	6	$1\frac{13}{16}$
10	$4\frac{1}{8}$	$5\frac{1}{2}$	3.50	$5\frac{1}{2}$	$6\frac{7}{8}$	7	2
12	5	7	4.25	$6\frac{5}{8}$	$8\frac{5}{8}$	8	$2\frac{3}{8}$
15	5	7	4.25	$6\frac{7}{8}$	$8\frac{7}{8}$	$9\frac{1}{2}$	$2\frac{5}{8}$

TABLE 2-10 (Continued)

Diameter	A	B	Telescoping Length T	C	D	R	X
			$\frac{1}{5}$-Bend Elbows				
2	$2\frac{3}{4}$	3	2.50	$4\frac{15}{16}$	$5\frac{3}{16}$	3	$2\frac{7}{16}$
3	$3\frac{1}{4}$	$3\frac{1}{2}$	2.75	$5\frac{13}{16}$	$6\frac{1}{16}$	$3\frac{1}{2}$	$3\frac{1}{16}$
4	$3\frac{1}{2}$	4	3.00	$6\frac{7}{16}$	$6\frac{15}{16}$	4	$3\frac{7}{16}$
5	$3\frac{1}{2}$	4	3.00	$6\frac{3}{4}$	$7\frac{1}{4}$	$4\frac{1}{2}$	$3\frac{3}{4}$
6	$3\frac{1}{2}$	4	3.00	$7\frac{1}{8}$	$7\frac{5}{8}$	5	$4\frac{1}{8}$
8	$4\frac{1}{8}$	$5\frac{1}{2}$	3.50	$8\frac{1}{2}$	$9\frac{7}{8}$	6	5
10	$4\frac{1}{8}$	$5\frac{1}{2}$	3.50	$9\frac{1}{4}$	$10\frac{5}{8}$	7	$5\frac{3}{4}$
12	5	7	4.25	$10\frac{13}{16}$	$12\frac{13}{16}$	8	$6\frac{9}{16}$
15	5	7	4.25	$11\frac{15}{16}$	$13\frac{15}{16}$	$9\frac{1}{2}$	$7\frac{11}{16}$
			$\frac{1}{6}$-Bend Elbows				
2	$2\frac{3}{4}$	3	2.50	$4\frac{1}{2}$	$4\frac{3}{4}$	3	2
3	$3\frac{1}{4}$	$3\frac{1}{2}$	2.75	$5\frac{1}{2}$	$5\frac{1}{2}$	$3\frac{1}{2}$	$2\frac{1}{2}$
4	$3\frac{1}{2}$	4	3.00	$5\frac{13}{16}$	$6\frac{5}{16}$	4	$2\frac{13}{16}$
5	$3\frac{1}{2}$	4	3.00	$6\frac{1}{8}$	$6\frac{5}{8}$	$4\frac{1}{2}$	$3\frac{1}{8}$
6	$3\frac{1}{2}$	4	3.00	$6\frac{3}{8}$	$6\frac{7}{8}$	5	$3\frac{3}{8}$
8	$4\frac{1}{8}$	$5\frac{1}{2}$	3.50	$7\frac{5}{8}$	9	6	$4\frac{1}{8}$
10	$4\frac{1}{8}$	$5\frac{1}{2}$	3.50	$8\frac{3}{16}$	$9\frac{9}{16}$	7	$4\frac{11}{16}$
12	5	7	4.25	$9\frac{5}{8}$	$11\frac{5}{8}$	8	$5\frac{3}{8}$
15	5	7	4.25	$10\frac{1}{2}$	$12\frac{1}{2}$	$9\frac{1}{2}$	$6\frac{1}{4}$

[a]All dimensions in inches.

Acid-Resistant Hub and Spigot Drain Pipe

Figure 2-15 and Table 2-11 give the dimensions for acid-resistant drain pipe.

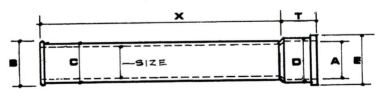

Figure 2-15 Acid-Resistant Drain Pipe—Metallic

TABLE 2-11 Hub and Spigot Acid-Resistant Drain Pipe[a]

Size	A	B	C	D	E	T	X (ft)	Wt (lb)
$1\frac{1}{2}$	$2\frac{3}{4}$	$2\frac{3}{8}$	2	$3\frac{3}{8}$	$3\frac{3}{4}$	$2\frac{1}{4}$	3	17
2	$3\frac{1}{4}$	$2\frac{7}{8}$	$2\frac{5}{8}$	$3\frac{13}{16}$	$4\frac{5}{16}$	$2\frac{1}{2}$	4	32
3	$4\frac{1}{4}$	$3\frac{7}{8}$	$3\frac{5}{8}$	$4\frac{15}{16}$	$5\frac{5}{16}$	$2\frac{3}{4}$	5	57
4	$5\frac{1}{4}$	$4\frac{7}{8}$	$4\frac{5}{8}$	$5\frac{15}{16}$	$6\frac{5}{16}$	3	5	73
5	$6\frac{1}{4}$	6	$5\frac{3}{4}$	7	$7\frac{3}{8}$	3	5	108
6	$7\frac{1}{4}$	7	$6\frac{5}{8}$	$8\frac{1}{8}$	$8\frac{1}{2}$	3	5	136

[a]All dimensions in inches except as noted.

QUARTER-BEND AND T-BRANCH PIPE FITTINGS

Finally, Fig. 2-16 and Table 2-12 show the dimensions for quarter-bend and T-branch pipe fittings.

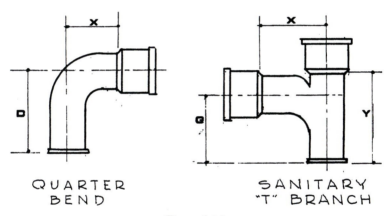

QUARTER
BEND

SANITARY
"T" BRANCH

Figure 2-16

TABLE 2-12 Quarter-Bend and T-Branch Fittings[a]

Size	D	K	(lb)	G	X	Y	Wt (lb)
$1\frac{1}{2}$	$5\frac{3}{4}$	$3\frac{1}{4}$	6	$6\frac{1}{4}$	$3\frac{1}{4}$	$8\frac{3}{8}$	9
2	6	$3\frac{1}{2}$	7	7	$3\frac{1}{2}$	9	12
3	7	4	12	$7\frac{1}{2}$	4	10	17
4	8	$4\frac{1}{2}$	17	8	5	11	25
5	$8\frac{1}{2}$	5	21	$8\frac{1}{2}$	5	12	31
6	9	$5\frac{1}{2}$	31	9	$5\frac{1}{2}$	13	47

[a]All dimensions in inches except as noted.

SELF-TESTING REVIEW QUESTIONS

1. A 1-in.-diameter pipe is actually only 1 in. in nominal size. What are its actual inside and outside diameters?
2. Name four pipe fittings.
3. The laying length of a single-hub cast iron soil pipe is how many feet?
4. What is the telescoping length of an 8-in.-diameter cast iron hub and spigot soil pipe?

3

VALVES; SPECIFIC GRAVITY

Valves are used to control the flow of fluids in a piping system. There are numerous types of valves designed to perform specific functions.

TYPES OF VALVES

Gate Valve

The *gate valve* is used primarily to halt the flow of fluids in a pipe. When the gate (Fig. 3-1) is lifted, a free, unobstructed flow passes through the valve. This type of valve is used mostly when only infrequent operation is needed. Some of the more important gate valves are the following:

Solid wedges
Split wedges
Double-disk parallel seat
Rising stem
Quick-opening gate

Globe Valve

The *globe valve* is used to throttle or control the quantity of flow. It is designed to cause a change of direction of the liquid flowing through

TABLE 3-2 Bronze Globe and Angle Valves

Pipe Size											
in.	$\frac{1}{8}$	$\frac{1}{4}$	$\frac{3}{8}$	$\frac{1}{2}$	$\frac{3}{4}$	1	$1\frac{1}{4}$	$1\frac{1}{2}$	2	$2\frac{1}{2}$	3
mm	3	6	10	15	20	25	32	40	50	65	80
Valve:											
a											
in.	$2\frac{3}{8}$	$2\frac{3}{8}$	$2\frac{3}{8}$	$2\frac{9}{16}$	$3\frac{1}{16}$	$3\frac{11}{16}$	$4\frac{5}{16}$	$4\frac{11}{16}$	$5\frac{5}{8}$	$6\frac{5}{8}$	$7\frac{3}{4}$
mm	60	60	60	65	78	94	110	119	143	168	197
b											
in.	$3\frac{3}{8}$	$3\frac{3}{8}$	$3\frac{3}{8}$	$3\frac{3}{8}$	$4\frac{3}{4}$	$5\frac{11}{16}$	$6\frac{1}{8}$	$7\frac{3}{16}$	$7\frac{15}{16}$	$10\frac{3}{16}$	$11\frac{3}{16}$
mm	86	86	86	86	121	145	156	183	202	259	284
c											
in.	$2\frac{3}{8}$	$2\frac{3}{8}$	$2\frac{3}{8}$	$2\frac{3}{8}$	$2\frac{3}{4}$	$2\frac{3}{4}$	3	$3\frac{11}{16}$	$4\frac{1}{32}$	5	6
mm	60	60	60	60	70	70	76	94	102	127	152
d											
in.	—	$1\frac{3}{16}$	$1\frac{3}{16}$	$1\frac{5}{16}$	$1\frac{9}{16}$	$1\frac{7}{8}$	$2\frac{3}{16}$	$2\frac{3}{8}$	$2\frac{13}{16}$	$3\frac{3}{16}$	$3\frac{7}{8}$
mm	—	30	30	33	40	48	56	60	71	81	98

Source: The Walworth Company.

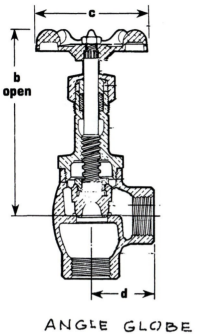
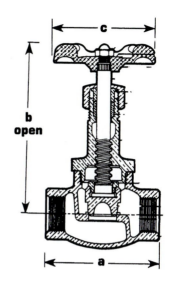

ANGLE GLOBE   GLOBE VALVE

Figure 3-2

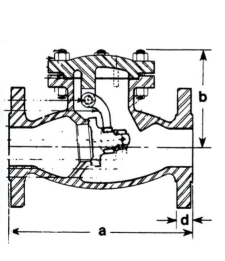
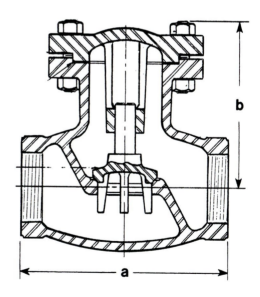

SWING CHECK VALVE   LIFT CHECK VALVE

Figure 3-3

TABLE 3-3 Swing Check Valves

Pipe size												
in.	$\frac{1}{2}$	$\frac{3}{4}$	1	$1\frac{1}{2}$	2	$2\frac{1}{2}$	3	4	6	8	10	12
mm	15	20	25	40	50	65	80	100	150	200	250	300
Valve:												
a (2377)												
in.	6	7	$8\frac{1}{2}$	$9\frac{1}{2}$	$10\frac{1}{2}$	$11\frac{1}{2}$	$13\frac{1}{2}$	14	$17\frac{1}{2}$	21	$24\frac{1}{2}$	28
mm	152	178	214	241	267	292	317	356	444	533	622	711
b (2377)												
in.	$4\frac{3}{4}$	$5\frac{1}{4}$	$5\frac{1}{2}$	5	$5\frac{1}{2}$	6	$6\frac{3}{4}$	8	$9\frac{1}{2}$	$12\frac{1}{4}$	14	$16\frac{1}{2}$
mm	121	133	140	127	140	152	171	203	241	311	356	419

Source: The Walworth Company.

TABLE 3-4 Lift Check Valves

Pipe Size					
in.	$\frac{1}{2}$	$\frac{3}{4}$	1	$1\frac{1}{2}$	2
mm	15	20	25	40	50
Valve:					
a(2550-A)					
in.	$3\frac{1}{4}$	$4\frac{1}{4}$	5	$6\frac{1}{2}$	$7\frac{1}{2}$
mm	95	108	127	165	191
b					
in.	$3\frac{3}{4}$	$3\frac{3}{4}$	$4\frac{5}{8}$	$5\frac{1}{2}$	$5\frac{7}{8}$
mm	95	95	118	140	149

Source: The Walworth Company.

adjusted to relieve pressure at a given point. The relief valve (Fig. 3-4) is often called a *safety valve*, the distinction being that safety valves are usually used for steam or other gases, and relief valves are used for liquids.

VALVE END CONNECTIONS

The *threaded-end* valve represents a common type of valve connection. Threaded connection between pipe and valves are found in brass, iron,

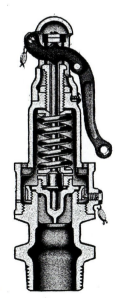

Figure 3-4 Relief Valve

Threaded Ends   Solder Ends   Figure 3-5

steel, and many other alloy piping materials. Threaded ends are used for ordinary pressures, but their use is usually limited to the smaller pipe size.

Solder-end joints for valves are used with copper tubing for plumbing and heating lines and for many low-pressure industrial lines (Fig. 3-5).

Welded ends on valves are available in two types: butt-welded and socket-welded ends, the socket-welded ends usually being limited to the smaller sizes. Welded-end valves are obtainable only in steel and are used for higher-pressure and higher-temperature service and on lines not requiring frequent dismantling.

FERROUS VALVES

Figure 3-6 and Table 3-5 show the dimensions of ferrous valves.

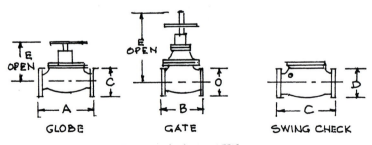

Figure 3-6 Ferrous Valves

TABLE 3-5 Dimensions of Ferrous Valves[a]

150 lb

Size	A	B	C	D	E	F
2	8	7	8	6	$13\frac{3}{4}$	$16\frac{1}{4}$
$2\frac{1}{2}$	$8\frac{1}{2}$	$7\frac{1}{2}$	$8\frac{1}{2}$	7	$14\frac{1}{2}$	$17\frac{1}{2}$
3	$9\frac{1}{2}$	8	$9\frac{1}{2}$	$7\frac{1}{2}$	$16\frac{1}{2}$	21
4	$11\frac{1}{2}$	9	$11\frac{1}{2}$	9	$19\frac{3}{4}$	26
5	14	10	13	10	23	31
6	16	$10\frac{1}{2}$	14	11	$24\frac{1}{2}$	$34\frac{1}{2}$
8	$19\frac{1}{2}$	$11\frac{1}{2}$	$19\frac{1}{2}$	$13\frac{1}{2}$	26	$42\frac{1}{2}$
10	—	13	$24\frac{1}{2}$	16	—	$51\frac{1}{2}$
12	—	14	—	19	—	$59\frac{3}{4}$
14	—	15	—	21	—	$70\frac{1}{4}$

300 lb

Size	A	B	C	D	E	F
2	$10\frac{1}{2}$	$8\frac{1}{2}$	$10\frac{1}{2}$	$6\frac{1}{2}$	$17\frac{3}{4}$	$18\frac{1}{4}$
$2\frac{1}{2}$	$11\frac{1}{2}$	$9\frac{1}{2}$	$11\frac{1}{2}$	$7\frac{1}{2}$	19	$21\frac{1}{4}$
3	$12\frac{1}{2}$	$11\frac{1}{8}$	$12\frac{1}{2}$	$8\frac{1}{4}$	$20\frac{1}{2}$	25
4	14	12	14	10	$24\frac{3}{4}$	31
5	$15\frac{3}{4}$	15	$15\frac{3}{4}$	11	$26\frac{1}{2}$	$34\frac{1}{2}$
6	$17\frac{1}{2}$	$15\frac{7}{8}$	$17\frac{1}{2}$	$12\frac{1}{2}$	$29\frac{3}{4}$	$38\frac{1}{2}$
8	22	$16\frac{1}{2}$	21	15	$35\frac{1}{2}$	48
10	$24\frac{1}{2}$	18	$24\frac{1}{2}$	$17\frac{1}{2}$	—	59
12	—	$19\frac{3}{4}$	28	$20\frac{1}{2}$	—	$66\frac{1}{4}$
14	—	$22\frac{1}{2}$	—	23	—	$74\frac{3}{4}$

400 lb

Size	A	B	C	D	E	F
2	$11\frac{1}{2}$	$11\frac{1}{2}$	$11\frac{1}{2}$	$6\frac{1}{2}$	21	$20\frac{1}{4}$
$2\frac{1}{2}$	13	13	13	$7\frac{1}{2}$	$23\frac{3}{8}$	$22\frac{1}{8}$
3	14	14	14	$8\frac{1}{4}$	$25\frac{5}{8}$	$24\frac{5}{8}$
4	16	16	16	10	$28\frac{7}{8}$	$29\frac{3}{8}$
5	18	18	18	11	—	$35\frac{1}{8}$
6	$19\frac{1}{2}$	$19\frac{1}{2}$	$19\frac{1}{2}$	$12\frac{1}{2}$	36	$38\frac{3}{4}$
8	$23\frac{1}{2}$	$23\frac{1}{2}$	$23\frac{1}{2}$	15	48	$48\frac{5}{8}$
10	$26\frac{1}{4}$	$26\frac{1}{4}$	$26\frac{1}{4}$	$17\frac{1}{2}$	$58\frac{1}{4}$	$58\frac{3}{4}$
12	—	30	30	$20\frac{1}{2}$	—	66
14	—	$33\frac{1}{2}$	—	23	—	—

600 lb

Size	A	B	C	D	E	F
2	$11\frac{1}{2}$	$11\frac{1}{2}$	$11\frac{1}{2}$	$6\frac{1}{2}$	19	$18\frac{1}{4}$
$2\frac{1}{2}$	13	13	13	$7\frac{1}{2}$	$21\frac{1}{4}$	$22\frac{1}{4}$
3	14	14	14	$8\frac{1}{4}$	$23\frac{1}{2}$	$25\frac{3}{4}$
4	17	17	17	$10\frac{3}{4}$	$27\frac{1}{2}$	32
5	20	20	20	13	$30\frac{3}{8}$	$36\frac{3}{4}$
6	22	22	22	14	35	$42\frac{3}{4}$
8	26	26	26	$16\frac{1}{2}$	$45\frac{3}{8}$	$52\frac{1}{4}$
10	31	31	31	20	54	$62\frac{1}{4}$
12	—	33	33	22	—	70
14	—	—	—	$23\frac{3}{4}$	—	$77\frac{1}{4}$

[a] All dimensions in inches.

SPECIFIC GRAVITY

Specific gravity is the ratio of the weight or mass of a given volume of a substance to that of an equal volume of another substance—water for liquids and solids, air or hydrogas for gases, used as a standard. For liquids and solids, for example, we know that weight of water is 0.0361 lb per cubic inch. If an equal volume of a solid, say aluminum, which weighs 0.0975 lb per cubic inch, is divided by the weight of water per cubic inch, the specific gravity of the aluminum will be

$$\text{specific gravity} = \frac{0.0975}{0.0361} = 2.70$$

Tables 3-6 to 3-8 give the specific gravity of metals, gases, and liquids, respectively.

TABLE 3-6 Specific Gravity of Metals

Metal	Specific Gravity	Weight per cubic inch
Aluminum	2.7	0.098
Brass	8.4	0.296
Bronze	8.8	0.317
Copper	8.8	0.321
Iron, steel	7.8	0.282
Zinc	7.0	0.254

TABLE 3-7 Specific Gravity of Gases at 60°F

Acetylene	0.91
Ammonia	0.596
Butane	2.067
Butene	1.93
Carbon dioxide	1.53
Carbon monoxide	0.967
Chlorine	2.486
Dry Air	1.000
Ethane	1.05
Helium	0.138
Hydrogen	0.0696
Nitrogen	0.9718
Oxygen	1.1053

TABLE 3-8 Specific Gravity of Liquids at 68°F

Liquid	Specific Gravity
Water	1
Acetone	1.08
Alcohol, butyl	0.81
Aniline	1.02
Benzene	0.88
Brine (25% NaCl)	1.18
Butyl acetate	0.88
Calcium chloride, 25%	1.23
Chlorobenzene	1.12
Chromic acid, 10%	1.07
Chromic acid, 50%	1.50
Ethylene bromide	2.18
Ferric chloride, 20%	1.18
Ferric chloride, 46%	1.50
Hydrochloric acid, 37%	1.18
Hydrogen peroxide, 30%	1.11
Kerosene at 85°F	0.82
Nitric acid, 30%	1.18
Oil, lubricating SAE 10-20-30 at 115°F	0.94
Phenol	1.07
Phosphoric acid, 50%	1.34
Sulfuric acid, 50%	1.40
Urea	1.36
Zinc chloride, 50%	1.61

SELF-TESTING REVIEW QUESTIONS

1. What type of valve is used primarily to hold the flow of fluid in a pipe?
2. What valve is used to throttle or control the quantity of fluid flow?
3. Name four types of globe valves.
4. The valve that prevents the backflow of the fluid in a pipe is known by what name?
5. Solder-end joints for valves are used with what kind of piping?
6. What is the weight of water per cubic inch?
7. To find the specific gravity of a metal, by what must the metal be divided?
8. What is the specific gravity of copper?

4

PLASTIC PIPING

USES FOR PLASTIC PIPING

Plastic piping is used for industrial and residential plumbing, for municipal water treatment, for chemical and food processing, for natural gas distribution and supply, for shipboard installation, and for laboratory and industrial waste disposal.

CHARACTERISTICS OF PLASTIC PIPE

The reason for all the listed uses lies in the fact that plastic piping has outstanding resistance to nearly all acids, salt solutions, and other corrosive liquids. Plastic material does not corrode, rust, scale, or pit, inside or outside the pipe. It does not rot, and it resists growth of bacteria, algae, and fungi that could cause offensive odors or create serious sanitation problems.

Since most plastics are nonconductive, they are not subject to galvanic or electrolytic action, a major cause of failure when metal pipe is installed undergound.

Plastic pipe is strong and tough and weighs only one-half to one-sixth as much as metal pipe. This makes it easier to handle, join, and install.

Plastic pipe can be fabricated by solvent welding, fusion welding, threading, and flanging. Each has special advantages for specific plastic materials and particular jobs. The word "plastic" does not indicate a single material; there are a variety of plastic compounds designed for particular and special uses.

Plastic materials are generally classified in two basic groups: thermoplastics and thermosets. *Thermoplastics* can be re-formed repeatedly by applying heat, whereas *thermosets*, once they have been cured, have fixed shapes and cannot be melted down and shaped for reuse.

TYPES OF PLASTIC PIPE

PVC (Polyvinyl chloride), type 1, grade 1

This thermoplastic material is considered one of the most economical and versatile materials used for piping. Its applications are for water service, process piping (liquid and gases), and industrial and laboratory chemical waste drainage.

CPVC (chlorinated polyvinyl chloride), type IV, grade 1, meeting the specifications of ASTM D-1784

This material has high impact strength, is tough, and can be used at temperatures up to 180°F. It is also used for carrying drinking water, irrigation, and in drain, waste, and vent piping. It can be joined by threading or by solvent welding.

FEP (fluorinated ethylene propylene)

This product requires that steel pipe and fittings be lined with FEP plastic intended to be used for conveying acids, gases, solvents, and other corrosive materials. The pipes and fittings treated with FEP linings are of the following diameters (in inches):

$$\tfrac{1}{2}, \ \tfrac{3}{4}, \ 1, \ 1\tfrac{1}{2}, \ 2, \ 2\tfrac{1}{2}, \ 3, \ 4, \ 5, \ 6, \ 8, \ 10, \ 12$$

This standard product covers pipe and fittings in two series: (1) based on a rated working pressure of 150 psi and (2) based on a rated working pressure of 300 psi.

The FEP linings in the steel pipe have a minimum wall thickness of 0.050 in., and the planed gasket faces are not less than 0.040 in. in thickness.

Polyethylene

This material has good chemical resistance qualities but is relatively low in mechanical strength. It is satisfactory when used at temperatures below 120°F. There are two types of this pipe, I and II, of low and medium density, which are used in chemical laboratory drainage lines, for drinking water pipe, and for piping used for irrigation.

Polypropylene

This is the lightest thermoplastic piping material, but has higher strength and better general chemical resistance than polyethylene, and may be used at temperatures up to 180°F. Polypropylene is an excellent material for laboratory and industrial drainage piping where acids and solvents are involved. This piping is also used in the petroleum industry.

PVDF (polyvinylidene fluoride)

This is a fluorocarbon material, which is strong, tough, and abrasive resistant. It resists distortions and retains its strength up to 280°F. It is resistant to most acids and organic solvents and is therefore well suited for carrying wet or dry chlorine. No other solid thermoplastic piping components can approach the combination of strength, chemical resistance, and working temperatures of PVDF. This piping material can be joined by the thermoseal fusion process, threading, or flanging.

PLASTIC PIPE SUPPORT SPACING

Tables 4-7 through 4-11 give the distances for which pipe carrying water (specific gravity 1.00) must be supported, for the given diameters and temperatures for both schedule 40 and schedule 80 pipe systems.
When heavier fluids are carried in the pipe, the support spacing should be multiplied by the following correction factors:

Specific Gravity	1.0	1.1	1.2	1.4	1.6	2.0	2.5
Correction Factor	1.0	0.98	0.96	0.93	0.90	0.85	0.80

These data are for uninsulated lines. For insulated lines the spans in the tables are to be reduced to 70% of the given values. Continuous support is required for spans of less than 2 ft.

TABLE 4-1 Weight of Pipe: Schedule 80[a]

Figure 4-1

Nominal Pipe Size	PVC Type 1 Pounds per:		CPVC Pounds per:		Polypropylene Pounds per:		PVDF Pounds per:		Outside Diameter (in.)	Inside Diameter (in.)	Wall Thickness (in.)
	1 ft	20 ft	1 ft	20 ft	1 ft	20 ft	1 ft	20 ft			
$\frac{1}{4}$	0.10	2.0	0.12	2.4	—	—	—	—	0.540	0.302	0.119
$\frac{1}{2}$	0.21	4.2	0.24	4.8	0.14	2.8	0.24	4.8	0.840	0.546	0.147
$\frac{3}{4}$	0.28	5.6	0.33	6.6	0.19	3.8	0.33	6.6	1.050	0.742	0.154
1	0.40	8.0	0.49	9.8	0.27	5.4	0.49	5.8	1.315	0.957	0.179
$1\frac{1}{4}$	0.57	11.4	0.67	13.4	0.38	7.6	—	—	1.660	1.278	0.191
$1\frac{1}{2}$	0.69	13.8	0.81	16.2	0.45	9.0	0.81	1.62	1.990	1.500	0.200
2	0.95	19.0	1.09	21.8	0.62	12.4	1.13	2.36	2.375	1.939	0.218
$2\frac{1}{2}$	1.45	29.0	1.65	33.0	—	—	—	—	2.875	2.323	0.276
3	1.94	38.8	2.21	44.2	1.27	25.4	—	—	3.500	2.900	0.300
4	2.83	76.6	3.23	64.6	1.85	37.0	—	—	4.500	3.826	0.337
6	5.41	108.2	6.17	123.4	3.60	72.0	—	—	6.625	5.761	0.432
8	8.22	164.4	9.06	181.2	—	—	—	—	8.625	7.625	0.500
10	12.28	245.6	—	—	—	—	—	—	10.750	9.564	0.593
12	17.10	342.0	—	—	—	—	—	—	12.750	11.376	0.687

[a]Schedule number $= 1000 \times \dfrac{P(\text{internal pressure), psi}}{S(\text{allowable fiber stress), psi}}$

TABLE 4-2 Weight of Pipe: Schedule 40[a]

Nominal Pipe Size	PVC Type 1		CPVC		Outside Diameter (in.)	Inside Diameter (in.)	Wall Thickness (in.)
	Pounds per:		Pounds per:				
	1 ft	20 ft	1 ft	20 ft			
$\frac{1}{2}$	0.16	3.2	0.19	3.8	0.840	0.622	0.109
$\frac{3}{4}$	0.22	4.4	0.25	5.0	1.050	0.824	0.113
1	0.32	6.4	0.38	7.6	1.315	1.049	0.133
$1\frac{1}{4}$	0.43	8.6	0.51	10.2	1.660	1.380	0.140
$1\frac{1}{2}$	0.52	10.4	0.61	12.2	1.900	1.610	0.145
2	0.70	14.0	0.82	16.4	2.375	2.067	0.154
$2\frac{1}{2}$	1.10	22.0	1.29	25.8	2.875	2.469	0.203
3	1.44	28.8	1.69	33.8	3.500	3.068	0.216
4	2.05	41.0	2.33	46.6	4.500	4.026	0.237
6	3.61	72.2	4.10	82.0	6.625	6.065	0.280
8	5.45	109.0	—	—	8.625	7.981	0.322
10	7.91	118.2	—	—	10.750	10.020	0.365
12	10.35	207.0	—	—	12.750	11.938	0.406

[a]Schedule number $= 1000 \times \dfrac{P(\text{internal pressure}), \text{psi}}{S(\text{allowable fiber stress}), \text{psi}}$

Pipe supports are determined by pipe size, schedule, temperature, loading, and type of material. For thermoplastic piping, point supports must not be used, but a wider bearing surface is desirable. Supports must not restrain movements due to expansion and contraction. Where heavier piping loads occur, such as at valves, extra support should be provided. Some pipe support hangers are shown in Figs. 4-11 and 4-12.

INSULATION ON PIPE

Insulation on pipe is required when temperature becomes a problem. The thickness of insulation around a pipe varies according to the need and the size of the pipe. Since insulation is soft, it is important that metal supports called *saddles* be installed at the points of support.

A typical section through an insulated pipe and saddle is shown in Fig. 4-13. The saddle is spot-welded to the pipe as illustrated. In the installation, dimensions are taken from the center of the pipe to the bottom of the saddle.

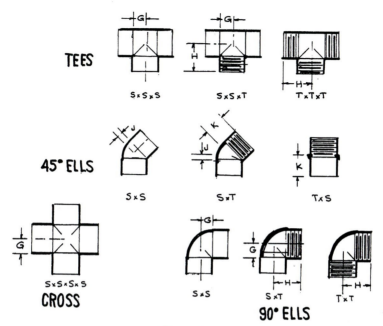

TEES — S × S × S, S × S × T, T × T × T

45° ELLS — S × S, S × T, T × S

CROSS — S × S × S × S

90° ELLS — S × S, S × T, T × T

Figure 4-2

TABLE 4-3 Standard-Weight Pressure Fittings for I.P.S. Schedule 40 Pipe[a,b]

Size	H	G	K	J
$\frac{1}{4}$	$1\frac{1}{8}$	$\frac{3}{8}$	1	$\frac{1}{4}$
$\frac{1}{2}$	$1\frac{1}{4}$	$\frac{1}{2}$	1	$\frac{1}{4}$
$\frac{3}{4}$	$1\frac{9}{16}$	$1\frac{5}{16}$	$1\frac{5}{16}$	$\frac{5}{16}$
1	$1\frac{27}{32}$	$\frac{23}{32}$	$1\frac{7}{16}$	$\frac{5}{16}$
$1\frac{1}{4}$	$2\frac{5}{32}$	$\frac{29}{32}$	$1\frac{11}{16}$	$\frac{3}{8}$
$1\frac{1}{2}$	$2\frac{11}{32}$	$1\frac{1}{32}$	$1\frac{13}{16}$	$\frac{7}{16}$
2	$2\frac{5}{8}$	$1\frac{1}{4}$	$1\frac{21}{32}$	$\frac{5}{8}$
$2\frac{1}{2}$	$3\frac{9}{16}$	$1\frac{9}{16}$	3	$\frac{3}{4}$
3	$3\frac{7}{8}$	$1\frac{7}{8}$	3	$\frac{13}{16}$
$3\frac{1}{2}$	$4\frac{1}{4}$	$2\frac{1}{4}$	$3\frac{15}{16}$	$\frac{15}{16}$
4	$4\frac{3}{8}$	$2\frac{3}{8}$	3	1
5	$5\frac{15}{16}$	$2\frac{15}{16}$	$4\frac{3}{8}$	$1\frac{3}{8}$
6	7	$3\frac{1}{2}$	$5\frac{1}{4}$	$1\frac{3}{4}$

[a]Schedule number =

$$1000 \times \frac{P(\text{internal pressure), psi}}{S(\text{allowable fiber stress), psi.}}$$

[b]All dimensions in inches.

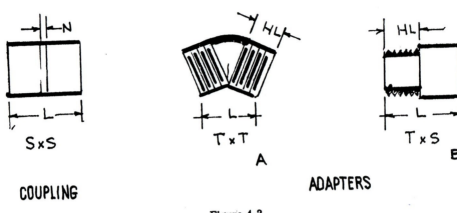

Figure 4-3

TABLE 4-4 Standard-Weight Pressure Fittings for I.P.S. Schedule 40 Pipe[a,b]

Size	G	Coupling		Adapter A		Adapter B	
		L	N	HL	L	HL	L
1/4	3/8	1 19/32	3/32	21/32	1 1/4	25/32	1 17/32
1/2	1/2	1 19/32	3/32	27/32	1 19/32	29/32	1 31/32
3/4	1 5/16	2 3/32	3/32	7/8	1 7/8	31/32	1 31/32
1	23/32	2 11/32	3/32	1 3/32	2 7/32	1 3/16	2 5/16
1 1/4	29/32	2 19/32	3/32	1 3/32	2 11/32	1 7/32	2 15/32
1 1/2	1 1/32	2 23/32	3/32	1 1/8	2 7/16	1 1/4	2 9/16
2	1 1/4	2 27/32	3/32	1 5/32	2 17/32	1 9/32	2 21/32
2 1/2	1 9/16	4 3/16	3/16	1 1/4	3 3/4	1 17/32	3 21/32
3	1 7/8	5 3/16	3/16	1 13/16	3 3/16	1 29/64	3 29/32
3 1/2	2 1/4	5 1/4	1/4	1 15/16	3 15/16	2 1/32	4 1/32
4	2 3/8	5 1/4	1/4	1 31/32	3 11/32	2 3/64	4 3/64
5	2 15/16	6 1/4	1/4	2 3/32	5 1/32	2 7/32	5 7/32
6	3 1/2	7 1/4	1/4	2 5/32	5 21/32	2 3/16	5 11/16

[a] Schedule number $= 1000 \times \dfrac{P(\text{internal pressure, psi})}{S(\text{allowable fiber stress, psi})}$

[b] All dimensions in inches.

TABLE 4-5 Schedule 40 Fittings[a,b]

(a) 90° Elbows, 45° Elbows, and Tees

Nominal Pipe Size	Center to End A	Center to Socket X	Weight (lb)
90° Elbows			
$\frac{1}{2}$	$1\frac{3}{8}$	$\frac{1}{2}$	0.08
$\frac{3}{4}$	$1\frac{3}{4}$	$\frac{3}{4}$	0.12
1	$1\frac{7}{8}$	$\frac{3}{4}$	0.19
$1\frac{1}{4}$	$2\frac{3}{16}$	$\frac{15}{16}$	0.28
$1\frac{1}{2}$	$2\frac{7}{16}$	$1\frac{1}{16}$	0.33
2	$2\frac{13}{16}$	$1\frac{5}{16}$	0.37
$2\frac{1}{2}$	$3\frac{5}{16}$	$1\frac{9}{16}$	0.53
3	$3\frac{3}{4}$	$1\frac{7}{8}$	0.81
4	$4\frac{5}{8}$	$2\frac{3}{8}$	1.87
45° Elbows			
$\frac{1}{2}$	$1\frac{1}{8}$	$\frac{3}{4}$	0.07
$\frac{3}{4}$	$1\frac{5}{16}$	$\frac{5}{16}$	0.09
1	$1\frac{1}{2}$	$\frac{3}{8}$	0.16
$1\frac{1}{4}$	$1\frac{11}{16}$	$\frac{7}{16}$	0.25
$1\frac{1}{2}$	$1\frac{7}{8}$	$\frac{1}{2}$	0.30
2	$2\frac{1}{8}$	$\frac{5}{8}$	0.44
$2\frac{1}{2}$	$2\frac{7}{16}$	$\frac{11}{16}$	0.50
3	$2\frac{11}{16}$	$\frac{13}{16}$	0.81
4	$3\frac{5}{16}$	$1\frac{1}{16}$	1.43
Tees			
$\frac{1}{2}$	$1\frac{3}{8}$	$\frac{1}{2}$	0.11
$\frac{3}{4}$	$1\frac{3}{4}$	$\frac{3}{4}$	0.17
1	$1\frac{7}{8}$	$\frac{3}{4}$	0.26
$1\frac{1}{4}$	$2\frac{3}{16}$	$\frac{15}{16}$	0.38
$1\frac{1}{2}$	$2\frac{7}{16}$	$\frac{11}{16}$	0.50
2	$2\frac{13}{16}$	$1\frac{5}{16}$	0.72
$2\frac{1}{2}$	$3\frac{5}{16}$	$1\frac{9}{16}$	1.00
3	$3\frac{3}{4}$	$1\frac{7}{8}$	1.37
4	$4\frac{5}{8}$	$2\frac{3}{8}$	2.50

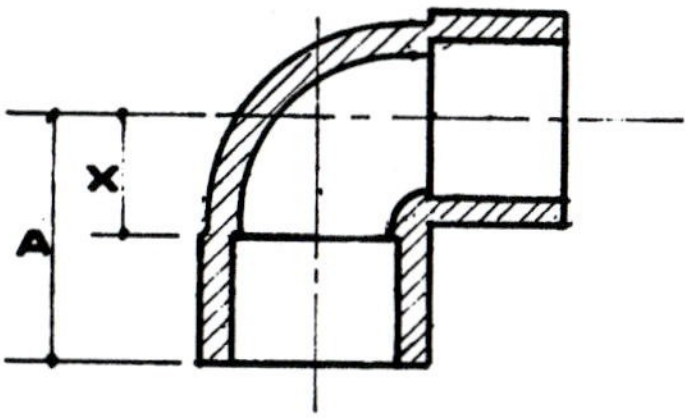

Figure 4-4 90° Elbow

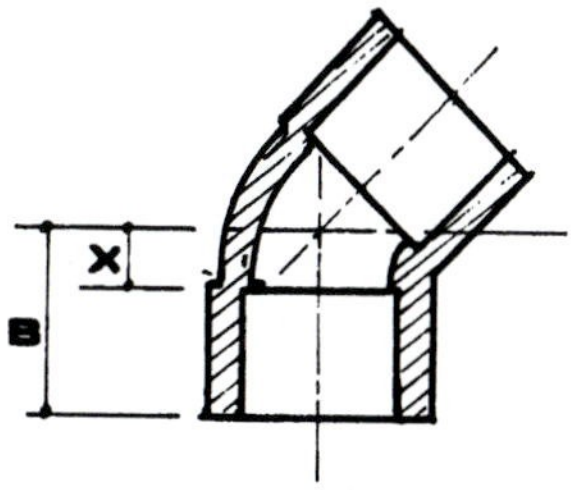

Figure 4-5 45° Elbow

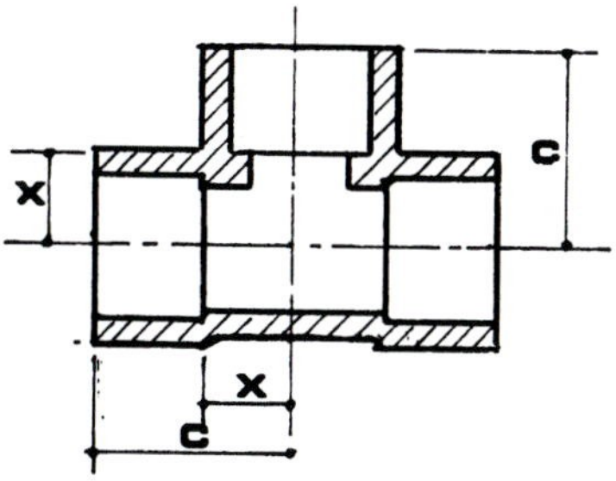

Figure 4-6 Tee

TABLE 4-5 (Continued)

(b) 90° Street Ell

Nominal Pipe Size	A	B	Weight (lb)	Standard Package
$\frac{1}{2}$	$1\frac{3}{8}$	$1\frac{5}{8}$	0.06	25
$\frac{3}{4}$	$1\frac{11}{16}$	$1\frac{7}{8}$	0.09	25
1	$1\frac{7}{8}$	$2\frac{1}{8}$	0.17	25
$1\frac{1}{4}$	$2\frac{3}{16}$	$2\frac{7}{16}$	0.25	25
$1\frac{1}{2}$	$2\frac{7}{8}$	$2\frac{11}{16}$	0.35	25
2	$2\frac{3}{4}$	$3\frac{1}{4}$	0.58	25

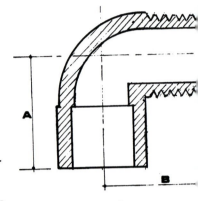

Figure 4-7 90° Street Ell

(c) Caps and Couplings

Nominal Pipe Size	End to End D	Socket to End or X	Weight (lb)
Caps			
$\frac{1}{2}$	$1\frac{1}{4}$	$\frac{3}{8}$	0.04
$\frac{3}{4}$	$1\frac{3}{8}$	$\frac{3}{8}$	0.06
1	$1\frac{1}{2}$	$\frac{3}{8}$	0.10
$1\frac{1}{4}$	$1\frac{1}{16}$	$\frac{7}{16}$	0.16
$1\frac{1}{2}$	$1\frac{13}{16}$	$\frac{7}{16}$	0.22
2	$1\frac{15}{16}$	$\frac{7}{16}$	0.31
$2\frac{1}{2}$	3	$1\frac{1}{4}$	0.45
3	$3\frac{1}{4}$	$1\frac{3}{8}$	0.52
4	$3\frac{7}{8}$	$1\frac{5}{8}$	0.94
Couplings			
$\frac{1}{2}$	2	$\frac{1}{4}$	0.06
$\frac{3}{4}$	$2\frac{1}{4}$	$\frac{1}{4}$	0.09
1	$2\frac{1}{2}$	$\frac{1}{4}$	0.14
$1\frac{1}{4}$	$2\frac{3}{4}$	$\frac{1}{4}$	0.24
$1\frac{1}{2}$	3	$\frac{1}{4}$	0.25
2	$3\frac{1}{4}$	$\frac{1}{4}$	0.44
$2\frac{1}{2}$	$3\frac{3}{4}$	$\frac{1}{4}$	0.56
3	4	$\frac{1}{4}$	0.63
4	$4\frac{3}{4}$	$\frac{1}{4}$	1.16

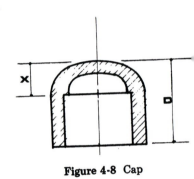

Figure 4-8 Cap

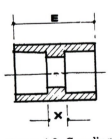

Figure 4-9 Coupling

[a] All dimensions in inches except as noted.
[b] All pipe is made of PVC.

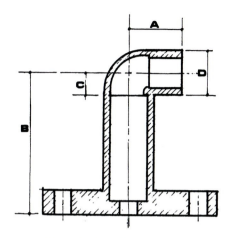

Figure 4-10 Schedule 80 Fitting

TABLE 4-6 Schedule 80 Fittings: 90° Elbow[a,b]

Nominal Pipe Size	O.D. D	Threaded Diameter A	Socket Diameter A	Socket Diameter C	Flanged Diameter B
PVC					
$\frac{1}{4}$	$\frac{7}{8}$	$\frac{15}{16}$	$\frac{15}{16}$	$\frac{5}{16}$	—
$\frac{1}{2}$	$1\frac{5}{16}$	$1\frac{3}{8}$	$1\frac{3}{8}$	$\frac{1}{2}$	$2\frac{7}{16}$
$\frac{3}{4}$	$1\frac{1}{2}$	$1\frac{3}{4}$	$1\frac{3}{4}$	$\frac{3}{4}$	3
1	$1\frac{7}{8}$	$1\frac{7}{8}$	$1\frac{7}{8}$	$\frac{3}{4}$	3
$1\frac{1}{4}$	$2\frac{1}{4}$	$2\frac{3}{16}$	$2\frac{3}{16}$	$\frac{15}{16}$	$3\frac{5}{8}$
$1\frac{1}{2}$	$2\frac{1}{2}$	$2\frac{7}{16}$	$2\frac{7}{16}$	$1\frac{1}{16}$	4
2	3	$2\frac{13}{16}$	$2\frac{13}{16}$	$1\frac{5}{16}$	$4\frac{1}{2}$
$2\frac{1}{2}$	$3\frac{5}{8}$	$3\frac{5}{16}$	$3\frac{5}{16}$	$1\frac{9}{16}$	$5\frac{5}{16}$
3	$4\frac{3}{8}$	$3\frac{3}{4}$	$3\frac{3}{4}$	$1\frac{7}{8}$	$5\frac{7}{8}$
4	$5\frac{1}{2}$	$4\frac{5}{8}$	$4\frac{5}{8}$	$2\frac{3}{8}$	$7\frac{3}{16}$
CPVC					
$\frac{1}{4}$	$\frac{7}{8}$	$\frac{15}{16}$	$\frac{15}{16}$	$\frac{5}{16}$	—
$\frac{1}{2}$	$1\frac{5}{16}$	$1\frac{3}{8}$	$1\frac{3}{8}$	$\frac{1}{2}$	$2\frac{7}{16}$
$\frac{3}{4}$	$1\frac{1}{2}$	$1\frac{3}{4}$	$1\frac{3}{4}$	$\frac{3}{4}$	3
1	$1\frac{7}{8}$	$1\frac{7}{8}$	$1\frac{7}{8}$	$\frac{3}{4}$	$3\frac{3}{16}$
$1\frac{1}{4}$	$2\frac{1}{4}$	$2\frac{3}{16}$	$2\frac{3}{16}$	$\frac{15}{16}$	$3\frac{5}{8}$

TABLE 4-6 (Continued)

| Nominal Pipe Size | O.D. D | Threaded Diameter A | Socket | | Flanged Diameter B |
			Diameter A	Diameter C	
CPVC					
$1\frac{1}{2}$	$2\frac{1}{2}$	$2\frac{7}{16}$	$2\frac{7}{16}$	$1\frac{1}{16}$	4
2	3	$2\frac{13}{16}$	$2\frac{13}{16}$	$1\frac{5}{16}$	$4\frac{1}{2}$
$2\frac{1}{2}$	$3\frac{5}{8}$	3	$3\frac{5}{16}$	$1\frac{9}{16}$	$5\frac{7}{8}$
3	$4\frac{3}{8}$	$3\frac{3}{4}$	$3\frac{3}{4}$	$1\frac{7}{8}$	$7\frac{3}{16}$
4	$5\frac{1}{2}$	$4\frac{5}{8}$	$4\frac{5}{8}$	$2\frac{3}{8}$	$9\frac{13}{16}$
Polypropylene					
$\frac{1}{4}$	—	—	—	—	—
$\frac{1}{2}$	$1\frac{5}{16}$	$1\frac{3}{8}$	$1\frac{3}{8}$	$\frac{1}{2}$	$2\frac{7}{16}$
$\frac{3}{4}$	$1\frac{1}{2}$	$1\frac{3}{4}$	$1\frac{3}{4}$	$\frac{3}{4}$	3
1	$1\frac{7}{8}$	$1\frac{7}{8}$	$1\frac{7}{8}$	$\frac{3}{4}$	$3\frac{3}{16}$
$1\frac{1}{4}$	$2\frac{1}{4}$	$2\frac{3}{16}$	$2\frac{3}{16}$	$\frac{15}{16}$	$3\frac{5}{8}$
$1\frac{1}{2}$	$2\frac{1}{2}$	$2\frac{7}{16}$	$2\frac{7}{16}$	$1\frac{1}{16}$	4
2	3	$2\frac{13}{16}$	$2\frac{13}{16}$	$1\frac{5}{16}$	$4\frac{1}{2}$
$2\frac{1}{2}$	—	—	—	—	—
3	$4\frac{3}{8}$	$3\frac{3}{4}$	$3\frac{3}{4}$	$1\frac{7}{8}$	$5\frac{7}{8}$
4	$5\frac{1}{2}$	$4\frac{5}{8}$	$4\frac{5}{8}$	$2\frac{3}{8}$	$7\frac{3}{16}$
PVDF					
$\frac{1}{4}$	—	—	—	—	
$\frac{1}{2}$	$1\frac{5}{16}$	$1\frac{3}{8}$	$1\frac{3}{8}$	$\frac{1}{2}$	
$\frac{3}{4}$	$1\frac{1}{2}$	$1\frac{11}{16}$	$1\frac{11}{16}$	$\frac{3}{4}$	
1	$1\frac{7}{8}$	$1\frac{7}{8}$	$1\frac{7}{8}$	$\frac{3}{4}$	
$1\frac{1}{4}$	$2\frac{1}{4}$	—	—	—	
$1\frac{1}{2}$	$2\frac{1}{2}$	$2\frac{1}{8}$	$2\frac{3}{8}$	$1\frac{1}{16}$	
2	3	$2\frac{3}{4}$	$2\frac{3}{4}$	$1\frac{5}{16}$	
$2\frac{1}{2}$	—	—	—	—	
3	$4\frac{5}{8}$	—	—	—	
4	$5\frac{1}{2}$	—	—	—	

[a] Schedule number $= 1000 \times \dfrac{P(\text{internal pressure}), \text{psi}}{S(\text{allowable fiber stress}), \text{psi}}$

[b] All dimensions in inches.

TABLE 4-7 Pipe Support Spacing for PVC Schedule 40[a,b]

Pipe Diameter (in)	Temperature (°F)				
	60	80	100	120	140
$\frac{1}{4}$	3.75	3.50	3.0	2.5	2.0
$\frac{1}{2}$	4.25	4.0	3.5	3.0	2.5
$\frac{3}{4}$	4.5	4.25	4.0	3.5	3.0
1	5.0	4.75	4.5	3.75	3.25
$1\frac{1}{4}$	5.25	5.0	4.75	4.0	3.50
$1\frac{1}{2}$	5.5	5.25	5.0	4.25	3.75
2	6.0	5.5	5.0	4.50	4.00
$2\frac{1}{2}$	6.75	6.25	5.75	4.75	4.25
3	7.25	6.75	6.25	5.25	4.50
4	7.75	7.50	6.75	6.00	4.75
6	8.75	8.50	7.75	6.50	5.25
8	9.75	9.25	8.50	7.75	6.00
10	10.25	9.75	9.00	8.00	6.75
12	11.00	10.25	9.75	8.25	7.25

[a]Schedule number = 1000 $\times$ $\dfrac{P(\text{internal pressure}), \text{psi}}{S(\text{allowable fiber stress}), \text{psi}}$

[b]All dimensions in feet except as noted.

TABLE 4-8 Pipe Support Spacing for PVC Schedule 80[a,b]

Pipe Diameter (in.)	Temperature (°F)				
	60	80	100	120	140
$\frac{1}{4}$	4.25	4.00	3.75	3.00	2.75
$\frac{1}{2}$	4.50	4.25	4.00	3.75	3.00
$\frac{3}{4}$	4.75	4.50	4.25	4.00	3.50
1	5.00	4.75	4.50	4.25	3.75
$1\frac{1}{4}$	6.00	5.00	4.75	4.50	4.25
$1\frac{1}{2}$	6.50	5.50	5.25	5.00	4.75
2	6.75	5.75	5.50	5.25	5.00
$2\frac{1}{2}$	7.25	6.75	5.75	5.50	5.25
3	7.75	7.50	7.00	6.25	5.50
4	9.00	8.75	7.25	6.50	5.75
6	9.75	9.50	8.50	7.75	6.50
8	11.00	10.25	9.75	8.75	7.00
10	11.50	10.50	10.25	9.50	7.75
12	12.50	12.25	11.50	10.25	8.75

[a]Schedule number = 1000 $\times$ $\dfrac{P(\text{internal pressure}), \text{psi}}{S(\text{allowable fiber stress}), \text{psi}}$

[b]All dimensions in feet except as noted.

TABLE 4-9 Pipe Support Spacing for CPVC Schedule 40[a,b]

Pipe Diameter (in.)	Temperature (°F)							
	60	80	100	120	140	160	180	200
$\frac{1}{4}$	3.875	3.75	3.50	3.25	2.75	2.50	2.125	1.75
$\frac{1}{2}$	4.50	4.25	4.00	3.75	3.25	2.75	2.50	2.00
$\frac{3}{4}$	5.00	4.75	4.50	4.25	3.75	3.25	2.75	2.25
1	5.50	5.00	4.75	4.50	4.00	3.75	3.50	2.50
$1\frac{1}{4}$	6.25	5.75	5.50	5.00	4.25	3.50	3.25	2.75
$1\frac{1}{2}$	7.25	6.25	5.75	5.25	4.50	3.75	3.50	2.87
2	7.00	6.50	6.25	5.50	5.25	4.50	3.75	3.00
$2\frac{1}{2}$	7.75	7.50	7.00	6.25	5.75	5.00	4.25	3.25
3	8.00	7.75	7.50	7.00	6.25	5.50	4.50	3.50
4	8.50	8.25	7.75	7.50	6.50	5.75	5.00	3.75
6	8.75	8.50	8.25	7.75	7.00	6.25	5.50	4.25
8	9.50	9.00	8.75	8.25	7.50	7.00	6.00	4.50

[a]Schedule number = $1000 \times \dfrac{P(\text{internal pressure), psi}}{S(\text{allowable fiber stress), psi}}$

[b]All dimensions in feet except as noted.

TABLE 4-10 Pipe Support Spacing for CPVC Schedule 80[a,b]

Pipe Diameter (in.)	Temperature (°F)							
	60	80	100	120	140	160	180	200
$\frac{1}{4}$	4.25	4.00	3.75	3.50	3.25	3.00	2.75	2.25
$\frac{1}{2}$	5.00	4.87	4.75	4.50	4.00	3.75	3.00	2.25
$\frac{3}{4}$	5.50	5.25	5.00	4.75	4.50	4.00	3.25	2.50
1	6.25	5.75	5.50	5.25	4.75	4.25	3.50	2.75
$1\frac{1}{4}$	6.50	6.25	6.00	5.50	5.00	4.50	3.75	3.00
$1\frac{1}{2}$	6.75	6.50	6.25	5.75	5.25	4.75	4.25	3.25
2	7.25	7.00	6.50	6.25	5.75	5.00	4.50	3.50
$2\frac{1}{2}$	8.25	8.00	7.75	7.25	6.50	5.75	4.75	3.75
3	9.00	8.75	8.25	7.75	7.00	6.25	5.00	4.00
4	10.00	9.50	8.75	8.25	7.25	6.50	5.75	4.50
6	10.25	10.00	9.25	8.75	8.00	7.25	6.25	4.75
8	10.50	10.25	10.00	9.25	8.75	7.75	6.75	5.50

[a]Schedule number = $1000 \times \dfrac{P(\text{internal pressure), psi}}{S(\text{allowable fiber stress), psi}}$

[b]All dimensions in feet except as noted.

Source: NIBCO Inc., Elkhart, IN 46515.

TABLE 4-11 Pipe Support Spacing for Polypropylene Schedule 80[a,b]

Pipe Diameter (in.)	Temperature (°F)						
	60	80	100	120	140	150	160
$\frac{1}{2}$	5.25	4.75	4.50	3.75	2.00	—	—
$\frac{3}{4}$	5.50	5.25	4.50	3.75	2.00	—	—
1	5.75	5.50	5.00	4.25	2.00	—	—
$1\frac{1}{4}$	6.25	5.75	5.25	4.50	2.25	—	—
$1\frac{1}{2}$	6.50	6.00	5.50	4.50	2.25	—	—
2	6.75	6.50	5.75	4.75	2.25	—	—
3	7.25	6.75	6.25	5.25	2.25	—	—
4	7.75	7.25	6.50	5.50	4.00	2.00	—
6	8.50	8.00	7.25	6.50	5.25	2.75	2.00

[a] Schedule number $= 1000 \times \dfrac{P(\text{internal pressure), psi}}{S(\text{allowable fiber stress), psi}}$

[b] All dimensions in feet except as noted.

Source: NIBCO Inc., Elkhart, IN 46515.

SPLIT PIPE RING

ADJUSTABLE SWIVEL RING

ADJUSTABLE WROUGHT PIPE RING

ADJUSTABLE SWIVEL SPLIT RING

Figure 4-11

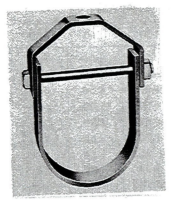

**ADJUSTABLE
WROUGHT
CLEVIS RING**

**PIPE HANGER
FLANGE**

**SWIVEL HANGER
FLANGE**

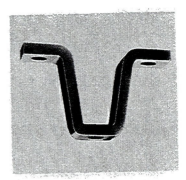

BEAM ATTACHMENT

Figure 4-12

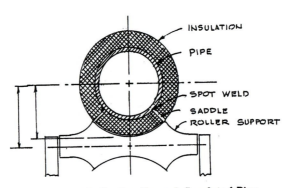

INSULATION

PIPE

SPOT WELD

SADDLE

ROLLER SUPPORT

Figure 4-13 Section through Insulated Pipe

PRESSURE LOSSES IN A PIPING SYSTEM

Friction in Pipe

Whenever a fluid flows through a piping system there is a head loss, or resistance to flow caused by the fluid velocity, the inside surface roughness of the pipe, and the total inside surface area of the pipe. Tables 4-12 and 4-13 give friction losses in feet, and gallons per minute passing through the pipe, for various pipe diameters.

Friction in Fittings and Valves

A common method of expressing the friction losses in pipe fittings and valves in relation to pipe is in equivalent pipe length. This is the length of pipe required to give the same friction loss as the same size fitting or valve. Tables 4-14 and 4-15 give the equivalent pipe length in feet for various sizes of a number of standard fittings and valves.

Example:

Suppose that we wanted to find the pressure loss through a 2-in. schedule 40 90° elbow, at 70 gal per minute.

Solution: From Table 4-14 we find the equivalent length of a 2-in. 90° elbow to be 5.5 ft of pipe. From Table 4-12 the friction head in feet, for 70 gal, of 5.5 ft of pipe would be

$$\frac{5.5}{100} \times 7.76 = 0.43 \text{ ft of head}$$

which is the loss through a 2-in. schedule 40 90° elbow. For a schedule 80 90° elbow, use Table 4-13.

$$\frac{5.5}{100} \times 10.80 = 0.59 \text{ ft of head}$$

which is the head loss through a 2-in. schedule 80 90° elbow.

BITUMINOUS FIBER DRAIN AND SEWER PIPE

Pipe diameters and lengths of this type of sewer pipe are shown in Fig. 4-14. A pipe diameter of

   2 in. comes 5 ft long
   3 in. comes 8 ft long

TABLE 4-12 GPM and Friction Loss for Thermoplastic Pipe: Schedule 40

Gallons Per Minute	Velocity (ft/sec)	Friction Head (ft)	Friction Loss (lb/sq in.)	Velocity (ft/sec)	Friction Head (ft)	Friction Loss (lb/sq in.)
	½-in. Pipe Diameter			1-in. Pipe Diameter		
1	1.13	2.08	0.90	—	—	—
2	2.26	4.16	1.80	0.77	0.55	0.24
5	5.64	23.44	10.15	1.93	1.72	0.75
7	7.90	43.06	18.64	2.72	3.17	1.37
10	11.28	82.02	35.51	3.86	6.02	2.61
15	4-in. Pipe Diameter			5.79	12.77	5.53
20	0.51	0.03	0.013	7.72	21.75	9.42
25	0.64	0.04	0.017	9.65	32.88	14.22
30	0.77	0.06	0.026	11.58	46.08	19.95
35	0.89	0.08	0.035	—	—	—
40	1.02	0.11	0.048	6-in. Pipe Diameter		
45	1.15	0.13	0.056	—	—	—
50	1.28	0.16	0.069	0.56	0.02	0.009
60	1.53	0.22	0.095	0.67	0.03	0.013
70	1.79	0.30	0.13	0.79	0.04	0.017
	1½-in. Pipe Diameter			2-in. Pipe Diameter		
1	—	—	—	—	—	—
2	0.33	0.07	0.03	—	—	—
5	0.81	0.22	0.09	0.49	0.066	0.029
7	1.13	0.38	0.17	0.69	0.11	0.048
10	1.62	0.72	0.31	0.98	0.21	0.091
15	2.42	1.53	0.66	1.46	0.45	0.19
20	3.23	2.61	1.13	1.95	0.76	0.33
25	4.04	3.95	1.71	2.44	1.15	0.50
30	4.85	5.53	2.39	2.93	1.62	0.70
35	5.66	7.36	3.19	3.41	2.15	0.93
40	6.47	9.43	4.08	3.90	2.75	1.19
45	7.27	11.73	5.08	4.39	3.43	1.49
50	8.08	14.25	6.17	4.88	4.16	1.80
60	9.70	19.96	8.65	5.85	5.84	2.53
70	—	—	—	6.83	7.76	3.36

[a]Schedule number = $1000 \times \dfrac{P(\text{internal pressure}),\ \text{psi}}{S(\text{allowable fiber stress}),\ \text{psi}}$

[b]All dimensions in feet except as noted.

Source: NIBCO Inc., Elkhart, IN 46515.

TABLE 4-13 GPM and Friction Loss for Thermoplastic Pipe:
Schedule 80[a,b]

Gallons per Minute	Velocity (ft/sec)	Friction Head (ft)	Friction Loss (lb/sq in.)	Velocity (ft/sec)	Friction Head (ft)	Friction Loss (lb/sq in.)
	$\frac{1}{2}$-in. Pipe Diameter			1-in. Pipe Diameter		
1	1.48	4.02	1.74	—	—	—
2	2.95	8.03	3.48	0.94	0.88	0.38
5	7.39	45.23	19.59	2.34	2.75	1.19
7	10.34	83.07	35.97	3.28	5.04	2.19
10	—	—	—	4.68	9.61	4.16
15	4-in. Pipe Diameter			7.01	20.36	8.82
20	0.57	0.04	0.017	9.35	34.68	15.02
25	0.72	0.06	0.026	11.69	52.43	22.70
30	0.86	0.08	0.035	14.03	73.48	31.82
35	1.00	0.11	0.048	—	—	—
40	1.15	0.14	0.061	6-in. Pipe Diameter		
45	1.29	0.17	0.074	—	—	—
50	1.43	0.21	0.091	0.63	0.03	0.013
60	1.72	0.30	0.13	0.75	0.04	0.017
70	2.01	0.39	0.17	0.88	0.05	0.022
	$1\frac{1}{2}$-in. Pipe Diameter			2-in. Pipe Diameter		
1	—	—	—	—	—	—
2	0.38	0.10	0.04	—	—	—
5	0.94	0.30	0.13	0.56	0.10	0.04
7	1.32	0.55	0.24	0.78	0.15	0.07
10	1.88	1.04	0.45	1.12	0.29	0.13
15	2.81	2.20	0.95	1.68	0.62	0.27
20	3.75	3.75	1.62	2.23	1.06	0.46
25	4.69	5.67	2.46	2.79	1.60	0.69
30	5.63	7.95	3.44	3.35	2.25	0.97
35	6.57	10.58	4.58	3.91	2.99	1.29
40	7.50	13.55	5.87	4.47	3.83	1.66
45	8.44	16.85	7.30	5.03	4.76	2.07
50	9.38	20.48	8.87	5.58	5.79	2.51
60	11.26	28.70	12.43	6.70	8.12	3.52
70	—	—	—	7.82	10.80	4.68

[a]Schedule number = 1000 $\times \dfrac{P(\text{internal pressure}), \text{psi}}{S(\text{allowable fiber stress}), \text{psi}}$

[b]All dimensions in feet except as noted.

Source: NIBCO Inc., Elkhart, IN 46515.

TABLE 4-14 Equivalent Length of Pipe for Friction in Fittings[a]

Pipe Diameter (in.)	90° Standard Elbow	45° Standard Elbow	90° Long-Radius Elbow	90° Street Elbow	45° Street Elbow	Square Corner Elbow	Standard with Flow through Run	Tee with Flow through Branch
¼	0.9	0.5	0.6	1.5	0.8	1.7	0.6	1.8
½	1.6	0.8	1.0	2.6	1.3	3.0	1.0	4.0
¾	2.1	1.1	1.4	3.4	1.8	3.9	1.4	5.1
1	2.6	1.4	1.7	4.4	2.3	5.0	1.7	6.0
1¼	3.5	1.8	2.3	5.8	3.0	6.5	2.3	6.9
1½	4.0	2.1	2.7	6.7	3.5	7.6	2.7	8.1
2	5.5	2.8	4.3	8.6	4.5	9.8	4.3	12.0
2½	6.2	3.3	5.1	10.3	5.4	11.7	5.1	14.3
3	7.7	4.1	6.3	12.3	6.6	14.6	6.3	16.3
4	10.1	5.4	8.3	16.8	8.7	19.1	8.3	22.1
6	15.2	8.1	12.5	25.3	13.1	28.8	12.5	32.2
8	20.0	10.6	16.5	33.3	17.3	37.9	16.5	39.9
10	25.1	13.4	20.7	41.6	21.7	47.6	20.7	50.1
12	29.8	15.9	24.7	49.7	25.9	56.7	24.7	59.7

[a] All dimensions in feet except as noted.

TABLE 4-15 Equivalent Length of Pipe for Friction in Valves When Valves are Fully Open[a]

Pipe Diameter (in.)	Globe Valve				Angle Valve		Gate Valve
	Conventional		Y-Pattern		Conventional		
	With no Obstruction Flat Bevel, or Plug-Type Seat	With Wing or Pin-Guided Disk	With Stem 60° from Run of Pipe Line	With Stem 45° from Run of Pipe Line	With No Obstruction in Flat, Bevel, Plug-Type Seat	With Wing or Pin-Guided Disk	Conventional Wedge Disk, Double Disk, or Plug Disk
$\frac{1}{4}$	10.3	13.7	5.3	4.4	4.4	6.1	0.4
$\frac{1}{2}$	17.6	23.3	9.1	7.5	7.5	10.4	0.7
$\frac{3}{4}$	23.3	30.9	12.0	10.0	10.0	13.7	0.9
1	29.7	39.3	15.3	12.7	12.7	17.5	1.1
$1\frac{1}{4}$	39.1	51.8	20.1	16.7	16.7	23.0	1.5
$1\frac{1}{2}$	45.6	60.4	23.5	19.5	19.5	26.8	1.7
2	58.6	77.5	30.1	25.0	25.0	34.5	2.2
$2\frac{1}{2}$	69.95	92.6	36.0	29.8	29.8	41.2	2.7
3	86.9	115.1	44.7	37.1	37.1	51.1	3.3
4	114.1	151.0	58.7	48.6	48.6	67.1	4.4
6	171.8	227.4	88.4	73.3	73.3	101.1	6.6
8	226.1	299.3	116.4	96.4	96.4	133.0	8.6
10	283.9	375.8	146.1	121.1	121.1	167.0	10.9
12	338.2	447.7	174.1	144.3	144.3	199.0	12.9

[a] All dimensions in feet except as noted.

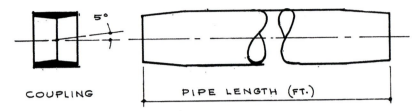

ORANGEBURG PIPE
ONE TAPERWELD COUPLING INCLUDED WITH EACH LENGTH

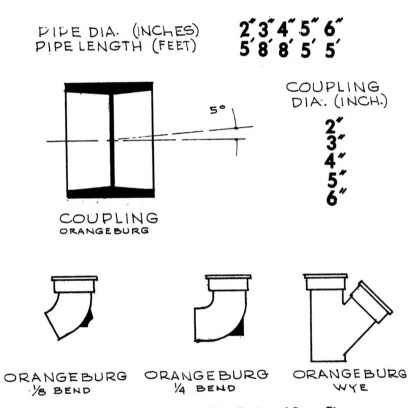

| PIPE DIA. (INCHES) | 2″ | 3″ | 4″ | 5″ | 6″ |
| PIPE LENGTH (FEET) | 5′ | 8′ | 8′ | 5′ | 5′ |

COUPLING
DIA. (INCH.)

2″
3″
4″
5″
6″

COUPLING
ORANGEBURG

ORANGEBURG   ORANGEBURG   ORANGEBURG
⅛ BEND   ¼ BEND   WYE

Figure 4-14 Bituminized Fiber Drain and Sewer Pipe

4 in. comes 8 ft long
5 in. comes 5 ft long
6 in. comes 5 ft long

Fittings for this pipe are furnished in ⅛ bends, ¼ bends, and in wye fittings. One coupling is furnished with each length of pipe.

SELF-TESTING REVIEW QUESTIONS

1. Name three kinds of plastic pipe.
2. List some of the outstanding characteristics of plastic pipe.
3. FEP (fluorinated ethylene propylene) pipe is intended to be used for conveying what materials?
4. What is a disadvantage of polyethylene pipe?
5. Name three advantages of PVDF pipe.
6. What is a common method of expressing friction losses in pipe fittings and valves?

5

THE DRAINAGE SYSTEM

The purpose of the sanitary drainage system is to collect the waste matter from toilets (w.c.'s) and the wastewater from other fixtures, such as the lavatory, kitchen sink, shower, tub, and dishwasher, and to convey it into the vertical plumbing stack. From the stack the waste is led into the horizontal house drain inside the building, and then into the house sewer outside the building, and finally into the public sewer in the street, or into a septic tank where no public sewer exists in the area.

PUBLIC AND HOUSE SEWERS

The *public sewer* pipe is located in the center of the street below the frost line (Fig. 5-1) and has a minimum fall or pitch of $1\frac{1}{4}$ in. for every 5 ft of length (which is $\frac{1}{4}$ in. per foot).

The *house sewer* is the length of pipe running from the public sewer to within 3 to 5 ft of the house. From this point the house drain continues inside the house also with a minimum pitch of $1\frac{1}{4}$ in. for every 5 ft of run, as recommended by most plumbing codes. Where this is impractical, due to the depth of a street sewer or the arrangement of the structural features of a building, piping 4 in. or larger in diameter may have a slope of not less than $\frac{1}{8}$ in. per foot if approved by the local administrative authority.

The minimum pipe diameter of the house sewer is 3 in. Larger

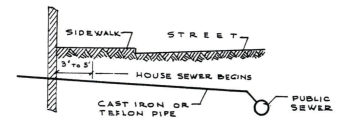

Figure 5-1 House and Public Sewer

sizes are required when a greater number of fixture units are served. Cast iron is the strongest pipe that can be used and is generally specified when the pipe passes under a driveway. Where building codes allow the use of plastic pipe or fiber pipe, they should be used since they are lighter and easier to handle. Most building codes further provide that if and when a house sewer line passes within 10 ft of a potable water supply line under pressure, the house sewer line must be leakproof. For cast iron, it means that the joints are to be leaded and caulked or hubless fittings are to be used. For plastic or fiber pipe, the joints must be welded and both pipes must be solid and not perforated.

HOUSE DRAIN AND SOIL, WASTE, AND VENT STACKS

The horizontal pipe inside the house into which the soil and waste stacks drain is called the *house drain* (Fig. 5-2). Just as the house sewer, the house drain must have a minimum pitch or slope of $\frac{1}{4}$ in. per foot unless similar conditions exist as described for the house sewer. Its minimum diameter is 3 in. Depending on the type of house, the house drain may be located under the cellar slab, or under the first-floor slab for a cellarless house, or it may be suspended from the ceiling joists of the cellar, or the pipe may be installed against the wall of the cellar. Location is, of course, determined by the depth of the public sewer in relation to the grade level of the house since both the house drain and house sewer require a continuous slope of $\frac{1}{4}$ in. per foot. In any case, before a house drain and house sewer are installed, it is necessary to know the invert elevation of the public sewer and the invert elevation where the house drain leaves the building. This information can be gotten from the local building or plumbing department. The *invert elevation* is the distance from the grade to the bottom of the inside diameter of the pipe. Where the house drain and the house sewer connect, the invert elevation must be less than that of the public sewer in order to provide the minimum pitch of the house sewer.

The *soil, waste, and vent stack* is the vertical pipe that connects

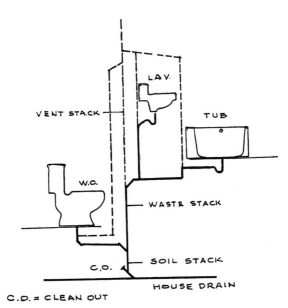

Figure 5-2 House Drain and Soil, Waste, and Vent Stack

to the house drain. It is advisable to group fixtures closely together so that only one stack is necessary since it is the most expensive part of a plumbing system. A *soil stack* receives the soil matter from a toilet, while a *waste stack* receives the wastewater from the lavatory, sink, tub, and shower. The stack above this point becomes a *vent stack*. Vent stacks are used only to allow air to enter the system.

FIXTURES, TRAPS, BRANCHES, AND BRANCH VENTS

The plumbing fixtures, such as the lavatory, the toilet bowl, the tub and shower, and the kitchen sink are called *fixtures*. Each fixture is equipped with a trap and vent. The *trap*, Fig. 5-3, filled with water, prevents foul gases in the plumbing pipes from entering the rooms, and the *vent* for the trap prevents the trap water from being siphoned out.

The *branches* of a plumbing system are the horizontal piping

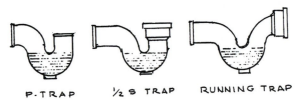

Figure 5-3 Fixture Traps

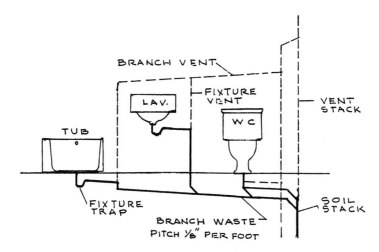

Figure 5-4 Branches and Branch Vents

running from the vertical stack to the fixtures. Fixture *branch vents*, on the other hand, are the horizontal piping that run from near the fixture trap, then above the fixture to the vent stack, as shown in Fig. 5-4. Branch vents are slightly graded so that the condensate that may collect in them can flow back into the branch lines.

Vent lines for fixtures are installed so that waste matter flowing through the fixture branch cannot clog up the vents. It is for this reason that branch vents are not connected directly to the crown of traps. Branch vents should never be taken from fixture branches below the hydraulic grade. *Hydraulic grade* is a line from the high water level of a fixture such as the lavatory to the branch connection at the soil stack (see Fig. 5-5).

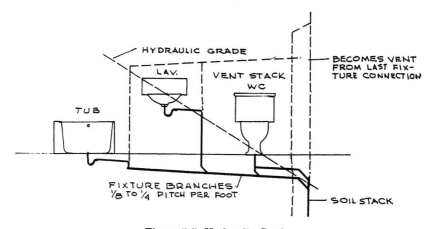

Figure 5-5 Hydraulic Grade

CLEANOUTS

Most building codes prescribe that each horizontal drainage pipe be provided with a *cleanout* (Fig. 5-6) at its higher terminal, with additional cleanouts for each run of piping that is more than 100 ft in total developed length. An additional cleanout is also required in a horizontal line whose direction changes 135°.

Further requirements are:

1. Install each cleanout so that it opens in a direction opposite to the flow of soil or waste.
2. Each 90° cleanout extension is extended from a Y-type fitting.
3. Each cleanout must be readily accessible unless installed under an approved cover plate.
4. Underfloor cleanouts in residential structures are not to be located more than 20 ft from an access door, trap door, or crawl space.
5. Cleanout fittings must not be smaller than those given for the following pipe diameters:

$1\frac{1}{2}$-in. pipe: $1\frac{1}{2}$-in.-diameter cleanout, $11\frac{1}{2}$ threads/in.

2-in. pipe: $1\frac{1}{2}$-in.-diameter cleanout, $11\frac{1}{2}$ threads/in.

$2\frac{1}{2}$-in. pipe: $2\frac{1}{2}$-in.-diameter cleanout, 8 threads/in.

3-in. pipe: $2\frac{1}{2}$-in. diameter cleanout, 8 threads/in.

4-in. pipe: $3\frac{1}{2}$-in. diameter cleanout, 8 threads/in.

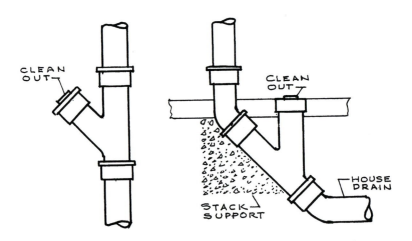

Figure 5-6 Cleanouts

TYPICAL DRAINAGE SYSTEM

A typical drainage system of two stacks is shown in Fig. 5-7. A cleanout is provided at the base of each stack connecting to the house drain under the basement floor. Two laundry tubs, trapped and vented, are in the basement. The first floor shows a sink, lavatory, and water closet (toilet bowl), while the second floor shows a water closet, lavatory, and tub. All fixtures are trapped and vented. Two stacks were used because of the separation of the fixtures. Long branch lines are mostly

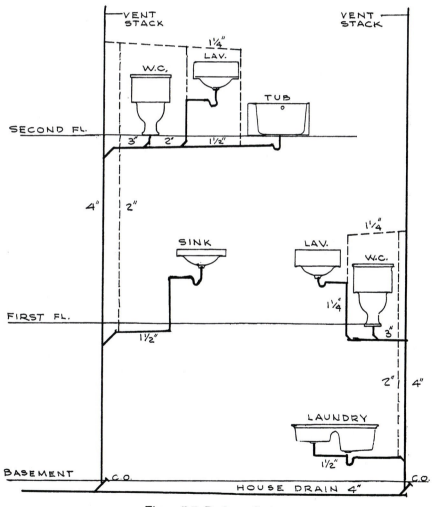

Figure 5-7 Drainage System

avoided so that the proper pitch of the branch lines can be held between the floor joists.

The pipe sizes indicated are typical for the average plumbing system but are subject to change to other sizes depending on the number of fixtures served.

SIZING OF DRAINAGE PIPING

Drainage piping such as the house sewer, house drain, stacks, branch drains, and vents are sized according to the number of fixture units they carry. A *fixture unit* (F.U.) is the number of gallons of water a fixture will drain in 1 minute. A lavatory, for example, can drain $7\frac{1}{2}$ gal per minute—that is, the drain pipe for the lavatory is of a diameter that can drain $7\frac{1}{2}$ gal per minute, although one lavatory requires only about 1 gal or less of water when washing one's face and hands. In other words, the rate of discharge of the water through the drain pipe of the lavatory is $7\frac{1}{2}$ gal per minute and is considered as one fixture unit. A bathtub is rated as two fixture units. This means that the drain pipe for the tub is of a size that will drain $2 \times 7\frac{1}{2}$ gal or 15 gal per minute. This system of assigning fixture units for all plumbing fixtures permits the sizing of the pipe.

When two or more fixtures drain into one pipe, the fixture units of each fixture must be added and the total will determine the pipe size. In Table 5-1 are given the equivalent fixture units of the listed fixtures, together with their drain pipe diameters.

Sizing of House Drain and House Sewer

In order to find the correct size of pipe required for the house drain and the house sewer, the total volume of discharge of water and waste must be determined, which means finding the total number of fixture units. Once this is known, the size of pipe can be read from Table 5-2.

For example, a building with a kitchen sink (2 F.U.), a dishwasher (2 F.U.), two water closets (8 F.U.), two lavatories (2 F.U.), a shower stall (domestic) (2 F.U.), a bathtub (2 F.U.), one floor drain (1 F.U.), a laundry tub with one or two compartments (2 F.U.) will have a total of 21 fixture units. If the pipes are laid with a fall of $\frac{1}{4}$ in. per foot, Table 5-2 shows that a 3-in. building drain is required.

Sizing of Vent Piping

Vent piping is sized by the number of fixture units they serve and also by the length of the vent, whether horizontal or vertical. Table 5-3

TABLE 5-1 Fixture Units, Drain, and Trap Diameters

Type of Fixture	Fixture Unit	Drain and Trap Size (in.)
Lavatory (wash basin)	1	$1\frac{1}{4}$
Lavatories (insets)	2	$1\frac{1}{2}$
Water closet (w.c.), flush tank	4	3
Water closet (w.c.), flushomatic	6	3
Dishwasher	2	$1\frac{1}{2}$
Bathtub	2	$1\frac{1}{2}$
Shower (single stall)	2	2
Kitchen sink	2	$1\frac{1}{2}$
Laundry tub	2	$1\frac{1}{2}$
Clothes washer	2	2
Sink (service)	3	2
Drinking fountain	1	$1\frac{1}{4}$
Floor drain	2	2
Urinal (stall)	2	2
Bidets	2	$1\frac{1}{2}$

TABLE 5-2 Maximum Number of Fixture Units that May Be Connected to any Portion of the Building Drain or Building Sewer at the Given Fall

Diameter of Pipe (in.)	$\frac{1}{16}$ in.	$\frac{1}{8}$ in.	$\frac{1}{4}$ in.	$\frac{1}{2}$ in.
2	—	—	21	26
$2\frac{1}{2}$	—	—	24	31
3	—	20[a]	27[a]	36[a]
4	—	180	216	250
5	—	390	480	575
6	—	700	840	1000
8	1400	1600	1920	2300
10	2500	2900	3500	4200
12	3900	4600	5600	6700

[a]Not over two water closets.

Source: IAPMO (International Association of Plumbing and Mechanical Officials).

TABLE 5-3 Maximum Unit Loading and Length of Drainage and Vent Piping

	Size of Pipe (in.)										
	1¼	1½	2	2½	3	4	5	6	8	10	12
Maximum units drainage piping[a]											
Vertical	1	2[b]	16[c]	32	48[d]	256	600	1380	3600	5600	8400
Horizontal	1	1	8	14	35[d]	216	428	720	2640	4680	8200
Maximum length (ft) drainage piping											
Vertical	45	65	85	148	212	300	390	510	750	—	—
Horizontal					Unlimited						
Vent piping Horizontal and Vertical											
Maximum units	1	8[c]	24	48	84	256	600	1380	3600	—	—
Maximum length (ft)	45	60	120	180	212	300	390	510	750	—	—

[a]Excluding trap arm.

[b]Except sinks and urinals.

[c]Except six unit traps or water closet.

[d]Only four w.c.'s or six traps allowed on any vertical pipe or stack and not to exceed three w.c.'s or six-unit traps on any horizontal branch or drain provided that any one of three discharges is separated from the other two by a minimum horizontal length of 15 ft whether connecting to vertical or horizontal piping.

Source: IAPMO (International Association of Plumbing and Mechanical Officials).

gives the pipe diameters for the maximum fixture unit loading and maximum length of drainage and vent piping.

Sizing Soil Stack and Soil Branch

Stacks and soil branches are sized similarly to the building drain and building sewer. That is, the maximum discharge in terms of fixture units must be determined; then the pipe diameter can be found from Table 5-4. The usual size of the soil stack is 4 in., although the smallest-diameter pipe that can be used is 3 in.

Final Sizing of Typical Drainage System

Table 5-5 gives the water flow in gallons per minute per pipe size for various types and numbers of fixtures.

SEPTIC TANK

When there is no public sewer, the house sewer may drain into a private sewer or *septic tank* (Fig. 5-8), located underground on the property it serves. The tank, usually constructed of concrete with smooth inside surfaces, retains the solids and digests this organic matter through a period of detention. The liquids in the tank discharge into the soil outside the tank through a system of open-joint piping into a seepage pit (Fig. 5-9) or a disposal area such as a leaching field (Fig. 5-10).

The size of a septic tank is based on the number of bedrooms within a dwelling and the estimated waste-sewage design flow rate, or the number of plumbing fixture units, whichever is greater. However, the capacity of the septic tank and its drainage system is limited by the nature of the soil or its porosity.

Seepage Pit

The *seepage pit* size is based on the quantity of liquid waste discharging into it, and also on the nature or the porosity of the surrounding soil. Seepage pits are circular in shape and must have an excavated diameter of at least 4 ft. The pit excavation may be lined with burned clay brick, concrete brick, field stone, or concrete circular-type cesspool blocks. If a pit is of a diameter of 6 ft or greater, approval must be secured from the proper authority. The wall thickness of the seepage pit must be at least 4 in. and the pit must have a minimum side wall, not including the arch, of 10 ft below the inlet.

TABLE 5-4 Horizontal Fixture Branches and Stacks

	Minimum Number of Fixture Units That May Be Connected to:		More Than Three Stories in Height	
Diameter Pipe (in.)	Any Horizontal Fixture Branch	One Stack of Three Stories in Height or Three Intervals	Total Soil Stack	Total at One Story or Branch Intervals
$1\frac{1}{4}$	1	2	2	1
$1\frac{1}{2}$	3	4	8	2
2	6	10	24	6
$2\frac{1}{2}$	12	20	42	9
3	20	30	60	16
4	160	240	500	90
5	360	540	1100	200
6	620	960	1900	350
8	1400	2200	3600	600
10	2500	3800	5600	1000
12	3900	6000	8400	1500

Source: IAPMO (International Association of Plumbing and Mechanical Officials).

TABLE 5-5 Flow and Pipe Size for Plumbing Fixtures

Number of Fixtures	Water Closets			Urinals			
	Pipe Size (in.)	Tank gpm	Flusho-meter gpm	Pipe Size (in.)	Tank gpm	Pipe Size (in.)	Flusho-meter gpm
1	$\frac{1}{2}$	8	30	$\frac{1}{2}$	6	1	25
2	$\frac{3}{4}$	16	50	$\frac{3}{4}$	12	$1\frac{1}{4}$	37
4	1	24	80	1	20	$1\frac{1}{4}$	45
8	$1\frac{1}{4}$	48	120	$1\frac{1}{4}$	32	$1\frac{1}{2}$	75
12	$1\frac{1}{2}$	60	140	$1\frac{1}{4}$	43	$1\frac{1}{2}$	85
16	$1\frac{1}{2}$	80	160	$1\frac{1}{4}$	56	2	100
24	2	96	200	$1\frac{1}{2}$	72	2	125
32	2	128	250	2	90	2	150
40	2	150	300	2	120	2	175

Number of Fixtures	Lavatories and Sinks		Bathtubs		Slop Sinks	
	Pipe Size (in.)	Faucet per gpm	Pipe Size (in.)	gpm	Pipe Size (in.)	Faucet per gpm
1	$\frac{1}{2}$	4	$\frac{3}{4}$	15	$\frac{3}{4}$	15
2	$\frac{1}{2}$	8	1	30	1	25
4	$\frac{3}{4}$	12	$1\frac{1}{4}$	40	$1\frac{1}{4}$	40
8	1	24	$1\frac{1}{2}$	80	$1\frac{1}{2}$	64
12	1	30	2	96	$1\frac{1}{2}$	84
16	$1\frac{1}{4}$	40	2	112	2	96
24	$1\frac{1}{4}$	48	3	144	2	120
32	$1\frac{1}{2}$	64	3	192	2	150
40	$1\frac{1}{2}$	75	3	240	3	200

Source: Rockwell International Municipal and Utility Division.

TABLE 5-6 Capacity of Septic Tank[a]

Single-Family Dwellings: Number of Bedrooms	Maximum Fixture Units Served	Minimum Septic Tank Capacity (gal)
1 or 2	15	750
3	20	1000
4	25	1200
5 or 6	33	1500

[a]One cubic foot = 7.48 gal.

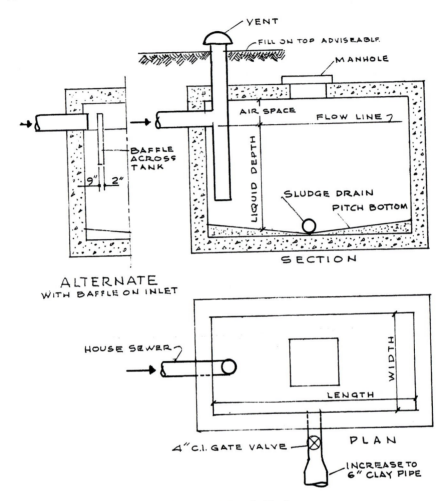

Figure 5-8 Septic Tank

Disposal Field

The pipe lines of a *disposal field* can be of clay tile laid with open joints, or perforated clay pipe, or perforated bituminous fiber pipe, or perforated high-density polyethylene pipe, or perforated ABS pipe, and PVC pipe. The trench in which the pipe is laid must first have a layer of clean stone, gravel, or slag varying in size from $\frac{3}{4}$ to $2\frac{1}{2}$ in. Drain lines must be covered with untreated building paper, straw, or similar porous material to prevent the closure of voids in the pipe with earth backfill.

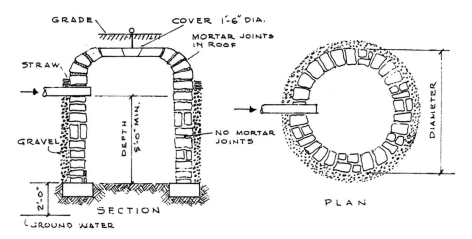

Figure 5-9 12-in. Stone Leaching Cesspool

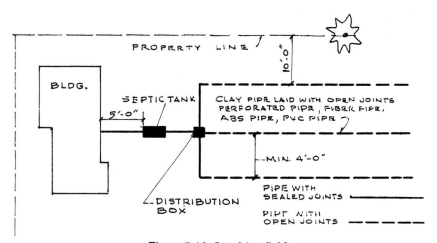

Figure 5-10 Leaching field

Distribution Box

Where two or more drain lines are installed, a *distribution box* is required to receive lateral pipe lines. The invert of the outlet pipe holes must be level and the invert of the inlet pipe must be at least 1 in. above the outlets. The box must be set on level compacted soil or on a concrete slab to ensure an equal flow to all outlet pipes. Lateral pipe from the distribution box to the disposal field must have watertight joints. The pipe from the septic tank to the distribution box also has to have watertight joints (see Fig. 5-11).

TABLE 5-7 Location of Sewage Disposal System[a]

Minimum Horizontal Distance from:	Septic Tank	Building Sewer	Disposal Field	Seepage Pit or Cesspool
Building	5	2	8	8
Private property	5	Clear[b]	5	8
Water supply wells	50	50	100	150
Streams	50	50	50	100
Trees	10	—	—	10
Seepage pits or cesspools	5	—	5	2
Disposal field	5	—	4	5
Domestic water service line	5	1	5	5
Distribution box	—	—	5	5
Pressure public water main	10	10	10	10

[a]All dimensions in feet.

[b]Trenches deeper than the footing of a building, and running parallel, must be at least $45°$ from the footing.

Source: Rockwell International Municipal and Utility Division.

TABLE 5-8 Soil Absorption Capacity for Listed Soils

Type of Soil	Required Square Feet of Leaching Area/100 Gal	Maximum Absorption Capacity (gal/sq ft) of Leaching Area for 24-Hr Period
1. Coarse sand or gravel	20	5
2. Fine sand	25	4
3. Sandy loam or sandy clay	40	2.5
4. Clay with sand or gravel	90	1.1
5. Clay with small amount of sand or gravel	120	0.83

TABLE 5-9 Septic Tank Size to Leaching Area

Required Square Feet of Leaching Area/100 Gal Septic Tank Capacity	Maximum Septic Tank Size Allowable (gal)
20–25	7500
40	5000
60	3500
90	3000

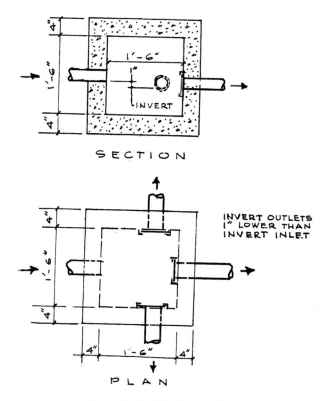

Figure 5-11 Distribution Box

SELF-TESTING REVIEW QUESTIONS

1. What part of the sanitary plumbing system is the house sewer?
2. What is the strongest pipe material used for the house sewer?
3. How does a soil stack differ from a waste stack?
4. What is meant by "invert elevation"?
5. Fixtures in a plumbing system have traps. Why?
6. How is the drainage piping sized?
7. What is the minimum septic tank capacity in gallons for a single-family dwelling of four bedrooms?
8. How many square feet of leaching area per 100 gal is required in a soil of clay with sand or gravel?

6

INSTALLING THE DRAINAGE SYSTEM

Although there are various installation procedures used by the plumber, the following steps seem to be preferred in most instances.

1. Install the toilet (w.c.) drain
2. Prepare and install cleanout assembly
3. Install house drain
4. Assemble and install the stack
5. Install branch lines and vent lines

Installing the Toilet (w.c.) Drain

When the toilet drain is installed under the floor joists (Fig. 6-1), a hub-top long ¼ bend, a vertical pipe, and a T-stack fitting are needed. These items are first joined on the floor, measured for correct lengths, and then permanently assembled. The toilet floor flange should not be installed until the entire stack is assembled with the house drain so that any slight adjustment of the assembled toilet drain can be made. Nailed brackets are used not only for temporary assembly but also as a permanent support for the cast iron pipe.

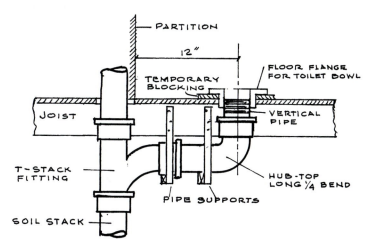

Figure 6-1 Cast Iron Pipe for Toilet Drain

Preparing and Installing Cleanout Assembly

Where the stack is to join the house drain, a cleanout is required. For cast iron pipe, the cleanout assembly will consist of a Y fitting with a cleanout ferrule and plug, and a $\frac{1}{8}$ bend as indicated in Fig. 6-2, detail A. Align the Y fitting and the $\frac{1}{8}$-bend assembly directly under the point where the stack is to enter the top of the Y fitting. Alignment is best

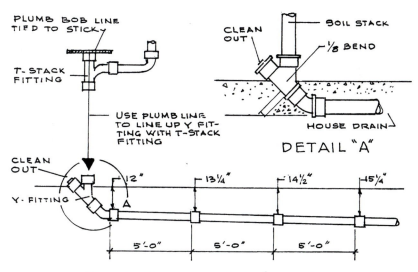

Figure 6-2 Pitch of House Drain, $\frac{1}{4}$ in. per Foot

achieved by letting a plumb bob and line from the center of the T-stack fitting of the toilet drain down to the center of the Y fitting of the cleanout assembly at the bottom of the stack.

Installing the House Drain

The house drain begins at the bottom of the soil stack, 12 in. below the floor level (Fig. 6-2), then, as stated before, pitches $\frac{1}{8}$ to $\frac{1}{4}$ in. per foot under the floor and extends 3 to 5 ft outside the building. The building drain trench should be dug 2 ft wide along a previously marked line to where it is to leave the building. The trench at the beginning, or at the foot of the stack, should be about 12 in. deep and then pitch $\frac{1}{4}$ in. per foot. The earth at the bottom of the trench must be compacted before the pipe lengths are placed.

Assembling and Installing the Stack

After the toilet drain and the house drain and cleanout assembly are installed, the soil stack is next in line (Fig. 6-3). Start the stack at the Y fitting of the cleanout assembly and bring the stack on up, connecting it into the toilet drain stack fitting. The length of pipe that is to fit into the toilet drain stack fitting will need to be cut. This is done by holding piece A in Fig. 6-4 against the other stack parts and marking for cutting.

Continue the stack over the stack fitting and up and out, at least 6 in. above the roof, provided that no window is within 10 ft of the vent. Most plumbing codes prescribe that a stack within 10 ft of a window must be brought at least 3 ft above the window.

Where the stack enters the ceiling, add an increaser and larger pipe diameter. These are required in colder climates to prevent blocking of the vent by frost.

Installing Branch Lines and Vent Lines

Branch lines, generally $1\frac{1}{2}$ in. in diameter, are started or installed from the stack to the fixtures. Branches must have a pitch of $\frac{1}{8}$ to $\frac{1}{2}$ in. per foot, and, must not be too long or too far away from the stack, especially if they are to be laid between the joists of the floor and ceiling below.

Vent lines permit air to circulate through the sanitary drainage system, and further exhaust sewer gas buildup above the roof. The vent for a trap must be installed as near to the top as possible but not on the crown of the trap, as stated earlier.

Where two similar fixtures discharge into the waste piping (Fig.

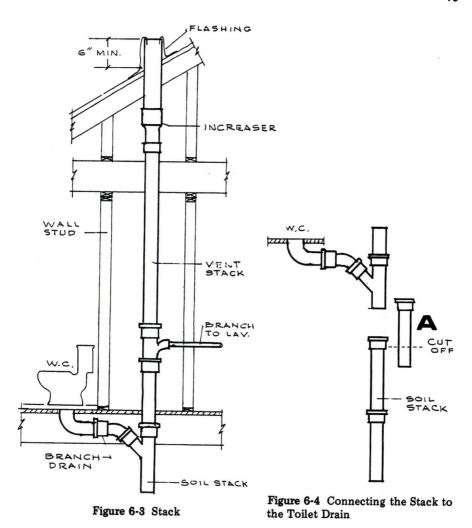

Figure 6-3 Stack

Figure 6-4 Connecting the Stack to the Toilet Drain

6-5), the vent is placed between the two fixtures that discharge into the horizontal waste branch and one common waste stack. The installation is made with a double combination Y and $\frac{1}{8}$ bend with deflectors.

HOW PIPE SIZES AFFECT PARTITION THICKNESS

Partition walls can be made wider than the usual 2 X 4 in. stud wall to accommodate drainage lines and the soil stack. The drainage line is led into notched studs as illustrated in section A-A of Fig. 6-6. There is,

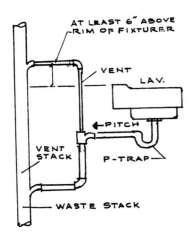

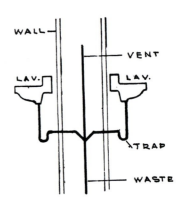

VENTING A LAVATORY
TO SOIL STACK

UNIT VENTS
FOR BACK TO BACK FIXTURES

Figure 6-5

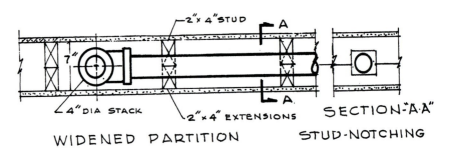

WIDENED PARTITION

STUD-NOTCHING

Figure 6-6

however, a limit to the depth to which a stud may be notched. On a nonbearing wall the stud may be notched one-half its width provided that a second stud is used, and this may only be done on the upper half of the stud. If stud notching is done on the lower half of the stud to a one-third depth, the stud must be reinforced.

When cast iron bell and spigot pipe is run in walls, partitions, and floors, enough width must be provided to accommodate the diameter of the bell of the bell-and-spigot pipe. In a 2 × 4 in. partition wall the actual dimensions of the stud are now $1\frac{1}{2}$ in. × $3\frac{1}{2}$ in., the new government-accepted standard for soft wood lumber. Similarly, a 2 in. × 8 in. floor joist actually measures $1\frac{1}{2}$ in. × $7\frac{1}{4}$ in. Following are nominal sizes and actual sizes of soft wood lumber.

Nominal Size (in.)	Actual Size (in.)
2 X 4	$1\frac{1}{2}$ X $3\frac{1}{2}$
2 X 6	$1\frac{1}{2}$ X $5\frac{1}{2}$
2 X 8	$1\frac{1}{2}$ X $7\frac{1}{4}$
2 X 10	$1\frac{1}{2}$ X $9\frac{1}{4}$
2 X 12	$1\frac{1}{2}$ X $11\frac{1}{4}$

Since the minimum width of a wall, partition, or floor is determined by the outside diameter of the bell, it becomes necessary to know the bell diameter for various pipe sizes. It should be remembered that given pipe diameters are usually inside diameters, and are expressed as nominal diameters. Following is a drawing of a section of a bell-and-spigot soil pipe (Fig. 6-7) and the dimensions of various sizes are given in Table 6-1. Compare the dimensions of the given pipe diameters with the illustration in Fig. 6-8.

HOW BEAM DEPTHS LIMIT SOIL RUNS

The minimum run, horizontally, from the water closet, including bend, between various size of wood joists, using 4-in. C.I. soil pipe is as follows (see Fig. 6-9):

For an 8-in.-deep floor joist, the run is 4 ft

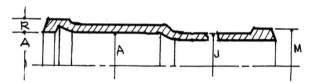

Figure 6-7 Bell-and-Spigot Soil Pipe Section

TABLE 6-1 Dimensions for Bell and Spigot Pipe

Size	I.D. of Hub A	O.D. of Barrel J	O.D. of Spigot M	Minimum R
2	2.94	2.25	2.62	0.37
3	3.94	3.25	3.62	0.43
4	4.94	4.25	4.62	0.43
5	5.94	5.25	5.62	0.43
6	6.94	6.25	6.62	0.43

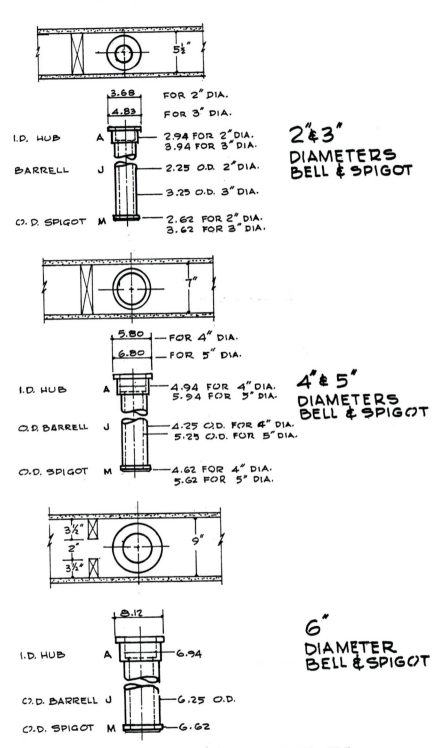

2" & 3" DIAMETERS BELL & SPIGOT

3.68 — FOR 2" DIA.
4.83 — FOR 3" DIA.

I.D. HUB — A — 2.94 FOR 2" DIA.
3.94 FOR 3" DIA.

BARRELL — J — 2.25 O.D. 2" DIA.
3.25 O.D. 3" DIA.

O.D. SPIGOT — M — 2.62 FOR 2" DIA.
3.62 FOR 3" DIA.

5½"

4" & 5" DIAMETERS BELL & SPIGOT

5.80 — FOR 4" DIA.
6.80 — FOR 5" DIA.

I.D. HUB — A — 4.94 FOR 4" DIA.
5.94 FOR 5" DIA.

O.D. BARRELL — J — 4.25 O.D. FOR 4" DIA.
5.25 O.D. FOR 5" DIA.

O.D. SPIGOT — M — 4.62 FOR 4" DIA.
5.62 FOR 5" DIA.

7"

6" DIAMETER BELL & SPIGOT

8.12

I.D. HUB — A — 6.94

O.D. BARRELL — J — 6.25 O.D.

O.D. SPIGOT — M — 6.62

3½"
2"
3½"
9"

Figure 6-8 How Pipe Sizes Affect Partition Walls

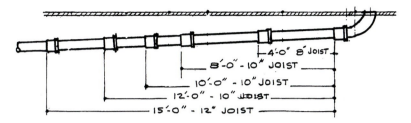

Figure 6-9 How Beam Depths Limit Soil Runs

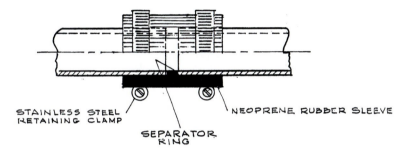

Figure 6-10 No-Hub Pipe Joint

For a 10-in.-deep floor joist, the run is 12 ft

For a 12-in.-deep floor joist, the run is 15 ft

NO-HUB PIPE JOINT

Cast iron pipe is also available with no-hub joints (Fig. 6-10). This type of joint can be used in place of the lead-and-oakum hub and spigot joint. The joint uses a neoprene rubber sleeve or gasket, a separator ring, and a stainless steel cover ring with clamps.

No-hub joints are relatively easy to make up and they can be used in narrower partitions and smaller spaces. Properly installed, they are trouble free and last a very long time.

SELF-TESTING REVIEW QUESTIONS

1. When the toilet drain is installed under the floor, name three fittings that make up that drain.
2. When should the toilet floor flange be installed?
3. What is required where the stack is to join the house drain?

4. What should be used to achieve perfect alignment between the center of the T-stack fitting of the toilet drain with the center of the Y fitting of the cleanout assembly?
5. Where does the house drain begin and where does it end?
6. The house drain is usually laid to what pitch?
7. How far above the roof must the stack be brought when it is 8 ft from a window?
8. Branch lines are generally of what diameter?

FIXTURE INSTALLATION

WATER CLOSET

It is not difficult to install a new toilet bowl (w.c.) and tank (Fig. 7-1) after the the old one is removed. There are a number of different types of bowls available: (1) the *washdown* type and (2) the *siphon* types, of which there are the reverse trap, the siphon jet, and the siphon action.

The two illustrated are the reverse-trap and the siphon-action-type water closet. Siphon water closets use a jet of water which speeds the siphon action. This type of bowl usually combines the closet and the flush tank in one unit.

The reverse-trap water closet is very similar to the siphon but has a smaller water area, passageway, and water seal.

One important dimension to consider is the *rough-in dimension*, which is the distance from the wall to the center of the hold-down bolts, as well as the center of the drain pipe, on top of which the hole of the new bowl must be aligned.

After the water in the old tank is removed and the water inlet and drain outlet are disconnected, the tank can be removed. Next, remove the old bowl by prying off the porcelain caps and by unscrewing the hold-down bolts. Carefully wrap both arms around the bowl, twisting and rocking it in order to pry it loose. Then lift the bowl up to clear the hold-down bolts and set the bowl aside. Stuff a rag into the drain pipe in the floor to prevent sewer gases from entering the

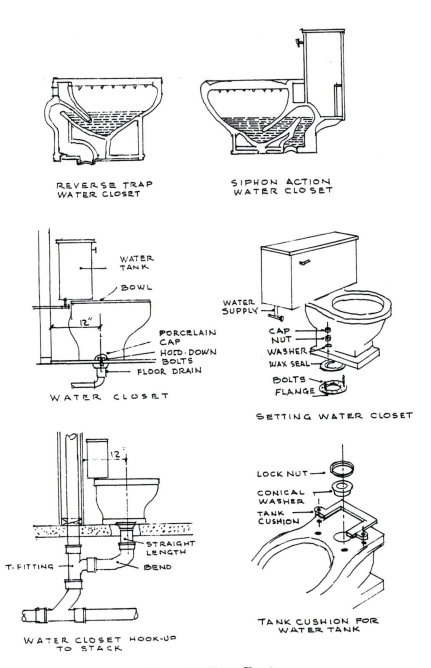

REVERSE TRAP
WATER CLOSET

SIPHON ACTION
WATER CLOSET

WATER TANK

BOWL

12"

PORCELAIN CAP

HOLD-DOWN BOLTS

FLOOR DRAIN

WATER CLOSET

WATER SUPPLY

CAP
NUT
WASHER
WAX SEAL

BOLTS
FLANGE

SETTING WATER CLOSET

12

STRAIGHT LENGTH

T-FITTING

BEND

WATER CLOSET HOOK-UP TO STACK

LOCK NUT

CONICAL WASHER

TANK CUSHION

TANK CUSHION FOR WATER TANK

Figure 7-1 Water Closet

room and to prevent anything from falling into the drain pipe opening. With a putty knife, scrape away all putty and wax around the floor flange.

Turn the new bowl upside down and install a new wax gasket around the horn of the bowl. Install the gasket with the sleeve away from the horn. When this is done, remove the rag from the drain pipe, and turn the bowl upright again and proceed to set it over the floor flange, allowing the hold-down bolts to enter the holes in the bottom of the bowl. Again with both arms, twist the bowl slightly in a side-to-side motion so that a good seal develops with the wax gasket and the sleeve and floor. Use a level across the top of the bowl for perfect alignment. Metal shims may be used if necessary. Next, screw the nuts on the bolts, but do not tighten them until the water tank is set on the top back end of the bowl.

Before placing the bowl-mounted tank, insert the beveled spud washer and tank cushion which comes with a new toilet bowl and water tank. Set the tank on the cushion and tighten the bolts of the tank to the toilet bowl. Adjust the tank and bowl with the wall and finally tighten down the hold-down bolts of the toilet bowl. Do not tighten too much, to prevent cracking the bowl.

FAUCETS

Single-Lever Mixing Unit

Installing a new single-lever mixing faucet (Fig. 7-2) in place of an old leaking faucet is not difficult. After turning off both hot and cold water shutoff valves, unfasten the coupling nuts of the tail piece and then with a basin wrench remove the locknut and washer under the sink. Then pull out the faucet assembly.

The new faucet not only improves the appearance of the kitchen sink, but also allows hot and cold water to be mixed by moving the mixing lever to the left or the right, at the same time lifting the lever up and backward to start the flow of water. The entire assembly is available in most plumbing supply or hardware stores. One important dimension that must be considered is the center-to-center distance of the holes in the kitchen sink into which the new faucet assembly is to be set. The mounting threaded studs of the new assembly unit must fit into the kitchen fixture holes. Washers and nuts applied onto the studs from under the sink will tighten the new assembly to the sink. The water supply tubes are then bent together so that they will slide through the center hole of the sink and into the new single-lever mixing faucet unit.

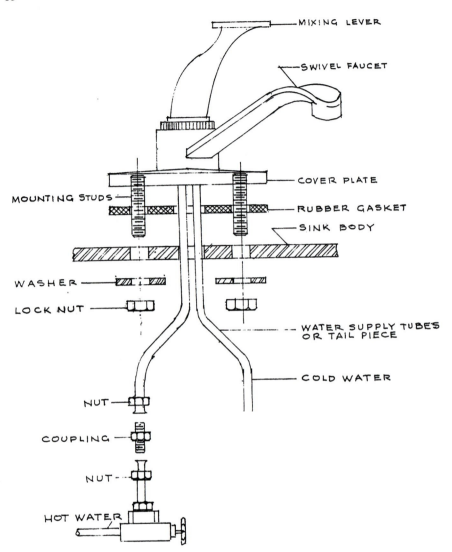

Figure 7-2 Single-Lever Mixing Unit on Kitchen Sink

Should a leak develop at the end of the spout, the two rubber valve seats and springs in the bottom of the faucet body can easily be replaced.

Replacing a Stem Washer

Leaking faucets are often caused by worn-out stem washers. To replace the old washer with a new one is an operation that can be done in a relatively short time with a screwdriver, a small wrench, and a pair of pliers.

The first thing to do is to turn off the water valve under the sink or lavatory. If there is no valve under the sink, the main water valve in the house must be turned off. This valve is usually near the water meter. Open the faucet and allow all the remaining water in the pipes to run out.

With a screwdriver pry off the decorative cap on the top center of the faucet handle and remove the screw that holds down the faucet handle, exposing the top part and knurled head of the stem. Be certain that the screwdriver fits the screw perfectly. Next, the stem and stem housing can be removed by turning with a wrench the hexagonal nut affixed to the stem housing.

Figure 7-3 shows a typical faucet stem assembly with its stem washer at the bottom of the stem. The stem washer fits into the washer housing and is held there by a brass round-head machine screw, as shown in the exploded detail. When screwed into the sink or lavatory frame, the stem housing is fixed and does not move. However, the stem, which is threaded to the inside of the stem housing can be raised off the valve seat, allowing for water to rush in. When the stem is turned clockwise, the stem washer is pressed onto the valve seat, shutting off the flow of water.

It should be remembered that there are numerous designs of faucet stems, long and short ones, but they all have one thing in common, which is that the stem washer will wear out in time. The life of the stem washer can be greatly prolonged by not tightening the faucet too much. Tighten only as much as necessary to stop the flow.

Faucet Assembly

When buying and installing a new faucet assembly, first determine the center-to-center distance of the holes in the lavatory basin. Most lavatory drillings are on 4-in. centers, but 8-in. centers are also quite common. The new faucet assembly must fit the drillings in the basin body (see Fig. 7-4).

First turn off the hot and cold water valves under the lavatory basin. If there are no valves, turn off the main house water supply. Open both faucets and let out any water still under pressure.

When the old faucet assembly is removed, clean off the surface around the drilled holes and the surface of the basin where the new gasket is to sit. Place the new gasket over the holes. If the assembly does not provide a gasket, plumber's putty should be spread around the faucet plate area. Next, insert the stem into the holes of the plate body and gasket. The stem will protrude through the basin body and

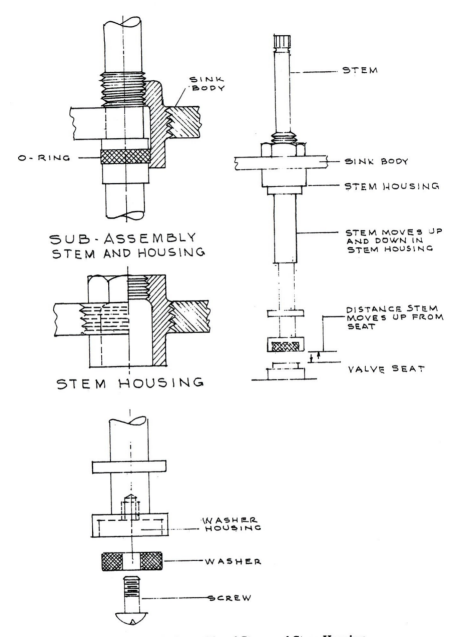

SINK BODY

O-RING

SUB-ASSEMBLY
STEM AND HOUSING

STEM HOUSING

STEM

SINK BODY

STEM HOUSING

STEM MOVES UP
AND DOWN IN
STEM HOUSING

DISTANCE STEM
MOVES UP FROM
SEAT

VALVE SEAT

WASHER
HOUSING

WASHER

SCREW

Figure 7-3 Assembly of Stem and Stem Housing

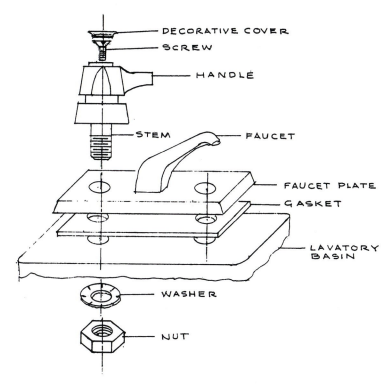

DECORATIVE COVER

SCREW

HANDLE

STEM

FAUCET

FAUCET PLATE

GASKET

LAVATORY BASIN

WASHER

NUT

Figure 7-4 Faucet Assembly

under the basin. From under the basin put on the stem washers and the nuts. The nuts can be tightened with a basin wrench.

Connect the hot and cold water lines by slipping the nuts of the supply lines over and onto the faucets. The bottom ends of the pipe are slipped into the fitting while the nuts are tightened at these connections. Care must be exercised not to overtighten the nuts, to prevent stripping the threads.

Next, turn on the water and check for leaks. Should a leak occur at the connections, a further slight tightening of the nuts will often remedy the problem.

DISHWASHER

The dishwasher is generally installed close to the kitchen sink (Fig. 7-5). A tee fitting must be installed on the hot water line under the sink. From the tee, a flexible copper tubing is brought to the dishwasher's

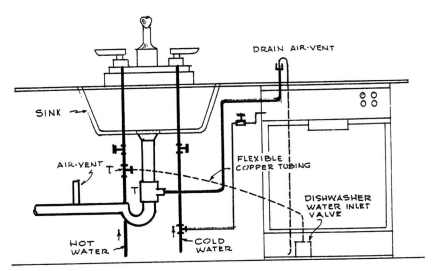

Figure 7-5 Dishwasher and Kitchen Sink

water valve and is connected according to the manufacturer's specifications.

A tee fitting must also be installed on the sink drainpipe above the trap. From the tee, a drain hose is run to the drain outlet of the dishwasher. A small pump will bring the dishwasher wastewater to the sink tee and out through the trap and waste line.

The operation of the dishwasher is automatically set for four cycles of washing after the dishes are stacked into the washer. Following are the four cycles:

1. Hot water mixed with dishwasher detergent washes the dishes.
2. The soiled water is pumped out.
3. Clean water is brought in as a rinsing action.
4. A heating element dries the dishes.

WATER TANK FOR WATER CLOSET

The homeowner can often correct most problems that occur within the flush tank, provided that he or she clearly understands the function or purpose of the various parts within the tank. Faulty or worn parts can be removed and easily replaced by purchasing new parts from a plumbing supply house. This is many times less costly than calling a plumber. Following are some of the common breakdowns that occur and how to go about correcting them. Refer to Fig. 7-6 for identification of parts.

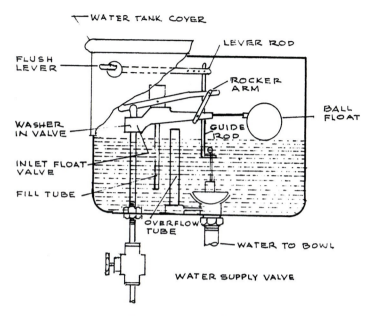

Figure 7-6 Water Tank

Flush Lever

If the problem is that the tank does not flush when the flush tank lever is pressed, remove the tank cover and raise the ball stopper to let the water out. Lift the flush lever up and down and see if the lever rod also moves at the same time. If it does not, check the connection between the handle and the lever arm, which may have loosened or disconnected. In some of the more modern tanks, the lever handle and lever rod are made of plastic and they may have broken. In this case purchase and install a new lever handle and lever rod of the same kind and size. Take the old parts to your plumbing supply house for comparison.

Guide Rods and Ball Stopper

The guide rods should first be checked to see if they are connected to each other and to the lever rod. There is an upper and a lower guide rod. Flush the tank and turn off the incoming cold water valve under the tank. Examine the guide rods carefully, also checking the rubber ball stopper assembly. Make certain that the upper guide rod is secured to the lever rod and that the lower rod is secured to the ball stopper.

The rubber ball stopper should be firm but not too soft in spots. It should not be rough or show cuts, wear marks, or have a hole in it. If the rods are found to be disconnected, simply connect them and the problem is solved. If the lower rod does not connect properly to the ball stopper, check to see if the threads on the rod and ball stopper are worn. In this case replace both rod and stopper.

Overflow Tube

The overflow tube can develop leaks and cause water to run continuously. To correct this problem, flush the tank and turn off the incoming cold water valve under the tank. Disengage the upper guide rod from the lever rod. Care must be taken not to damage the guide rod during its removal.

Lift out the entire guide rod and rubber ball stopper assembly. Do not try to shortcut this work, for trying to remove the overflow tube with the guide rods in place will cause distortion to the rods and a new problem will have been created. Next, remove the overflow tube by hand turning it counterclockwise while looking into the tank.

Get a new overflow tube of the same size from your supply store and install it in the same manner. Replace the ball stopper and guide rod assembly. Attach the upper guide rod to the lever rod. Turn on the water valve, allow the tank to fill, flush, and test for leaks.

Water Level in Tank

The water level in the tank should be inspected periodically. If the water level is at the same level as the overflow tube, a constant water loss will result over a period of time.

The water level in the tank will rise due to a slight turning of the ball float on its threaded stem, causing the ball to float somewhat higher and thereby raising the water level to the point of overflow.

The following observations, made over a period of years, show the loss of water in hundreds of cubic feet.

Water Used in Hundreds of Cubic Feet readings every two months

1982	1981	1980	1979	1978
13	16	7	8	8
13	7	7	6	8
22	6	5	6	7
18	11	8	8	7
11	10	7	8	8
13	8	6	7	8
90	58	40	43	46

In 1982, the total water used was 9,000 cubic feet. In 1978, the total water used was 4,600 cubic feet.

This water consumption study was based on the life-style of an elderly couple whose water use was consistent over the years. The increase in cubic feet of water, prompted the investigation. The cause was found to be a continuous flow of water into the overflow tube. By slightly bending the ballfloat arm downward, the incoming water was shut-off below the overflow tube.

Inlet Float Valve

When the flush tank inlet float valve is not functioning the water will be running continuously, causing overfilling of the tank. To correct this problem, proceed by draining the water from the tank. Then remove the bolts from the rocker arm and from the connecting piece screwed to the float arm. Take out the stopper plug and washer from the inlet float valve. Remove the fill tube by unscrewing it by hand.

Thoroughly clean the fill tube with a thin wire rod and replace it again by hand, turning it onto the float valve. Place a new washer at the top of the inlet float valve, and then replace the brass stopper plug. Replace the rocker arm and the connecting piece that fastens it to the float arm. Allow water into the tank, flush, and check that the fault has been corrected.

Ball Float

To check the ball float, flush the tank and shut off the incoming water valve. Carefully unscrew the ball float from the rod and inspect it for holes, cracks, or stripped threads. If there is any damage, replace it with a new ball float. Floats are available in copper or plastic. Secure the new float by holding the rod with one hand and screwing on the ball float with the other. Care should be taken not to bend the rod, or force the threaded parts. Hand-tightening the rod to the ball float is all that is necessary.

Reopen the water valve and fill the tank. Check to see that the ball float stops the inflow of water to the tank before the water level reaches the top of the overflow tube.

Water Supply Line Inlet

Leaks at the water supply line coming into the flush tank at the bottom of the tank are caused by worn-out washers. Sometimes a slight tightening of the nut will stop the leak, but it is important not to overtighten the nut. If the leak persists, empty the tank of water, and turn off the incoming water supply valve. Loosen the nuts both inside and outside the tank and replace the old washer with a new one. Turn on the nuts and tighten them, being careful not to overtighten them. Turn on the valve and allow the tank to fill. Check to see if the leaks have stopped.

FOOD WASTE DISPOSER

Most new houses are equipped with garbage disposers under the kitchen sink, provided that local codes sanction such installations. It was once believed that the disposer would clog up the drainage system, but this has since been proven not to be true because of the high pressure under which waste material is forced through the waste line.

Garbage disposers (Fig. 7-7) are made to fit sink drain openings. After setting the flange from the top into the sink opening, press it down until it grips the putty layer around the sink opening. From underneath the sink, place the gasket and clamping ring. Next, the mounting ring with three holes and mounting bolts is set into place. This is followed by the snap ring, which should be slipped over the flange and up until it snaps and fits into the groove. With the acutal parts at hand, these instructions will be much easier to follow.

Next, lift the main disposer unit from underneath the sink to the mounting assembly and turn the body flange counterclockwise until it engages the mounting assembly. Once the disposer is set, the plumbing connection can be made, and the unit be tightened into place.

The disposer drain pipe may be connected directly above the second sink trap, where codes permit. However, if this is done, a special directional tee, detail A (Fig. 7-7), is used.

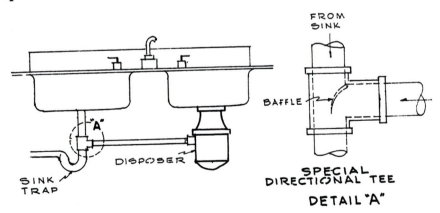

Figure 7-7 Food Waste Disposer

Care of Disposer

The food waste disposer is designed to grind up soft leftover foods as well as raw food cuttings resulting from food preparation. To keep the disposer in good working order, here are some helpful rules to follow:

1. Do not grind up bones, paper, foil, cardboard, rags, tea bags, strings, wire, broken glass, bottle caps, or broken dishes.
2. Use cold water when the unit is running—cold water solidifies oils and greases, which are then shredded and disposed.
3. Regular drain cleaners should not be used in a disposer; use only those specially advertised for such units, because they contain a peteroleum compound which takes care of oils and greases as well as a deodorant.
4. If the unit jams because something is preventing the cutter blades from turning, switch off the unit and try to loosen the cutter blades by turning them counterclockwise with a stick. A jammed unit will always trip as a safety precaution. Press the reset button after cleaning to start the unit again.

SELF-TESTING REVIEW QUESTIONS

1. Name two types of water closets.
2. The dimension from the wall to the center of the hold-down bolts of the water closet is what kind of dimension?
3. What must be done before replacing a stem washer in a leaking faucet?
4. What tools are required to replace a stem washer?
5. How can the life of a stem washer be prolonged?
6. Name the four cycles of the dishwasher.
7. When the water in a flush tank runs continuously, what is the most likely cause?
8. Leaks at the incoming supply line of the flush tank are caused by what?

8

WATER SUPPLY SYSTEM

The water system must provide an adequate supply of potable water to the fixtures at a suitable pressure. Most water supplies coming from an urban or suburban area are usually delivered already treated and are brought into the building at a good working pressure, between 30 and 80 pounds per square inch (psi). Higher pressure can put great strain on piping in the system and may cause leaking and damage to valves, faucets, and fixtures. Pressure below 30 psi is not sufficient to supply water to the upper floors of a building.

Where pressures are in excess of 80 psi, a pressure reducing valve, preceded by an adequate strainer, must be installed, and reduced to 80 psi or less, in accordance with the *Uniform Plumbing Code*. The *Code* further states that a water system provided with a pressure-regulating device or check valve at its source, or any water system containing water heating equipment, must be provided with a pressure relief valve set at a pressure of not more than 150 psi.

WATER SERVICE

The water service of a water supply system consists of the piping leading from the street main to the main valve just inside the house (Fig. 8-1). From there the water is conducted to both the hot water tank and to the fixtures through risers and branches.

From the street main, the water under pressure is forced into the

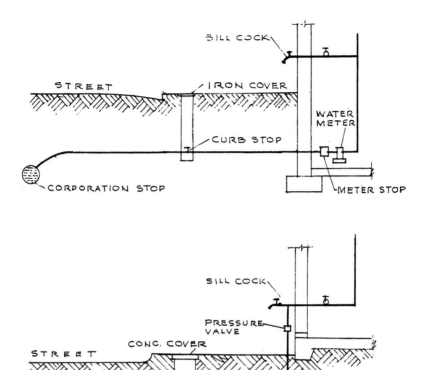

Figure 8-1 Water Service

service pipe, through a curb stop, a pressure reducing valve, then through the meter valve, the meter, the main shutoff valve, and into the main line which distributes the water to the fixtures.

The curb valve belongs to the city, town, or municipality and can be operated by a long-handled wrench. The meter is installed inside the house in the basement, or, in warm climates, it may be located outside the house. The meter valve is located just before the meter, and the main shutoff valve is directly after the meter.

WATER DISTRIBUTION WITHIN THE HOUSE

The water distribution system in a house starts at the water meter. From there it separates into two lines, one leading to the hot water heater and the other running across the basement ceiling and into risers and branches to the various fixtures throughout the house.

The cold water conducted into the hot water tank is heated

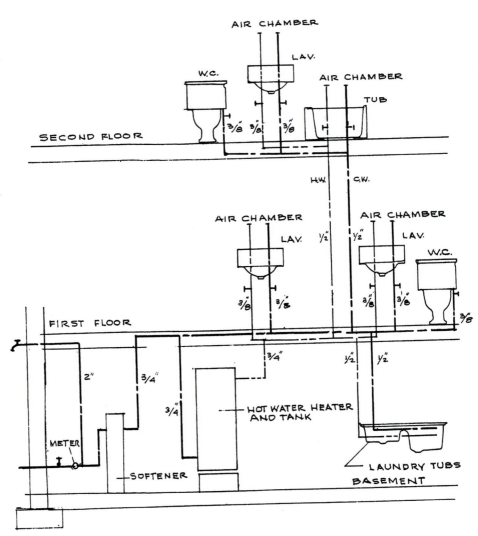

Figure 8-2 Water Distribution System

and is then conducted through the hot water piping to those fixtures that require hot water. Figure 8-2 shows a typical water distribution system within a two-story house with basement.

The hot water lines are represented by two short dashes followed by a long line. The cold water lines are represented by one short dash followed by a long line. Hot and cold lines are installed parallel to each other.

All fixtures receive hot and cold water, with the exception of the water closet, which receives cold water only.

DOMESTIC HOT WATER

By domestic hot water is meant the hot water delivered to fixtures, such as the kitchen sink, the lavatory, tub, shower, dishwasher, and washing machine. The hot water is produced in a storage tank-type heater, whose heating elements are at the bottom of the tank, in the case of a gas heater. For an electric heater, the heating elements are immersed in the tank water near the bottom of the tank and also near the top of the tank.

The gas heater is provided with fresh-air inlets and a flue to carry off exhaust fumes. The electric heater, on the other hand, does not require a flue since no fume-causing fuel is used.

TYPES OF WATER HEATERS

In residential heating, two types of hot water heaters may be used, and these are:

1. Fuel-burning (gas or oil) storage heater
2. Electric storage heater

The most common heaters in use today are the fuel-burning (gas or oil) heaters, with the solar heater making rapid advances.

The Gas-Fired Hot Water Storage Heater

The installation and maintenance of a hot water heater (Fig. 8-3) is part of the plumber's work, and, for him, is a relatively simple job. However, a hot water heater can be maintained by the mechanically inclined homeowner. Basically, the water heater consists of a storage tank and a burner unit at the bottom of the tank. Tank capacities range from 30 to 60 gal. A 40-gal tank is suitable for a 1250- or 1300-sq ft house that has two bathrooms.

The cold water supply comes in at the top of the tank through a dip tube inside the tank and is routed to the bottom, where it mixes with already heated water. A water temperature dial on the outside of the tank controls the desired temperature of the water within the tank. The water inside the tank enters the hot water supply line at the top of the tank, where it is led under pressure to the fixtures and appliances.

Relief Valves. There are two types of relief valves, the temperature type and the pressure type. The temperature-type valve opens to let in cold water when the water temperature rises above 200° F.

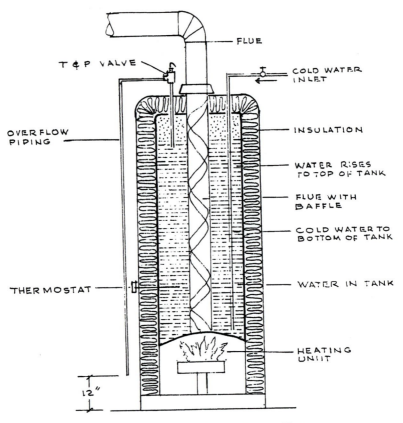

FLUE

T & P VALVE

COLD WATER
INLET

OVERFLOW
PIPING

INSULATION

WATER RISES
TO TOP OF TANK

FLUE WITH
BAFFLE

COLD WATER TO
BOTTOM OF TANK

WATER IN TANK

THERMOSTAT

HEATING
UNIT

12"

Figure 8-3 Gas-Fired Water Storage Heater

The pressure valve opens when the pressure inside the tank reaches 70 psi. Its purpose is to prevent the tank from bursting in the event that the thermostat fails to function and the water is overheated. A sensing element will detect a temperature rise and, together with pressure, opens the valve to release water or steam.

The T&P (temperature and pressure) valve installation requires a light coat of pipe-joint compound on its male threads. First, thread the valve into the tank and finger-tighten before tightening further with a wrench. Do not overtighten the valve.

Run a drain line pipe from the T&P valve outlet to an open sink or drain hole in the floor. The drain line must be the same size as the T&P valve opening, and its end must be open and unthreaded. Allow between 6 and 12 in. of air gap between the end of the pipe and the drain.

Magnesium anodes are installed in some of the newer tanks (Fig. 8-4). The purpose of these is to attract any particles in the water and thus help to keep the tank corrosion-free, adding to the life of the

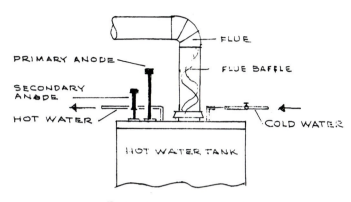

Figure 8-4 Anodes in Tank

water heater. The primary anode is already installed in the top of the tank when it is first acquired. The secondary anode is not installed but comes with the new heater and is packed inside the water heater carton. The anode is connected to a short piece of pipe which must be installed in the hot water supply outlet of the tank.

When you install the secondary anode, apply pipe-joint compound to the threads before placing it in the outlet. Tighten the pipe with a pipe wrench. The manufacturer of such tanks will not guarantee the tank if the anodes are not installed.

Drain Line. This line is needed due to the overflow from the water heater as it heats up. The drain line conveys the overflow water to a house drain or a sump pump. The line should not be run outside the house in freezing climates. Allow about 6 in. of air gap at the bottom of the pipe and the draining surface.

Gas Pilot Burners

Gas water heaters have pilot burners (Fig. 8-5) which burn continuously. The flame of the pilot light is projected on the thermocouple. If for any reason the pilot light goes out, the thermocouple causes the gas valve to close, preventing a supply of gas to the burner.

Electric Ignition

Instead of the gas jet ignition to light the gas burner, an automatic system, known as an electronic ignition system, may be used.

When the room thermostat calls for heat, the electronic current flows to an igniter circuit, which opens a pilot valve that brings gas to the pilot. A spark is provided to light the pilot gas.

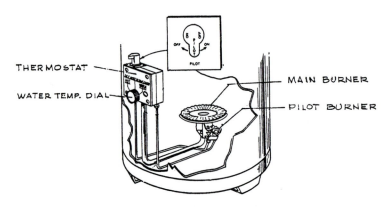

Figure 8-5 Gas Burner Unit

After the pilot is lit, sparking will stop. Flame is provided through a thermal sensing element and gas is furnished to the main burner, where it will be ignited by the pilot.

When the thermostat is satisfied and contacts open, the main burner and the pilot will go off. After about 1 minute the system will reset itself in preparation for the next cycle on a demand for heat. In some states the electronic igniter has become mandatory.

Inside the flue of the water tank are baffles running from the burner to the vent at the top of the tank. Baffles catch much of the escaping heat and transfer it to the interior of the tank to provide additional energy for heating water.

Gas Supply Piping

The gas supply piping to the gas furnace or boiler must be installed according to the latest recommendations of the "American National Standards for Installing of Gas Appliances and Gas Piping." Consult local codes or regulations for recommended sizes of pipe for the required gas volumes.

Furnace inputs up to 125,000 Btu/hr generally do not require a gas supply pipe size larger than 1 in. However, in no instance must a gas supply line be smaller than $\frac{1}{2}$ in., and further, a gas supply line must not serve more than one unit.

At the bottom of the gas supply riser a small stretch of pipe, called a *drip leg* (Fig. 8-6), should be installed to catch any dirt particles or moisture that may be carried in the pipe.

A manual gas shutoff valve should also be installed on the horizontal stretch of pipe leading into the boiler or furnace. A union joint provides easy access to the gas controls on the unit in the event of repairs.

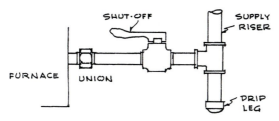

Figure 8-6 Gas Supply Piping to Furnace

Sizing the Gas Pipe. The size or diameter of the gas pipe depends on the volume of gas supplied and the pressure drop within the pipe length. The volume rate of gas in cubic feet per hour is determined by dividing the Btu per hour required by the furnace by the Btu per cubic foot of gas being used, a figure obtained from the local gas company. The cubic feet per hour value can then be used to determine the pipe size for gas of a specific gravity other than 0.60. The data used for the calculation are listed in Tables 8-1 and 8-2. Proceed as follows:

1. Multiply the cubic feet per hour required by the furnace by the multiplier found in Table 8-2.

TABLE 8-1 Capacity of Pipe[a]

Length of Pipe (ft)	Diameter of Pipe (in.)			
	$\frac{3}{4}$	1	$1\frac{1}{4}$	$1\frac{1}{2}$
15	172	345	750	1220
30	120	241	535	850
45	99	199	435	700
60	86	173	380	610

[a]Pressure drop, 0.3; specific gravity, 0.60. All values are cubic feet per hour.

Source: Uniform Plumbing Code, copyright 1982, International Association of Plumbing and Mechanical Officials (IAPMO).

TABLE 8-2 Multiplier Table

Specific Gravity	Multiplier	Specific Gravity	Multiplier
0.40	0.813	1.00	1.29
0.50	0.910	1.10	1.35
0.60	1.00	1.20	1.42
0.70	1.08	1.30	1.47
0.80	1.15	1.40	1.53
0.90	1.22	1.50	1.58

2. Find the pipe size for the length of the gas pipe run to the unit
   in Table 8-1. This procedure applies to the average piping installation where no more than about five fittings to the furnace are used.

Electric Water Storage Heater

The electric storage heater (Fig. 8-7) is clean and can be installed in
almost any part of the house. It does not require a flue for combustion
gases as do gas- or oil-fired heaters. Electric storage heaters use heating
elements to heat the water. The elements are immersed in the water
itself. Most electric water heaters with two elements have the same
size on the upper and lower areas of the heater [such as 4500 watts (W)
on a 30- or 40-gal unit]. They are connected in series; the top element
goes on first and heats the top water until the desired temperature is
reached, then the bottom element turns on.

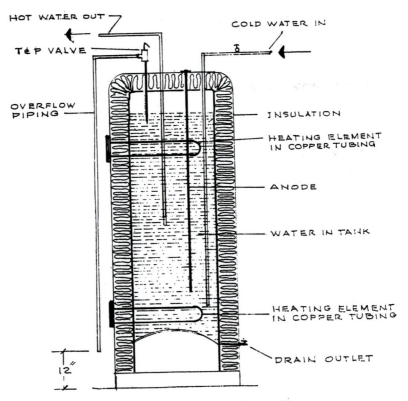

Figure 8-7 Electric Water Storage Heater

STORAGE CAPACITIES OF WATER HEATERS

Storage capacities of water heaters for the private home range from 20 to 60 gal.

Minimum	20 gal
Family of two	30 gal
Family of four	40 gal
with dishwasher and	
automatic washer	50 gal
Larger families	60 gal

Larger tanks are also available.

All tank-type storage heaters have a specification plate attached which contains pertinent information. As an example:

Capacity, 40 gal.
Natural gas
    input, 40,000 Btu/hr
Recovery, 38.7 gal/hr
Test Pressure, 300 psi
Work Pressure, 150 psi
Gas pressure in W.C. (water column)
    Minimum inlet, 5 in. W.C.
    Maximum inlet, 14 in. W.C.
    Manifold, 4.0 in. W.C.

The recovery per hour for a water heater is an important specification. The value of 38.7 gal/hr for a $100°F$ rise means that if cold water enters the tank at say $36°F$, in 1 hr we will get 38.7 gal of hot water at $100° + 36° = 136°F$.

Some manufacturers of hot water heaters may specify a recovery rate of $60°F$ instead of the usual $100°F$ rise. This will show that a heater with 40 gal recovery per hour for $60°F$ rise is equivalent to only about 24 gal recovery per hour for $100°F$ rise and is inferior to the specification claimed. It is often wise to seek out reputable manufacturers even if their products are somewhat more expensive.

The inside lining of a water heater is also quite important. The better the lining, the better the heater will be. Glass linings are perhaps the best and most durable, with copper running a close second. The least expensive water tank is the galvanized tank. It will last a long time provided that the water does not contain chemicals that will gradually erode the tank.

The average consumption of hot water in a home is shown below for various fixtures.

Washing machine	25 to 35 gal
Dishwasher (automatic)	4 to 5 gal
Dishwashing by hand	2 to 4 gal
Bathtub	10 to 15 gal
Shower	8 to 12 gal

CARE OF A WATER HEATER

The homeowner must from time to time perform two routine chores regarding the water heater:

1. Check the tank for sediment.
2. Check the relief valve

Sediment can form due to rusty or alkaline impurities in the water. An accumulation of these impurities can block the transmission of heat to the water and waste energy. Sediment does settle near the bottom of the tank and can therefore be drawn off through the drain valve near the bottom of the tank. Drain off a pail full of water to see if it is cloudy. This can be done once every two to three months to draw out all sediment.

Checking the relief valve is an important safety measure. Should the thermostat not function properly and too much pressure is built up in the tank, the valve will open automatically provided that it functions properly. Check the valve by periodically opening the lever and letting out some water or steam.

INSTALLING PIPING FOR A HOT WATER HEATER

When hooking up or installing a new hot water heater, certain basic steps ought to be followed to ensure a proper and safe installation.

1. List all the fittings needed to connect pipes for both hot and cold water, including the drain pipe for the T&P valve. These can be purchased in your local plumbing supply store.
2. Shut off the main house water valve.
3. Open a hot and cold water faucet to allow all water to drain out. Close the faucets after the pipes are drained.

4. Connect the cold water pipe to the cold water inlet of the heater in the following manner:
    (a) On top of the heater, the water inlet is marked "cold water supply" and the outlet is marked "hot water supply."
    (b) The dip tube must be in the cold water opening.
    (c) In using copper tubing, solder the tubing to an adapter before attaching the adapter to the water inlet. Do not solder the cold water connection, for it may harm the dip tube.
    (d) On the cold water inlet line, install a shutoff valve and union.
    (e) To restore cold water service, open the main house water valve. The valve on the cold water inlet line must always remain open.

Pipe Thread Compounds

Pipe thread compounds or sealants are made of a filler material held together by grease, oil, or resinous or plastic binders. Linseed oil is used as a binder in the preparation of some thread compounds. Barium oxide powder is particularly conducive to chemical inertness within the compound. Calcium carbonate, silicates, and lead are suitable for many applications.

Installing Copper Connectors

Copper connectors can be used between the incoming cold water and the hot water leaving the tank (see Fig. 8-8). Connectors require no cutting or threading. They replace nipples, elbows, tees, and adjust to any alignment. The homeowner can easily purchase and install the connectors by following a few simple steps.

1. First, shut off the gas, electric, or oil burner.
2. Turn off the cold water at the shutoff valve.
3. Bend the connector into the approximate shape to join the cold water supply to the inlet nipple of the water heater.
4. Bend another connector for the hot water outlet.
5. Make certain that all connections are in perfect alignment and finger-tighten before tightening with a wrench.
6. Plumbing water lines are sometimes used to ground electric currents. Since the copper connector is self-insulating, it breaks the electric path. To maintain continuity of ground, the connector must be bonded or jumped. Use approved clamps and connect No. 10 wire from the pipe on one side to the pipe on the other side.

1 COLD WATER VALVE
2 COPPER CONNECTORS
3 TEMP.-PRESSURE RELIEF VALVE
4 #10 WIRE

Figure 8-8 Flexible   Copper Connectors

7. Finally, light the gas pilot, turn on the water supply, and test the installation.

Filling the Hot Water Tank

When filling the hot water tank with water, the following steps are recommended.

1. Close the heater drain valve, which is located below the thermostat beneath the access cover.
2. Open the cold water supply valve to the heater. (*Note:* This valve must be left open when the heater is in use.)
3. Open a hot water faucet in the kitchen, bath, or laundry.
4. Fill the heater tank until water runs out of the open hot water faucet. This will let out the air in the tank and piping. Close the faucet after the water comes out. Remember, leave open the cold water valve to the tank.
5. Check all new piping installations for leaks; fix them if needed.

TREATMENT OF POTABLE WATER

The United States Environmental Protection Agency (EPA) has established minimum national drinking water standards which set limits on the amounts of certain substances found in drinking water. These substances are: chemicals, pesticides, bacteria, radioactivity, and cloudiness in water. If these substances are kept within proper amounts within the water, no immediate health threat is anticipated. Two substances that pose an immediate threat to health are bacteria, from human and animal wastes, and, nitrate in water above the national standard.

Natural water always contains impurities which can be detrimental to the plumbing system as well as to the health of the user. Water for drinking is therefore treated to counteract or neutralize these impurities by filtering, aeration, deionizing, and demineralizing the water.

WATER SOFTENERS

Water softeners are designed to take out large quantities of calcium and magnesium or bicarbonates that are contained in hard water. Hard water may also contain objectionable minerals such as iron and sulfur. Its constant use as drinking water may cause intestinal disorders, and its flow through piping will cause the formation of scale, adding resistance to the flow of the water.

Calcium and magnesium react with soaps, taking away the cleaning power of the soap. Iron in hard water may cause stains on clothing, while sulfur creates an objectionable odor and taste to the water.

A mineral known as *zeolite* is put into the water softener tank to exchange the calcium and magnesium for sodium (salt), which reacts favorably with soap. From time to time the sodium must be replaced by adding common salt to the softener. Drinking water treated in this manner has a salty taste and should be taken in moderation for those on a low-salt diet.

WATER PRESSURE

It might be well to point out the basic principles of hydraulics and why the water pressure at the bottom of a tank increases as the depth of the water in the tank increases.

One cubic foot of water weighs 62.4 lb and exerts a pressure of 62.4 lb per square foot at the bottom of a container. If the 1-cubic ft container were 2 ft high, the pressure at the bottom would be 2 X 62.4 or 124.8 lb per square foot. To express this in pounds per square inch, divide by 144, since 144 sq in. is equal to 1 sq ft. Therefore, 124.8 ÷ 144 = 0.866 psi.

Example:

Find the pressure per square foot at the bottom of a tank that is filled to a depth of 16 ft 6 in. (16.5 ft).

Solution:

$$P = 62.4 \times D$$

$$= 62.4 \times 16.5 = 1029.6 \text{ lb/sq ft, } or$$

$$P = \frac{62.4}{144} \times 16.5 = 7.15 \text{ psi}$$

The municipal water tower (Fig. 8-9) illustrates water pressure as it is available in buildings. The water level in the tower is 120 ft, which causes a pressure at the bottom of the tank of 51.9 psi, or

$$P = \frac{62.4}{144} \times D = \frac{62.4}{144} \times 120 = 51.9 \text{ psi}$$

This pressure also exists for the first house since it is at the same level as the bottom of the tank. In the second house, however, the water level in the tank is 120 + 40 ft = 160 ft.

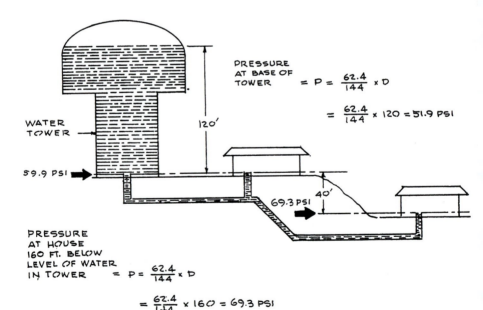

Figure 8-9 Pressure Head

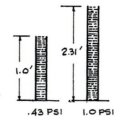

Figure 8-10 Pressure at Base of
Two Columns of Water

Pressure Head

It has been established that a column of water 1 ft high produces a pressure of 0.43 psi at the base of the column. Similarly, a 2.31-ft column of water produces a pressure at its base of 1 psi (Fig. 8-10).

To convert pressure head of water to pressure measured in psi, use the formula

$$P = H \times 0.43$$

Example:

How much pressure (psi) is exerted by a pressure head of 38 ft of water?

Solution:

$$P = 38 \times 0.43 = 16.34 \text{ psi}$$

To convert water pressure measured in pounds per square inch (psi) to pressure head, use the formula

$$H = 2.31 \times P$$

Example:

How much pressure head is required to create a pressure of 60 psi?

Solution:

$$H = 2.31 \times 60 = 138.6 \text{ ft}$$

Friction Loss

It can readily be seen that water pressure is affected by elevation. When designing a piping system another important factor to be considered is friction loss. Friction is the result of the fluid in the pipe rubbing against its inner surface. A rough inner pipe will cause more friction than a smooth pipe. Friction is also caused by fittings and valves.

To compute the friction loss of a piping system (Fig. 8-11), include the friction created by fittings and valves to the straight length of pipe (Table 8-3).

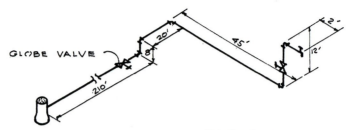

Figure 8-11 Computing Friction Loss

Example:

Find the head loss between the meter and the sill cock.

Solution: Find the total length of a $\frac{3}{4}$-in.-diameter standard pipe.

210 ft + 8 ft + 20 ft + 45 ft + 12 ft + 2 ft = 297.0 ft

Five 90° elbows (5 × 2.5 ft of pipe) = 12.5 ft

Two $\frac{3}{4}$-in. globe valves (2 × 20 ft of pipe) =   40.0 ft

Total (pipe, valves, elbows) = 349.5 ft

HOT WATER PIPE SIZING

There are two considerations that must be explored in the sizing of both hot and cold water pipe: (1) the flow rate of the water and (2) the friction loss in the pipes. The flow rate is measured in gallons per minute (gpm), and the friction loss is expressed in thousands of an inch for each foot of pipe length, which is 0.43 psi.

The quantity of water supplied to the fixtures is expressed in fixture units, as shown in Table 8-4.

If the maximum supply pipe is 200 ft or less, and where each piping system has 50 fixture units or less, the pipe is sized according to Table 8-5. When the piping system installation is sized according to Table 8-5, the following conditions must be taken into consideration:

1. Determine the total number of fixture units in the system.
2. Determine the difference in elevation between the meter and the highest fixture outlet.
3. Determine the length of the supply pipe from the meter to the highest fixture outlet.
4. Determine the incoming pressure of the piping system from the street main. Calculations are based on pressure not to exceed 100 psi pressure in the system.

TABLE 8-3 Allowance in Equivalent Length of Pipe for Friction Loss in Valves and Threaded Fittings[a]

Diameter of Fittings (in.)	Equivalent Length of Pipe for Various Fittings						
	90° Standard Elbow	45° Standard Elbow	90° T Standard	Coupling of straight Run of T	Gate Valve	Globe Valve	Angle Valve
$\frac{3}{8}$	1	0.6	1.5	0.3	0.2	8	4
$\frac{1}{2}$	2	1.2	3	0.6	0.4	15	8
$\frac{3}{4}$	2.5	1.5	4	0.8	0.5	20	12
1	3	1.8	5	0.9	0.6	25	15
$1\frac{1}{4}$	4	2.4	6	1.2	0.8	35	18
$1\frac{1}{2}$	5	3	7	1.5	1	45	22
2	7	4	10	2	1.3	55	28
$2\frac{1}{2}$	8	5	12	2.5	1.6	65	34
3	10	6	15	3	2	80	40
4	14	8	21	4	2.7	125	55
5	17	10	25	5	3.3	140	70
6	20	12	30	6	4	165	80

[a] All dimensions in feet except as noted.

Source: IAPMO (International Association of Plumbing and Mechanical Officials).

TABLE 8-4 Equivalent Fixture Units (Includes Combined Hot and Cold Water Demand)

Fixture	Private Use		Public Use	
	Number of Fixture Units	Gal	Number of Fixture Units	Gal
Bath tub (with or without shower overhead)	2	15	4	30
Hose bibb or side cock	3	22.5	5	37.5
Laundry tub or clothes washer (each pair of faucets)	2	15	4	30
Lavatory	1	7.5	2	15
Lawn sprinklers (standard type, each head)	1	7.5	1	7.5
Shower (each head)	2	15	4	30
Sink (bar)	1	7.5	2	15
Sink or dishwasher	2	15	4	30
Water closet (flush tank)	3	22.5	5	37.5
Water closet (flushometer valve)	6	45	10	75

TABLE 8-5 Fixture Unit Table for Determining Water Pipe and Meter Sizes for Flush Tank System

Pipe Diameter (in.)		Maximum Allowable Length (ft)					
Meter and Street Service	Building Supply and Branches	40	60	80	100	150	200
		Pressure Range: 30 to 45 psi					
$\frac{3}{4}$	$\frac{1}{2}$ a	6	5	4	4	3	2
$\frac{3}{4}$	$\frac{3}{4}$	18	16	14	12	9	6
$\frac{3}{4}$	1	29	25	23	21	17	15
1	1	36	31	27	25	20	22
1	$1\frac{1}{4}$	54	47	42	38	32	28
$1\frac{1}{2}$	$1\frac{1}{4}$	90	68	57	48	38	32
$1\frac{1}{2}$	$1\frac{1}{2}$	151	134	105	91	70	57
2	$1\frac{1}{2}$	210	162	132	110	80	64
$1\frac{1}{2}$	2	220	205	190	176	155	128
2	2	372	329	292	265	217	185
2	$2\frac{1}{2}$	445	418	390	370	330	300
		Pressure Range: 46 to 60 psi					
$\frac{3}{4}$	$\frac{1}{2}$ a	9	8	7	6	5	4
$\frac{3}{4}$	$\frac{3}{4}$	27	23	19	17	14	11
$\frac{3}{4}$	1	44	40	36	33	28	23
1	1	60	47	41	36	30	25
1	$1\frac{1}{4}$	102	87	76	67	52	44

TABLE 8-5 (Continued)

Pipe Diameter (in.)		Maximum Allowable Length (ft)					
Meter and Street Service	Building Supply and Branches	40	60	80	100	150	200
		Pressure Range: 46 to 60 psi					
1½	1¼	168	130	106	89	66	52
1½	1½	270	225	193	167	128	105
2	1½	360	290	242	204	150	117
1½	2	380	360	340	318	272	240
2	2	570	510	470	430	368	318
2	2½	680	640	610	580	535	500
		Pressure Range: over 60 psi					
¾	½ [a]	11	9	8	7	6	5
¾	¾	34	28	24	22	17	13
¾	1	63	53	47	42	35	30
1	1	87	66	55	48	38	32
1	1¼	140	126	108	96	74	62
1½	1¼	237	183	150	127	93	74
1½	1½	366	311	273	240	186	154
2	1½	490	395	333	275	220	170
1½	2	380[b]	380[b]	380[b]	380[b]	370	325
2	2	690[b]	670	610	560	478	420
2	2½	690[b]	690[b]	690[b]	690[b]	690[b]	650

[a]Building supply ¾ in. minimum.
[b]Maximum allowable load on meter.
Source: IAPMO (International Association of Plumbing and Mechanical Officials.

SIZE OF WATER METER AND BUILDING SUPPLY PIPE

Once the available pressure at the water meter is known, subtract ½ psi pressure for each foot of difference in elevation between the meter and the highest fixture outlet. Using the "Pressure Range" group within which this pressure will fall, from Table 8-5 select the length of column which is equal to or longer than the length required. Follow down the column to a fixture unit value equal to or greater than the total number of fixture units required by the installation. The sizes of meter and building supply pipe are given in the two left-hand columns.

SELF-TESTING REVIEW QUESTIONS

1. At what pressure may potable water be brought into a house?
2. What can be done to reduce the incoming pressure?

3. What stretch of piping is known as the water service?
4. How are a cold and a hot water line represented on a drawing?
5. Name two types of hot water heaters that may be used in residential heating.
6. What are the average tank capacities in gallons for a house?
7. Explain the purpose of a pressure relief valve on a hot water tank.
8. The size of a gas pipe to a gas-fired furnace depends on what two items?
9. What is the function of a water softener?
10. What are two conditions that must be explored in the sizing of hot and cold water pipe?

9

WATER HAMMER

SHOCK WAVES

In closing a faucet or valve abruptly, the running water in the pipe is brought to a sudden stop, causing the momentum of the water to be converted into shock waves. These shock waves produce a noise, called *water hammer*, and the energy of the wave also vibrates or shakes the pipe violently, which may rupture the pipe at its fittings, or crack the fittings. It is for this reason that malleable iron fittings are often recommended for water pipes.

PRESSURE RISE

The sudden closing of a faucet or valve also causes a momentary pressure rise in a piping system. The pressure rise increases with the velocity of the liquid, the length of the system from the fluid source, or with an increase in the speed with which it is started or stopped.

The pressure rise created by the water hammer effect is added to whatever fluid pressure exists in the piping system and although only momentary, this shock can be enough to burst pipes and break fittings and valves.

FORMULA THAT PREDICTS WATER HAMMER

A formula that closely predicts water hammer effect is

$$P = Cv$$

TABLE 9-1 Surge Wave Constants

Pipe Size (in.)	PVC Schedule 40	PVC Schedule 80	CPVC Schedule 40	CPVC Schedule 80
$\frac{1}{4}$	31.3	34.7	33.2	37.3
$\frac{3}{8}$	29.3	32.7	31.0	34.7
$\frac{1}{2}$	28.7	31.7	30.3	33.7
$\frac{3}{4}$	26.3	29.8	27.8	31.6
1	25.7	29.2	27.0	30.7
$1\frac{1}{4}$	23.2	27.0	24.5	28.6
$1\frac{1}{2}$	22.0	25.8	23.2	27.3
2	20.2	24.2	22.3	26.3
$2\frac{1}{2}$	21.1	23.7	21.2	25.0
3	19.5	23.2	20.6	24.5
4	17.8	21.8	18.8	22.9
6	15.7	20.2	16.8	21.3
8	14.8	18.8	15.8	19.8
10	14.0	18.3	15.1	19.3
12	13.7	18.0	14.7	19.2

Source: NIBCO Inc., Elkhart, IN 46515.

where P = maximum surge pressure,
C = surge wave constant for water (at $73°F$)
v = fluid velocity, ft/sec

Example:

For a liquid in a 2-in.-diameter Schedule 80 PVC pipe carrying 10 gal/min, the velocity in feet per second is 1.12 (refer to Table 4-13) and the surge wave constant is 24.2 (Table 9-1). What is the water hammer effect?

Solution:

$$P = 24.2 \times 1.12 = 27.1 \text{ psi}$$

The surge pressure (water hammer) is a maximum pressure rise for any fluid velocity, such as would be expected from instant closing of a valve. It would therefore yield a somewhat conservative figure for use with slow-closing actuated valves.

Correction Factors

For fluids heavier than water, the following correction should be made to the surge wave constant C:

$$C' = \frac{\text{S.G.} - 1}{2} = C + C$$

where C' = corrected surge wave constant

S.G. = specific gravity of liquid

Example:

A liquid with a specific gravity of 1.2 (ethylene chloride) in a 2-in.-diameter Schedule 80 PVC pipe has a surge wave constant of 24.2 (see Table 9-1). What is the corrected surge wave constant?

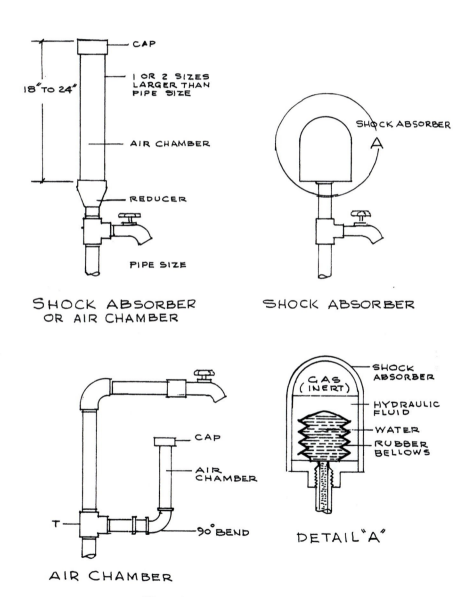

SHOCK ABSORBER OR AIR CHAMBER

SHOCK ABSORBER

AIR CHAMBER

DETAIL "A"

Figure 9-1 Types of Air Chambers

Solution:

$$C' = \frac{1.2 - 1}{2} \ (24.2) + 24.2$$

$$C' = \frac{0.2}{2} \ (24.2) + 24.2$$

$$C' = 0.1 \ (24.2) + 24.2$$

$$C' = 2.42 + 24.2$$

$$C' = 26.6 \text{ psi (corrected wave constant)}$$

AIR CHAMBERS

Water hammer can be eliminated by installing *air chambers* (Fig. 9-1). These are small lengths of vertical pipe about 18 in. long, capped at the top and attached to the line near a valve or faucet. The air chamber contains air which gets compressed when the water hammer wave hits it and acts as a cushion which greatly reduces the sound and impact.

When water hammer starts on a system that has been quiet before, it becomes quite obvious that the air chambers have filled with water, making them ineffective. To remedy this, close off the supply from the main water valve and open all faucets to drain out the water, thereby allowing air to enter the piping system. The air chambers will fill once again with air and become effective. Then close all faucets and turn on the main water valve.

SELF-TESTING REVIEW QUESTIONS

1. What causes water hammer?
2. What is the formula that predicts water hammer effect?
3. How can water hammer be eliminated?
4. How can we tell when air chambers are no longer operative?
5. How can air chambers be again made operative?

10

STORM WATER SYSTEM

SIZING GUTTERS

When it is necessary to find the size of a semicircular roof gutter, find
the area of the roof in square feet that the gutter is to serve, and then
determine the rainfall intensity in inches per hour for the particular
location of the building. Following are some of the established rainfall
intensities in inches per hour, lasting 5 minutes, for the localities
shown.

New York City	6 in.
Boston,	5 in.
Detroit, Mich.	6 in.
Memphis, Tenn.	5 in.
San Francisco	2 in.
Seattle, Wash.	4 in.

Once you have determined the rainfall intensity, look at Table 10-1
to find the nearest and next higher number of square feet of the roof
surface for the gutter pitch desired. The left column of the table will
give the diameter of the roof gutter.

TABLE 10-1 Size of Gutters

Diameter of Gutter (in.)	Maximum Rainfall (in./hr)				
	2	3	4	5	6

$\frac{1}{16}$-in. Slope

3	340	226	170	136	113
4	720	480	360	288	240
5	1,250	834	625	500	416
6	1,920	1,160	960	768	640
7	2,760	1,840	1,380	1,100	918
8	3,980	2,655	1,990	1,590	1,325
10	7,200	4,800	3,600	2,880	2,400

$\frac{1}{8}$-in. Slope

3	480	320	240	192	160
4	1,020	681	510	408	340
5	1,760	1,172	880	704	587
6	2,720	1,815	1,360	1,085	905
7	3,900	2,600	1,950	1,560	1,300
8	5,600	3,740	2,800	2,240	1,870
10	10,200	6,800	5,100	4,080	3,400

$\frac{1}{4}$-in. Slope

3	680	454	340	272	226
4	1,440	960	720	576	480
5	2,500	1,668	1,250	1,000	834
6	3,840	2,560	1,920	1,536	1,280
7	5,520	3,680	2,760	2,205	1,840
8	7,960	5,310	3,980	3,180	2,655
10	14,400	9,600	7,200	5,750	4,800

$\frac{1}{2}$-in. Slope

3	960	640	480	384	320
4	2,040	1,360	1,020	816	680
5	3,540	2,360	1,770	1,415	1,180
6	5,540	3,695	2,770	2,220	1,850
7	7,800	5,200	3,900	3,120	2,600
8	11,200	7,480	5,600	4,480	3,730
10	20,000	13,330	10,000	8,000	6,660

Source: IAPMO (International Association of Plumbing and Mechanical Officials).

SIZING VERTICAL PIPES OR LEADERS

When it is necessary to find the size of a leader, find the area of the roof in square feet served by the leader, and determine the rainfall intensity in inches per hour. From Table 10-2, find the nearest and

TABLE 10-2 Sizing of Roof Drains and Rainwater Piping for Varying Inches of Rainfall (Quantities Given Are Roof Areas in Square Feet)

Rainfall (in./hr)	Size of Drain or Leader (in.)[a]					
	2	3	4	5	6	8
1	2,880	8,800	18,400	34,600	54,000	116,000
2	1,440	4,400	9,200	17,300	27,000	58,000
3	960	2,930	6,130	11,530	17,995	38,660
4	720	2,200	4,600	8,650	13,500	29,000
5	575	1,760	3,680	6,920	10,800	23,200
6	480	1,470	3,070	5,765	9,000	19,315
7	410	1,260	2,630	4,945	7,715	16,570
8	360	1,100	2,300	4,325	6,750	14,500
9	320	980	2,045	3,845	6,000	12,890
10	290	880	1,840	3,460	5,400	11,600
11	260	800	1,675	3,145	4,910	10,545
12	240	730	1,530	2,880	4,500	9,660

[a]Round, square, or rectangular rainwater pipe may be used and are considered equivalent when enclosing a scribed circle equivalent to the leader diameter.

Source: IAPMO (International Association of Plumbing and Mechanical Officials).

next higher number of square feet of the roof surface. The size of the leader is found above the square feet of roof surface.

SIZING HORIZONTAL RAINFALL PIPING

In finding the diameter of a horizontal storm drain pipe, determine the maximum rainfall in inches per hour and the total amount of drainage in square feet the pipe carries at the pitch or fall the pipe is laid. In Table 10-3, find the nearest and larger number of square feet the pipe carries, and opposite left, find the size of pipe in inches.

DESIGN OF STORM SYSTEM

To clarify the foregoing, let's assume a flat roof on an industrial building (Fig. 10-1), measuring 58 X 80 ft, or a total of 4640 sq ft of roof surface. It was decided to use four roof drains, one at each corner of the building. At the front and rear of the building are cantilevered roofs over door openings and over a series of show windows which are also provided with roof drains. The front overhang is 2 ft X 58 ft, or a total of 116 sq ft. The rear overhang roof measures 8 ft X 16 ft, or a total of 128 sq ft.

The main roof is provided with a roof fill, creating a slight pitch to each of the four drains so that one-fourth of the amount of storm

TABLE 10-3　Size of Horizontal Rainwater Piping

Size of Pipe (in.)	Maximum Rainfall (in./hr)				
	2	3	4	5	6
	$\frac{1}{8}$-in. Pitch				
3	1,644	1,096	822	657	548
4	3,760	2,506	1,880	1,504	1,253
5	6,680	4,453	3,340	2,672	2,227
6	10,700	7,133	5,350	4,280	3,566
8	23,000	15,333	11,500	9,200	7,600
10	41,400	27,600	20,700	16,580	13,800
12	66,600	44,400	33,300	26,650	22,200
15	109,000	72,800	59,500	47,600	39,650
	$\frac{1}{4}$-in. Pitch				
3	2,320	1,546	1,160	928	773
4	5,300	3,533	2,650	2,120	1,766
5	9,440	6,293	4,720	3,776	3,146
6	15,100	10,066	7,550	6,040	5,033
8	32,600	21,733	16,300	13,040	10,866
10	58,400	38,950	29,200	23,350	19,450
12	94,000	62,600	47,000	37,600	31,350
15	168,000	112,000	84,000	67,250	56,000
	$\frac{1}{2}$-in. Pitch				
3	3,288	2,295	1,644	1,310	1,096
4	7,520	5,010	3,760	3,010	2,500
5	13,360	8,900	6,680	5,320	4,450
6	21,400	13,700	10,700	8,580	7,140
8	46,000	30,680	23,000	18,400	15,320
10	82,800	55,200	41,400	33,150	27,600
12	133,200	88,800	66,600	53,200	44,400
15	238,000	158,800	119,000	95,300	70,250

Source: IAPMO (International Association of Plumbing and Mechanical Officials).

water will flow into each drain. The water from the drains flows down pipes called *leaders*. The leaders are piped together, as shown, and are placed under the floor slab of the building before the concrete slab is poured. The system is provided with cleanouts (c.o.) and cleanout deck plates (c.o.d.p.). From the house drain the water flows into a public sewer.

To find the diameter of each pipe, the area of the roof surface that drains into the pipes must be known. For example, if the main roof has an area of 4640 sq ft, each of the four main roof drains will collect one-fourth of the area of storm water, which is 1160 sq ft.

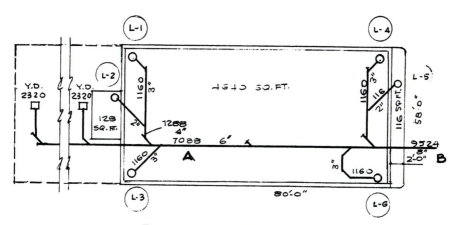

Figure 10-1 Storm Water System

Leader Sizes

To begin, first size all the leaders or the vertical pipe leading from the roof to the horizontal piping under the floor slab. Leader 1 collects one-fourth of the main roof area, or 1160 sq ft. In Table 10-2, find a rainfall of 4 in. in the left column and by moving to the right find the nearest and next larger number of square feet to 1160. The nearest number is 2200. Above this number read a 3-in.-diameter pipe. Therefore, leaders 1, 3, 4, and 6 are 3 in. in diameter. Leaders 2 and 5, of 128 and 116 sq ft, require a 2-in.-diameter pipe.

Horizontal Drain Pipe Sizes

Where the horizontal drain pipe from leader 1 and leader 2 meet, the pipe following carries the number of square feet for both leaders. This becomes 1160 sq ft, plus 128 sq ft, or a total of 1288 sq ft. Refer to Table 10-3 for finding the pipe size. Again assuming a rainfall of 4 in. and with an area of 1288 sq ft, the nearest next larger number of square feet, for a fall or pitch of $\frac{1}{4}$ in. per foot is shown as 2650 sq ft. Read the pipe size of 4 in. in the left column. Similarly, the pipe at A collects all the square feet of drainage from leaders 1, 2, and 3 and from two yard drains, making a total of 7088 sq ft. The nearest and next larger number of square feet in Table 10-3 is 7550 sq ft, which calls for a pipe size of 6 in.

Finally, the drain pipe at B collects all roof areas and yard areas, or a total of 9524 sq ft. From Table 10-3, the pipe size is found to be 8 in.

UNDERGROUND DRAINAGE

Rain or storm water falling on paved yards, courts, schoolyards, public parking areas, and similar places must be drained into a storm water drainage system, if such is available, or into underground drainage basins, located on the property to be drained.

Drainage basins are usually made in three sections: the drain ring, the solid ring, and the dome (Fig. 10-2). The water runs either into the opening at the top of the dome or it is collected in a series of yard drain inlets, or catch basins, which are connected by pipes to the underground drainage basin.

The lower ring of the underground basin is provided with drain hole openings designed especially to let the water seep into the earth without allowing the openings to become clogged with earth. Drainage also takes place at the open bottom of the underground basin.

Drain rings and solid rings are available in 4-, 6-, 8-, and 10-ft diameters. The height of the individual rings are either 2 ft or 4 ft 6 in. They can be stacked as needed.

Drainage Requirements

There are basic rules regarding draining projects, approved by planning boards and town engineers. These are:

1. All storm water must be contained on the site.
2. Where soil conditions and all other requirements of the town

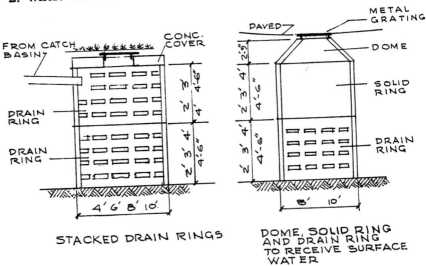

STACKED DRAIN RINGS

DOME, SOLID RING AND DRAIN RING TO RECEIVE SURFACE WATER

Figure 10-2 Underground Basins

TABLE 10-4 Runoff Factors

Pavement (grade 5% or less)	0.90
Pavement (grade in excess of 5%)	0.95
Seeded (grade 5% or less)	0.08
Seeded (grade in excess of 5%)	0.17
Roof deck	1.00
Other areas (minimum)	0.30

engineer so justify, an underground basin must be selected in accordance with the runoff factors shown in Table 10-4.

3. Computation for cubic footage of rainfall must be determined as follows: required capacity in feet is equal to the area in square feet to be drained, multiplied by the proper runoff factor, multiplied by 0.17 ft (2 in., the depth of the rainfall in a certain locality).

4. An underground basin with drainage openings should be designed, allowing for ground absorption, as follows:

total capacity = area (sq ft) $\times$ runoff factor $\times$ 0.17 (2-in. rainfall)

5. Selection of underground basin should be guided as follows:

Standard 8-ft-diameter basin contains 42 cu ft for each foot of height.

Standard 10-ft-diameter basin contains 67 cu ft for each foot of height.

No credit for drainage should be given for basin height above the level of inlet pipes.

Example:

Find the equivalent drainage for the following developed land area and flat-roof building.

Area (sq ft)	Use	Material	Runoff Factor	Drainage (sq ft)
7,300	Parking	Paving	0.90	6,570
6,400	Building	Roof deck	1.00	6,400
4,000	Landscaping	Seeded (graded 5% or less)	0.08	320
1,200	Undeveloped	Earth	0.30	360
18,900	Total	Equivalent drainage		13,850

Solution: Total capacity: 13,850 sq ft $\times$ 0.17 ft (runoff) = 2354.5 cu ft

$$\frac{2354.5}{42 \text{ cu ft}} = 56 \text{ lineal feet}$$

Using a 4-ft-high basin 8 ft in diameter, divide the height (linear feet) by 4 ft, or 56/4 = 14 sections. To stack up 14 sections in one basin is not practical. However:

$$14 \text{ sections} \div 2 \quad = 7 \text{ basins}$$

$$14 \text{ sections} \div 3 \quad = 5 \text{ basins (approx.)}$$

$$14 \text{ sections} \div 4 \quad = 4 \text{ basins (approx.)}$$

$$14 \text{ sections} \div 4.5 = 3 \text{ basins}$$

COMBINED STORM WATER AND SANITARY DRAIN

The storm and sanitary drainage system must be entirely separate from each other, except where a combined public sewer is available for disposal of such drainage. To find the diameter of the pipe where the sanitary and the storm sewer pipes join (Fig. 10-3), add to the storm-drained area an allowance in square feet for each fixture unit on the sanitary system. In other words, the total number of fixture units (21 in our example) must be transposed into an equivalent number of square feet of drainage that must be added on to the drained area of the storm system.

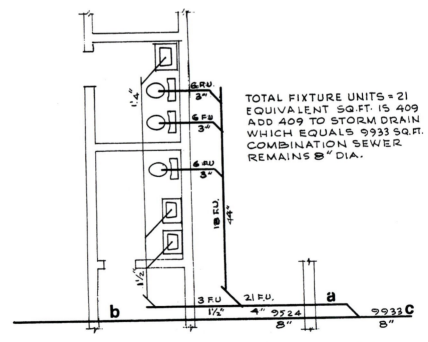

Figure 10-3 Sanitary Sewer A with Storm Sewer Line B, and Combination Sewer C

Example:

Add to the drained area of 9524 sq ft shown on the drawing the following number of square feet, found in the following manner:

30 sq ft for each of the first 6 fixture units
20 sq ft for each of the next 4 fixture units
14 sq ft for each of the next 10 fixture units
9 sq ft for each of the next 10 fixture units

$$\begin{array}{r} \text{Total fixture units} = 21 \\ - 6 \\ \hline 15 \\ - 4 \\ \hline 11 \\ - 10 \\ \hline 1 \end{array}$$

Solution:

$$\begin{array}{r} 30 \times 6 = 180 \text{ sq ft} \\ 20 \times 4 = 80 \text{ sq ft} \\ 14 \times 10 = 140 \text{ sq ft} \\ 9 \times 1 = 9 \text{ sq ft} \\ \hline 409 \text{ sq ft} \end{array}$$

Add the 409 sq ft to the 9524 sq ft of the storm system, a total of 9933 sq ft.

The additional equivalent square feet has not changed the pipe diameter requirement of the combination sewer. See Table 10-3 for a rainfall of 4 in. and pipe pitch of $\frac{1}{8}$ in. per foot. The nearest largest square feet is 11,500, making the required pipe size 8 in. in diameter.

SELF-TESTING REVIEW QUESTIONS

1. What is the established rainfall intensity in inches per hour lasting 5 minutes in Detroit, Michigan?
2. Find the diameter of the horizontal storm drain pipe when the rainfall is four inches per hour and the total amount of drainage is 6375 sq ft. The drain pipe is laid $\frac{1}{4}$ in. per foot.
3. Explain how rain leaders are sized.
4. What is a drainage basin?
5. Drain rings and solid rings are available in what diameters?
6. How is a combination storm water and sanitary drain sized?

11

SOLAR HEATING

The basic principles of solar heating and cooling rely on a basic fact. During summer, the sun appears high in the sky, and its rays fall almost straight down on us. In the winter, as the earth tilts away from the sun, the sun appears lower on the horizon, its path farther to the south.

One of the easiest and most effective ways to use solar energy is to take advantage of the natural course of the sun. If a building faces south, the sun's warming rays will shine directly into it during the winter, providing natural heat. During the summer, the structure will stay cooler if the windows are shielded from the sun by overhangs. A critical factor is the way the building faces.

The principle of natural solar heating and cooling was well understood by the early Greeks. Entire cities were laid out on an east-west axis so that one long side of each building faced south. By the first century A.D., the Romans had glass and built their famous baths with large south-facing windows, to warm the rooms with sunlight.

A classic example of natural solar design is Mesa Verde, Colorado, where the Indians built their adobe homes among the cliffs of the mesa. During the winter, the sun would shine directly into the cliff dwellings and warm them naturally. The thick adobe walls stored the heat of the day and at night the warmth would radiate into the living space. During the summer, when the sun is high, the overhanging cliffs would shade the structures to keep them cool. The Indians of Mesa Verde built their homes about A.D. 1200. Today, about 800 years later, their natural heating and cooling system is still working.

SOLAR WATER HEATING INDUSTRY

At the turn of the century favorable economies prompted the birth of the solar water heating industry in southern California. In 1914, soft coal sold at $13 a ton in California, twice the national average. Natural gas cost more than 10 times what it costs today, and electricity cost more than gas. Whatever fuel was used, heating water for the home was an expensive proposition.

Sunlight, on the other hand, was plentiful and free. Solar water heating systems were introduced in 1891. The early models were simply shallow water tanks mounted on the roof of the house with plumbing leading to the kitchen and bathroom. In 1909, southern Californians were introduced to the "Day and Night" Solar Water Heater. By adding a separate insulated hot water storage tank, the solar-heated water stayed heated day and night.

In 1930, rooftops in Los Angeles and such nearby towns as Pasadena and Monrovia were dotted with solar collectors. The solar industry was also booming in Florida and parts of the Southwest. But as electricity, natural gas, and other fuels became more readily available and dropped in price, the use of solar energy declined.

Now the pendulum has swung again. Fuels, although still available, are higher priced, and shortages are predicted in the coming years.

ESSENTIALS OF THE SOLAR HEATING SYSTEM

To understand how sunshine works to heat the home or office, imagine a garden hose that has been laying in the sun for several hours. When the faucet is turned on, out comes hot water—not the cool water one would expect. The sun's energy is absorbed by the hose and is transmitted as heat to the water inside it. The hose acts as a solar collector.

The four functional elements (Fig. 11-1) of the solar heating system are:

The collector
The storage
The distribution
The controls

Sunlight falling on the *collector* heats it just as it heats the garden hose, and the collector in turn raises the temperature of the water or

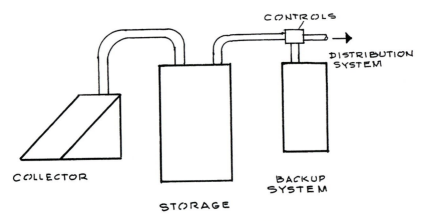

Figure 11-1 Elements of the Solar Heating System

air that carries the heat to where it is used. The *storage* system is where the heated water or air is stored for later use at night or on cloudy days. The *distribution system* delivers the warmed liquid or air from the collector to storage, and from storage to where it is needed in the building. The *controls* are used to regulate the flow of heat.

SOLAR WATER HEATERS

The solar water heater functions by passing water through a device called the *collector*, which converts the sun's energy into heat and raises the temperature of the water flowing through the collector. Instead of pure water, an antifreeze solution consisting of water and either ethylene glycol, alcohol, or propylene glycol may be desirable in freezing climates.

The flat-plate collector is ideal for the domestic hot water heater that requires a water temperature between 110 and 150°F, up to 200°F.

The collector (Fig. 11-2) consists of a metal plate and tubing which is soldered to the metal plate. The collector plate absorbs heat and transfers it to the liquid in the tubing. Collector plates can be of copper, aluminum, or steel, but both tubing and collector plate must be of the same materials so that their rates of expansion and contraction are the same.

The box containing the collector plate and tubing should be well insulated to shield the plate from the weather, that is, winds and rain, and to reduce heat loss. The tubing and plate are painted a flat black for additional absorption of the sun's energy. Light colors tend to reflect or throw off heat, whereas dark colors absorb heat.

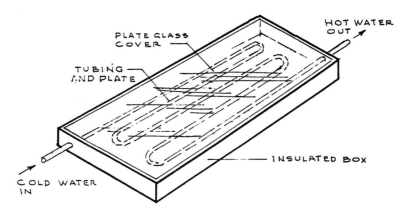

Figure 11-2 Solar Collector

The collector box is covered with a sheet of plate glass to permit the sun's rays to strike the metal collector plate and thus reduce the loss of reradiated heat back to the atmosphere. In cold climates a double layer of glass should be installed to prevent heat loss by convection when very cold air strikes the transparent surface.

When installing the collector on a pitched roof, for best results it should be tilted perpendicular to the rays of the sun. This is possible only if motorized equipment is used on the collector to follow the sun's path.

However, fixed collectors, those remaining in one position, should face south whenever possible. Those facing southeast or southwest work about 70 to 75% as well as those facing directly south.

The collector should be mounted as close as possible to the storage tank to reduce pipe lengths and hence friction losses within the pipe. All piping must be insulated.

How Water Circulates Through Pipe

Water circulates through the pipes of the collector to where it is needed by two methods. One is the forced method, or by the use of a circulation pump (Fig. 11-3), where friction of the circulating water in the pipe is of no consequence. The other is by the thermosyphon method, which is a natural circulation caused by the hotter water moving away from the colder water (Fig. 11-4). Hot water, which is lighter than cold water, rises to the top of the storage tank and replaces cold water drawn into the collector. The thermosyphon system will not work unless the storage tank's bottom is at least 2 to 3 ft above the top of the solar collector.

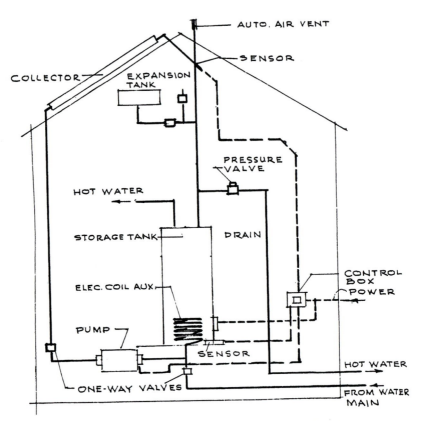

Figure 11-3 Solar Water Heating System: Forced Circulation

SIZING TANK AND COLLECTOR

One of the first considerations in sizing a storage tank is the gallons of hot water required per person within the family. This, of course, can vary from 20 to 5 gal per person per day depending on the family's lifestyle. The size of the tank is proportional to the number of people using the hot water. Allowances must be made for tank heat losses, for storage during bad weather, and for some reserve. This requires an additional 10% increase in the size of the tank in gallons.

Example:

Assuming a family of four using 10 gal per person per day, what size of tank would this family require?

Solution:

tank (gal.) size = 2 (reserve factor) × number of people × gal/person/day × 1.1
(heat loss factor, 10% increase in size of tank)

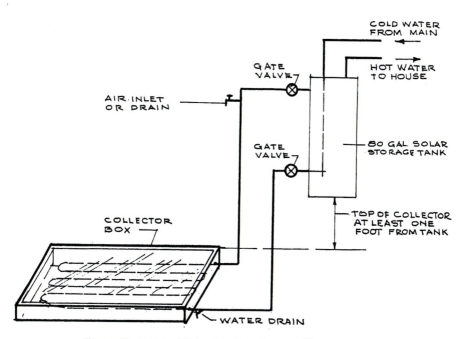

Figure 11-4 Solar Water Heating System: Thermosyphon

Thus:

$$2 \times 4 \times 10 \times 1.1 = 88 \text{ gal}$$

To size the collector area needed for an 88-gal tank, use Table 11-1.

In northern states an 88-gal tank will require a collector size of $1.5 \times 88 = 132$ sq ft.

In central states an 88-gal tank will require a collector size of $1 \times 88 = 88$ sq ft.

TABLE 11-1 Collector Area Per Gallon Of Water Stored
in Various Parts of the Country

Northern States: $1\frac{1}{2}$ Sq Ft	Central States: 1 Sq Ft	Southern States: $\frac{1}{2}$ Sq Ft
Washington	Utah	Southern California
Montana	Colorado	Arizona
North Dakota	South Dakota	New Mexico
Minnesota	Nebraska	Texas
Illinois	Iowa	Mississippi
New York	Ohio	Alabama
New Hampshire	Indiana	Georgia
Vermont	Virginia	South Carolina
Maine	Pennsylvania	Florida

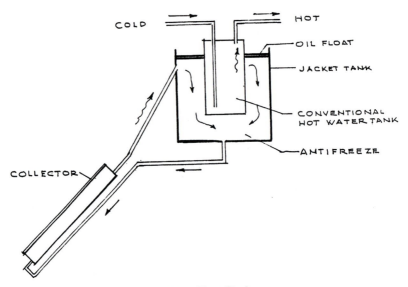

Figure 11-5 Heat Exchanger

In southern states an 88-gal tank will require a collector size of
0.5 × 88 = 44 sq ft.

Heat Exchangers

To keep the water in a collector from freezing in cold climates, several
things can be done. The water can be drained when freezing weather
is contemplated, warm water can be circulated through the collector,
the collector can be heated electrically, or a heat exchanger can be used.
By far the best way to prevent the freezing of the water in the collector
pipes is by the use of a heat exchanger. The heat exchanger is simply a
separate hot water loop added into the continuous flow system (Figs.
11-5 and 11-6). This separate loop allows the water in the collector
loop to be treated with an antifreeze. Therefore, a separate sealed container is necessary for drinking water which is in thermal contact with
the hot fluid that circulates in the collector.

ACTIVE SOLAR FORCED-AIR HEATING SYSTEM

In this system, the flat-plate collector collects hot air which is circulated
into a storage compartment containing a bed of rocks (Fig. 11-7).
The rocks become heated and when the heat is needed, it is drawn
off through a duct into a backup system and finally distributed through
the various rooms by a standard-type duct system such as that used in

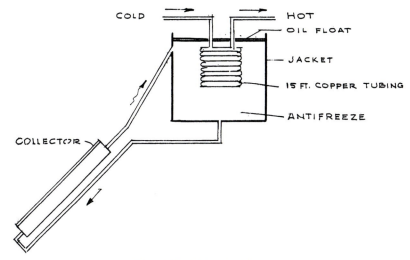

Figure 11-6 Heat Exchanger

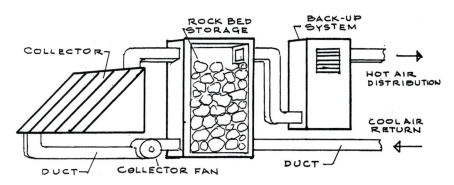

Figure 11-7 Active Solar Forced-Air Heating System

a warm air heating system. Cooler and recirculated air is drawn in at the bottom of the rock bed storage and again circulated into the collector for reheating.

SOLAR TRACKING SYSTEM

In the solar tracking system, collectors begin to track the sun's image as soon as the morning sunlight strikes them. The system's main pump is activated when an adequate amount of heat intensity is available, sending the coldest water from the bottom of the storage tank or tanks to the collector. Heated water returns to the storage tanks. Until sunset, collectors continue to track in accordance with these principles and water circulation is automatically controlled by a microcomputer (Fig. 11-8).

At the end of the day, the pump shuts down and collectors return to their face-down "park" position, ready for operation on the following morning. Protection against freezing is provided automatically and protection against boiling is provided by a cutoff which activates whenever stored water reaches a temperature of 185°F.

Collector lengths are 96 in. and 22 in. wide. Each collector weighs 40 lb. The collector itself is composed of a 28-gauge galvanized sheet metal body reinforced with cross bars. A rigid copper tube, selectively coated, is $1\frac{1}{4}$ in. X 105 in. A 5-mil (0.005-in.) metallized Mylar reflector assembly is attached in a concave shape with four aluminum strips and six retainer springs (Fig. 11-9). A 4-mil (0.004-in.) protective cover of DuPont Tedlar film is provided, offering spectral transmission properties superior to $\frac{1}{8}$-in. glass.

The electronic components of the solar tracking system consist of a gear reduction drive and photocells for up to 50 collectors. The drive box measures 30 in. X 8 in. X 8 in. and the photocells measure 5 in. X 8 in. X 2 in.

A control box assembly, complete with two pump relays, thermistor, and function switch, measures 12 in. X 12 in. X 4 in.

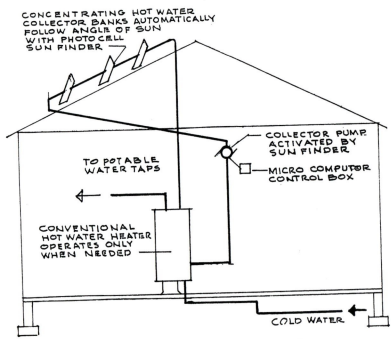

Figure 11-8 Solar Domestic Water Heating

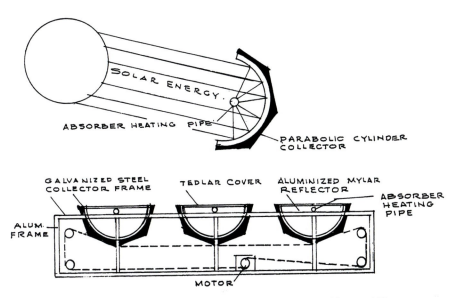

Figure 11-9 Parabolic Cylinder Collector (Courtesy of National Energy Alternatives, Inc.)

CHECKLIST FOR SOLAR WATER HEATING SYSTEM

To receive utility credits or low-cost financing for the installation of a solar/gas water heating system, gas companies require information such as that stated in the following typical checklist.

1. Does the system have the required permits?
2. Has the system been inspected and approved by the local building department?
3. Unless electricity is present by being used for water heating and if natural gas is available, is natural gas used for a backup system?
4. Has a method for flushing and draining the system been installed, unless prohibited by manufacturer's specifications?
5. On a closed-loop system, has a sampling or drain valve been provided in the collector loop?
6. Has a provision been made to permit independent operation of conventional backup systems; and in case of single-family gas backup systems, has valving been provided to enable both solar and conventional systems to operate independently?
7. Are flow directions indicated?
8. Is all plumbing in the solar system insulated, except where prohibited by local law? (All potable and nonpotable hot water

pipes must be insulated. All cold water pipes must be insulated for a distance of 2 linear feet from connection to hot water sources: $\frac{1}{2}$ in. wall thickness required indoors; $\frac{3}{4}$ in. wall thickness outdoors.)

9. Is insulation that is exposed to the weather protected from solar degradation and weathering?

10. Are joints in insulation either taped or glued according to manufacturer's specifications, if any?

11. Are exposed components other than solar collectors protected from freeze damage?
    (a) Air vent
    (b) Vacuum breaker
    (c) Temperature and pressure relief valve
    (d) Expansion tank
    (e) Other

12. If the system is a closed-loop system, has the contractor certified the kind of fluid in the closed system?
    (a) On nontoxic fluid systems, are closed-loop parts labeled with a warning to prevent the use of toxic fluids in the system?
    (b) On toxic fluid systems, are fluid lines marked with a warning label, "Danger, Water Not Drinkable—Poison"?

13. Is plumbing $\frac{3}{4}$-in. M copper or better?

14. Has piping been installed so that all freeze-protected plumbing slopes to drain?

15. Have dielectric unions been properly installed at all copper–ferrous joints?

16. Are all pipe runs, vertical and horizontal, adequately supported (fasteners at no greater than 5-ft intervals)?

17. Are temperature and pressure relief valves installed on the system in proper places? (On pressurized systems this is on the tanks. On closed-loop systems, it is on the tank and on the collector loop.)

18. Are the pressure and temperature relief valves discharged in a direction to eliminate any possible scalding or property damage?

19. Are all temperature and pressure relief valves from closed-loop systems installed in such a manner as to prevent damage to health and property? (These fluids are sometimes poisonous and proper disposal should be accounted for.)

20. In drain-down systems, has a vacuum relief valve been installed in the system? (Not applicable to closed-loop systems with expansion tanks.)

21. Are the collectors manifolded in a reverse-return, parallel manner (an equal flow path length through all collectors), or are other flow-balancing techniques employed?

22. Has the circulator pump been installed according to manufacturer's specifications?

23. Has the expansion tank been located on the suction side of the pump?

24. Are the following components located in such a manner as to allow access for cleaning, adjusting, servicing, examination, replacement, or repair?
    (a) Storage tank
    (b) Pump
    (c) Heat exchanger
    (d) Controller

25. Has the check valve for reverse flow prevention been installed in a proper manner?

26. Is the storage tank properly connected to the conventional water heater?

27. If supply water is in excess of 80 psi, or if it exceeds the working pressure rating of any system component, has an approved pressure regulator, preceded by an adequate strainer, been installed?

28. Has the completed system been installed in a neat and orderly fashion?

29. Is a device installed which indicates that the system is in operation?

30. Does the storage tank have a minimum insulation of R 12?

31. Does the conventional water heater have an extra insulation blanket or a minimum insulation of R 12?

32. Have the plumbing connections from the storage tank to the solar collectors been installed in a manner to promote thermal stratification?

33. If the storage tank is located outside, is its insulation material protected from weather and solar degradation?

34. Has a tempering valve or other temperature-limiting device been installed to limit the exit temperature of the hot water?

35. If the storage tank is installed in an attic, is it provided with a drip pan and an outlet to an adequate drain?

36. Have collectors been mounted with weep holes, if any, at the lowest end of the collector?

37. Is adequate drainage available in the collector array for leaks that may occur?

38. Has access to gutters, downspouts, and caulking been allowed for?

39. Are minor repairs and preventive maintenance allowed for in the collector installation?

40. Has flashing or a roof jack been installed to prevent water leakage at any piping penetration through the roof?

41. Are joints between the framework and the rest of the building caulked and/or flashed to prevent water leakage?

42. Are collectors installed so that water flowing off the collector surfaces cannot freeze and cause damage to roof or wall surface?

43. Using a solar sighter, do the collectors have a clear unobstructed view of the sun between the hours of 10:00 and 15:00 o'clock in December, or in the case of partial obstruction, has the system been adequately increased in size to provide a reasonable assurance of 60% annual contribution?

44. Is the rack constructed in a solid manner?

45. Has a minimum clearance of $1\frac{1}{2}$ in. been allowed between the collectors and the roof and the collectors and any side wall? (This does not apply when the collectors are integrated into the roof.)

46. Are control sensors located within inches of and near the bottom of the storage tanks?

47. Are control sensors located within 1 in. of and at the top of the solar collectors, outlet or within the collector box according to the manufacturer's specifications?

48. Are sensors for collectors and storage tank attached tightly for the best possible thermal transfer?

49. Is the system controller properly grounded? (Not applicable for systems of 30 volts or less.)

50. Have the control sensor and lead wiring been color-coded or otherwise labeled so that wires are readily traceable?

51. Has a qualified person in both solar and conventional water systems put the system through at least one startup cycle, including all modes of operation?

SELF-TESTING REVIEW QUESTIONS

1. Name the four functional elements of the solar heating system.
2. How does a solar water heater function?
3. Describe the construction of the collector.
4. Describe the two methods by which water circulates through pipes of the collector.
5. How are a hot water tank and a collector sized?
6. What is the function of a heat exchanger?
7. Describe the active solar forced-air heating system.
8. What is a tracking system?

12

FUELS FOR HEATING

Heating fuels are classified as follows:

1. Gases: natural, manufactured, and liquefied petroleum gas
2. Liquids: fuel oils
3. Solids: coal, coke, and briquettes

Gaseous Fuels

Natural gas, the richest of gases, contains 80 to 95% methane. Heating value is from 1000 to 1200 Btu per cubic foot.

The raw materials of manufactured gas are coal, oil, coke, and natural gas. They have a low calorific value, between 500 and 1000 Btu per cubic foot, primarily for industrial use.

Liquefied petroleum gas is a hydrocarbon mixture extracted from "wet" natural gas, known as propane, butane, or bottled gas. The word "wet" means that it contains more than 0.1 gal of gasoline per 1000 cu ft. Propane used for domestic heating contains 2516 Btu per cubic foot (per gallon), about $2\frac{1}{2}$ times the Btu content of natural gas.

Liquid Fuels

Fuel oils are hydrocarbon mixtures obtained from refined crude petroleum. For domestic heating, fuel oils are divided into:

No. 1 fuel oil

No. 2 fuel oil

The No. 1 fuel oil has the lowest viscosity. It is a distillate oil used in atomizing-type burners.

No. 2 fuel is a distillate oil used in domestic oil burners that does not require preheating. It is slightly heavier than the No. 1 fuel oil. Its Btu content is 139,000 Btu per gallon.

PS 300 and PS 400 are heating oils used on the West Coast. PS 300 is the lighter of the two and is used primarily for domestic heating purposes. The Btu content of No. 1 fuel oil per gallon is 137,400 Btu, while the No. 2 fuel oil per gallon is 139,600 Btu.

Solid Fuels

Coal. Coal is classified as follows:

Anthracite coal: a clean, hard coal containing 14,440 Btu per pound. Used primarily for industrial purposes and is exported to other countries for both domestic and industrial uses.

Bituminous coal: coal with an available heat range from 11,000 Btu per pound to a high of 14,000 Btu per pound. This coal is available in greater supply than anthracite.

Semibituminous coal: a soft coal that ignites slowly.

Lignite or brown coal: another coal that ignites slowly. It is classified midway between peat and bituminous coal. Contains about 7400 Btu per pound. It is considered a low-grade fuel.

Coke. Coke results from the solid residue remaining after the distillation of bituminous coals, or as a by-product of petroleum distillation. Also obtained from pitch. It ignites more quickly than anthracite and burns rapidly with little draft.

Briquettes. Briquettes are a solid fuel prepared from coal dust and finely crushed powdered coal. By adding a binder, such as pitch or coal tar, the dust particles are held together. Briquettes made with a pitch binder have the highest calorific value, exceeding that of coal.

FINDING THE BTU UNIT OF FUEL FOR OIL, GAS, AND ELECTRICITY

The total number of hours in the heating season depends on the location of the house. In northern areas the season is longer than in the more southerly states.

Assume that the heating season begins in an area, say, on November 1 and ends April 1. The total number of days for which heat may be required is 5 months or approximately 5 × 30 = 150 days × 24 hours per day = 3600 hours.

Winter Temperature Difference

The average winter temperature difference is found by subtracting the average low temperature from the average high temperature for the location in which the house is located.

The Btu Unit of Fuel

The Btu unit of fuel for oil, gas, and electricity is determined for each type, usually obtained from the local distributor of the fuel. For No. 2 oil the Btu unit per gallon is 139,600 Btu. For natural gas the Btu unit is 100,000 Btu per therm at 80% efficiency. For electricity the Btu unit is 3413 Btu per watt-hour at 100% efficiency.

Outside Design Temperature

The outside design temperature is the lowest temperature found to be in an area over a 5-year period. These design temperatures are available for a large number of localities in the United States.

The consumption of the fuels in gallons of oil, therms of natural gas, and kWh (kilowatt-hours) of electricity are found through the formulas given below.

Assume that the heat loss for a building is 20,700 Btu per hour. Then:

1. No. 2 oil, 139,600 Btu/gal, at 80% efficiency, 20,700 Btu loss, 73°F inside temperature:

$$\frac{20{,}700 \times 3600}{139{,}600 \times 0.80} \times \frac{73° - 40°}{70° - 0°} = 315 \text{ gal}$$

2. Natural gas, 100,000 Btu per therm, 80% efficiency:

$$\frac{20{,}700 \times 3600}{100{,}000 \times 0.80} \times \frac{73° - 40°}{70° - 0°} = 439 \text{ therms}$$

3. Electricity, 3413 Btu per kWh, 100% efficiency:

$$\frac{20{,}700 \times 3600}{3413} \times \frac{73° - 40°}{70° - 0°} \ 1028 \text{ kWh}$$

SELF-TESTING REVIEW QUESTIONS

1. Name the three basic types of heating fuels.
2. Which of the fuels is the richest in Btu per cubic feet?
3. What are the raw materials for manufactured gas?
4. Fuel oil No. 2 has what Btu content per gallon?
5. Anthracite coal contains how many Btu per pound?
6. What is coke?
7. Bituminous coal is available in what Btu range?
8. What are briquettes?

13

HEATING AND COOLING SYSTEMS

The water heated in the boiler is forced through the piping and the baseboard units, which give up the heat into the room (Fig. 13-1).

A pump, controlled by the room thermostat, circulates the heated water. The piping for this system may be of wrought iron, black steel, or copper pipe. Joints may be threaded, welded, or sweat-soldered when copper piping is used.

The size of the main as it leaves the boiler is usually about $1\frac{1}{4}$ to $1\frac{1}{2}$ in. in diameter, while risers to the second floor seldom exceed $\frac{3}{4}$ in. Branch pipes are $\frac{1}{2}$ in.

The one-pipe hot water system pumps about 8 to 10 gal of hot water per minute through the system and requires a $\frac{1}{8}$-hp 110-V motor.

A flow control valve is located at the first elbow on the main line leaving the boiler. Its purpose is to open under the influence of the pressure of the flowing water when the pump is operating, and to close and prevent gravity flow when the pump is off. If the hot water were allowed to circulate during pump-off periods, the radiators or convectors would overheat when the room was already too warm. A special flow fitting is also installed at the point where the water leaves the convector and joins the supply water to the next convector. The cooler water leaving the convector flows in the same pipe, with the hotter water

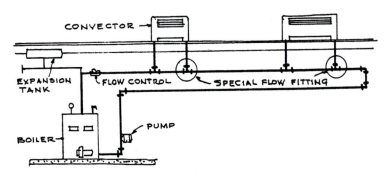

Figure 13-1 One-pipe forced hot water system

feeding the next convector. The special flow fitting is designed to lead the cooler and hotter water together in the same pipe without undue mixing.

Radiators may be of the baseboard type with fins, or they may be convectors that can be recessed in the wall. Each convector or baseboard heating unit is equipped with a control valve and air vent.

In operation, the one-pipe hot water system is filled slowly with water, with air vents open, until all air is vented from the system. Then the vents are closed and the control valves adjusted, and the system is ready for continuous operation.

The boiler water is kept at a desired temperature, usually between 180 and 200°F, by an aquastat located in the boiler. A room thermostat, sensing a falling temperature, starts the pump that circulates the hot water throughout the system. When the room has warmed to the desired temperature, the thermostat stops the pump and the flow valve swings shut, and the system furnishes no further heat until called upon again by the room thermostat.

EXPANSION TANKS

Expansion tanks on hot water systems are used to allow for the expansion of the water in the piping system when heated. Water expands with the rise of temperature and the additional volume thus created can flow into the expansion tank. Expansion tanks further trap air above their water level and compress it to an extent where all the water in the system will be under sufficient pressure to permit relatively high water temperatures to be carried in the boiler without danger of steam being formed. It is because of the latter function that expansion tanks are often called compression tanks.

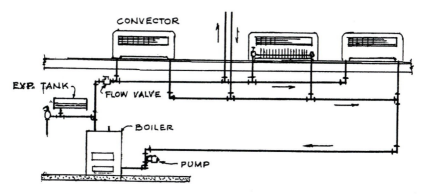

Figure 13-2 Two-pipe reversed-return hot water system

TWO-PIPE REVERSED-RETURN HOT WATER SYSTEM

In this system (Fig. 13-2) the hot water leaving the main of the first convector does not mix with the hot water main to the second convector. The somewhat cooler water leaving the first convector picks up all return water from all convectors before the water is brought back to the boiler. Circuits from boiler to each convector are of equal lengths; that is, the supply to the first convector plus its return are of the same length as the supply to the second convector and its return, and so on. All convectors receive the same amount of heat.

TWO-PIPE DIRECT-RETURN HOT WATER SYSTEM

In this system (Fig. 13-3) the hot water leaving the first convector nearest to the boiler is immediately returned to the boiler to be reheated. This is a relatively short circuit. The hot water supply to the second,

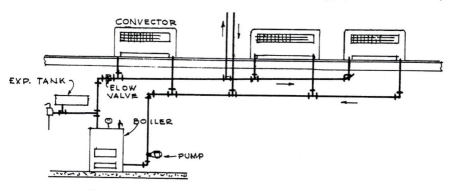

Figure 13-3 Two-pipe direct-return hot water system

third, fourth, and so on, convectors, each has its own immediate return, making the water travel to the first convector the shortest circuit and the water travel to the last convector the longest circuit. This system causes the first convector to overheat or receive more heat than the others, while the last convector, farthest from the boiler, or the longest circuit, receives the least amount of heat. To correct this condition, balancing cocks can be installed, or the proper pipe sizes can be used, or the radiators or convectors that receive a greater amount of heat can be proportionately reduced. This can be done by counting all the radiators except the first one on the circuit, and dividing this number into 10% (0.10). The answer is the percentage to add to each radiator or convector capacity so that the last radiator or convector on the circuit will have its capacity increased by about 10%.

SERIES-LOOP HOT WATER SYSTEM

In this system (Fig. 13-4) the hot water is pumped through a continuous pipe loop from boiler supply to boiler return. Baseboard heat-emitting units, strategically placed, give off the heat into the rooms. The pipe loop passes through each baseboard unit with the proper number of fins to supply the amount of radiation for which it was designed. Since the heat-emitting units are connected in series and are part of the main loop line, the same hot water supply passes through each successive

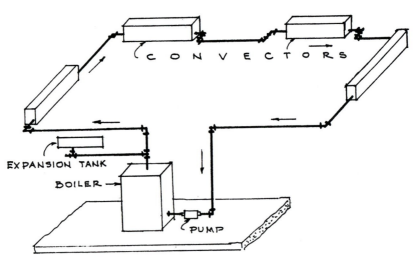

Figure 13-4 Series-loop hot water system

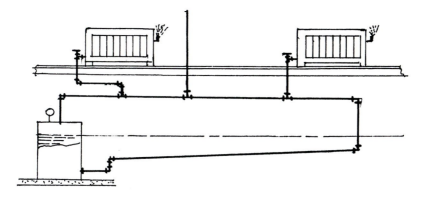

Figure 13-5 One-pipe steam system

convector. Accordingly, the convector closest to the boiler receives the hottest water, and those convectors farthest away receive somewhat cooler water. This problem can be remedied similar to that of the direct-return hot water system.

ONE-PIPE STEAM SYSTEM

The one-pipe steam system shown in Fig. 13-5 is one of the oldest systems and possibly still the cheapest to install. Other systems, however, are now favored over the one-pipe steam system.

The steam from the boiler, at a 5-lb pressure, rises in the pipes and into the heat-emitting units. When the units or radiators give off their heat to the rooms, the steam within the unit condenses, and the water thus formed settles at the bottom of the heating unit and flows back into the boiler by gravity, in the same pipe that carried the steam to the heating unit. It is for this reason that radiators or heating units, main steam pipes must be pitched slightly to allow for gravity flow.

The one-pipe steam system has a number of disadvantages based on our present-day standards. The system requires large pipe diameters, since steam and condensate travel in the same pipe in opposite directions. Often, the large pipes are exposed within the room, when running to upper floors. Radiators require air vents to allow air within the radiator to escape as the steam enters. When air vents get stuck, no heat can enter the radiator. Water hammer often occurs when condensate flows against the rising steam. Although not used in new private homes any longer, this system may still be used in factories and small public buildings.

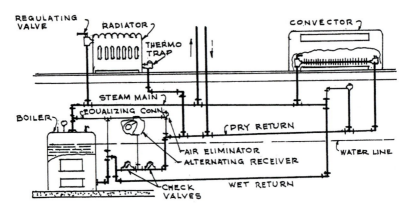

Figure 13-6 Two-pipe vapor system

TWO-PIPE VAPOR SYSTEM

The two-pipe vapor system requires vary low boiler pressure (1 to 2 oz) and a partial vacuum sufficient to circulate steam throughout the system (see Fig. 13-6). The steam enters the radiator at the top where a regulating valve controls the amount of heat. On baseboard unit heaters or convectors, the regulating valve is located where the steam enters the finned convector. After the radiator and/or the finned convector absorb and give up the heat to the rooms, condensate is formed which flows out through the thermostatic trap and back to the boiler. The thermostatic trap opens and closes, caused by the difference in temperature between the steam and the condensate. The steam, being hotter, closes the valve control element and does not allow the steam to escape. As soon as the steam changes to condensate, the heating element contracts within the valve and opens to allow the condensate to flow out. This action can be compared to a room thermostat. When the room cools, the thermostat signals for more heat. The thermostat causes the supply of heat to be turned off when the room has reached its predetermined temperature. The return condensate is brought back into the boiler through check valves and an alternating receiver. When the alternating receiver has received enough water, the head pressure is enough to force the water back into the boiler. The incoming check valve closes while the check valve nearest the boiler opens.

VACUUM SYSTEM

In this system (Fig. 13-7) the steam can be circulated at low pressure (under 5 lb), due to the constant vacuum maintained by a vacuum pump in the return main.

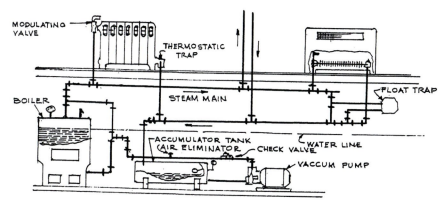

Figure 13-7 Vacuum system

The radiator temperature can be modulated within limited range. Radiators can also be placed below the water line, provided that the pump is placed still lower.

ELECTRIC HEATING SYSTEM

Electric heating is not much different from other systems. It has baseboard heaters and convectors like other hot water systems. Instead of circulating water, heating elements such as those on the electric kitchen range are used. The electric elements in baseboard heaters run the length of the heater, as shown in Fig. 13-8. There are no glowing coils because the elements are embedded in cast aluminum, and there are no fins to collect dust or lint.

An electric terminal box at one end allows for the electric connection. Baseboard electric heaters are available in many different

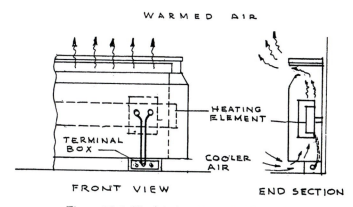

Figure 13-8 Electric baseboard heating unit

lengths, and when installed are made to fit snugly against the wall and floor and, at the same time, take the place of the room baseboard.

As in all heating systems, before the sizes of radiators, convectors, or baseboard heating units can be determined, it is necessary to find the heat loss in Btu required for that room. When this is known it is a simple matter to select a radiator, convector, or baseboard heating unit, for each is rated with its own number of Btu. A 3-ft-long baseboard convector, for example, can deliver 2560 Btu, and a 4-ft convector can deliver 3413 Btu. If the number of Btu required for a room is known, it is easy to select the number and length of convectors needed.

Example:

Suppose that a room has a heat loss of 8533 Btu per hour. How many and what length of baseboard convectors are needed to supply the Btu?

Solution: The answer can be found by taking out one 3-ft convector at 2560 Btu from the total of 8533 Btu. Take out another 2560 Btu from the remainder, and another 3413 Btu, and check what remains. This can be stated at follows:

$$
\begin{array}{rl}
8533 & \text{Btu required} \\
-\ 2560 & \text{one 3-ft convector} \\
\hline
5973 & \\
-\ 2560 & \text{another 3-ft convector} \\
\hline
3413 & \\
-\ 3413 & \text{one 4-ft convector} \\
\hline
0 &
\end{array}
$$

The unit of heat in electric heating is measured in watts of electric power. But how does the watt relate to the Btu?

1 Btu per hour is 0.293 W
1 kW is 1000 W
16,000 W is 16 kW

A room with a heat loss of 1707 Btu will need 1707 × 0.293 = 500 W of power to replace the lost Btu.

A small house with a heat loss of 38,010 Btu needs 38,010 × 0.293 = 11,137 W per hour to heat the house. An electric heating system for a small house is shown in Fig. 13-9, with baseboard heaters, pipe conduits, and service line. The baseboard heaters show the electric power (watts) needed to produce the Btu to warm the rooms. The pipe conduit, shown by the dashed line, houses the electric wires that feed the heaters. The service line is the electric line from the electric utility company.

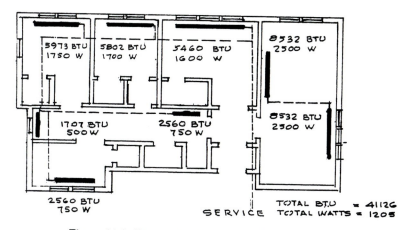

Figure 13-9 Electric heating system for small house

SUSPENDED-TYPE HEATERS

The suspended-type heater is fan-forced, and blows air through the electric element of the heater into the room. The amount of warmed air is expressed in cubic feet of air per minute (cfm). The heater may be hung from the ceiling or attached to the wall with steel brackets. Heaters can deliver from 700 to 4000 cu ft of air per minute. Suspended-type heaters are used where large areas as industrial or commercial areas are to be heated.

WARM AIR SYSTEM

The warm air system in use today is an outgrowth of the old gravity hot air system, with improvements that have made it one of the most popular types of residential heating systems. Unsightly round pipes or ducts, reaching in all directions from a clumsy centrally located furnace, and terminating in ugly floor or wall registers in the various rooms, have been replaced with small neat angular or round insulated ducts and streamlined wall grilles (Fig. 13-10).

Instead of dry hot air, emptying unguided into the room under gravity circulation, warm humidified air is forced through the system by a blower and distributed in measured amounts through directional outlets in each room.

The duct system is arranged to provide for the admission of outside air for ventilation in an amount equal to about 20% of the total air circulated in the winter months, but may also permit circulation of

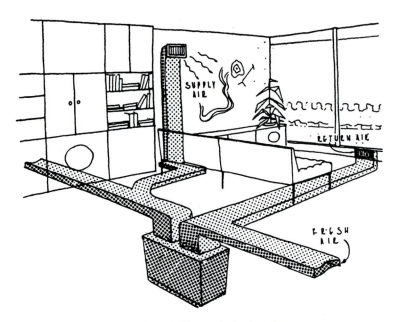

Figure 13-10 Warm air duct system

100% outdoor air in the spring, summer, or fall. In addition, the air is filtered at all times by inexpensive, throwaway filters located in the blower section adjacent to the furnace. A humidifier pan, automatically filled with city water, is located in the furnace unit, and has sufficient capacity to maintain a relative humidity of about 50% in the heated area.

The gas or oil burner, motor, blower, filters, and humidifier are all contained in an insulated metal jacket, giving the entire unit an acceptable appearance as part of a recreation room or utility room.

The forced warm air system for the average-size home is capable of supplying between four and six complete air changes per hour within the heated space. Warm, filtered, and humidified air leaves the heating unit at about 155°F and arrives at the room grille at about 140°F, having lost some of its heat through the metal ductwork.

Modern grilles are designed along clean, simple lines and may be finished to harmonize with any decorating scheme (Fig. 13-11). The matter of whether to place the supply grille high on the side wall, or near the floor, depends on the climate of the area in which the house is located.

In northern and colder climates, where cold floors can be a problem and where walls facing outside exposures must be thoroughly heated, supply air diffusers are best placed around the perimeter of outside-facing walls. The air diffuser can be located near the baseboard.

In warmer climates, however, where cooling air distribution is

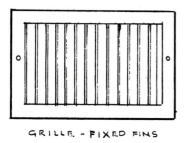

GRILLE - FIXED FINS   REGISTER · ADJUSTABLE LOUVER

Figure 13-11 Air diffusers

more important than heating air distribution, diffusers can be located on an inside wall as high as 6 ft above the floor or about 6 in. from the ceiling. In this location the outlets are high enough to blow air over the heads of occupants, and are also ideally placed for cool air supply should summer air conditioning be added to the system in the future. Adjustable bars across the face of the register direct the air in any required direction.

In addition to one or more supply outlets, each area except the kitchen and bathrooms contains a return air outlet, for the purpose of recirculating the return air (about 80% of the total).

No special construction is required where ducts run through partitions, as the ducts are sized to fit the standard stud wall space. For rooms larger than 10 X 10 ft, two or more supply registers are required.

Where one or more supply outlets are placed in every room to be heated, connecting rooms with open doorways can have a common return that may be located in a hallway or foyer. This is particularly true for smaller homes of 1500 sq ft or less.

The furnace unit may be placed wherever convenient within the house, or in an attached garage. Ducts may be run in the basement or in the attic space, or along the ceiling of the room being heated. If ducts are run above the ceiling, air outlets of special design may be mounted on the ceiling. There are a number of forced warm air furnaces of different design available which are (1) of horizontal design ideally suitable in an attic space; (2) the upflow or "high-boy" furnace, for small and confined closet areas; (3) the low boy, for a basement or a low ceiling area; and (4) the downflow, used in houses with under-the-floor type of distribution system. A typical low-boy blower furnace unit is shown in Fig. 13-12.

The temperature control system for a warm air heating system is somewhat similar to that used on a hot water installation. The room thermostat, upon demand for heat, starts the blower. But the blower can run only if the air temperature at the furnace outlet is between 90 and 175°F. This prevents circulation of air which is too cool to heat the room. If the air temperature at the furnace outlet drops below 90°F, the burner operates to heat the air to at least 90°F before

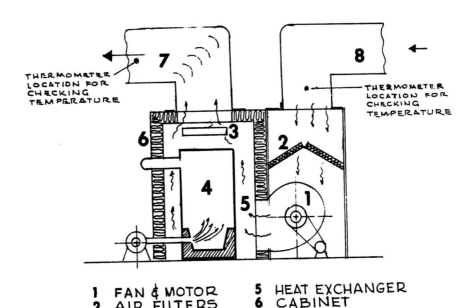

THERMOMETER LOCATION FOR CHECKING TEMPERATURE

1 FAN & MOTOR
2 AIR FILTERS
3 HUMIDIFIER
4 BURNER UNIT
5 HEAT EXCHANGER
6 CABINET
7 SUPPLY DUCT
8 RETURN DUCT

Figure 13-12 Detail of typical low-boy warm air blower-burner furnace

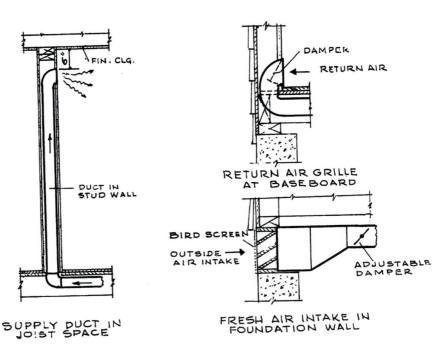

FIN. CLG.

DUCT IN STUD WALL

DAMPER

RETURN AIR

RETURN AIR GRILLE AT BASEBOARD

BIRD SCREEN

OUTSIDE AIR INTAKE

ADJUSTABLE DAMPER

SUPPLY DUCT IN JOIST SPACE

FRESH AIR INTAKE IN FOUNDATION WALL

Figure 13-13 Typical details of forced warm air system

the fan is allowed to start. When the room thermostat is satisfied, the blower and burner unit do not operate. Additional details of the forced warm air system are shown in Fig. 13-13.

AIR CONDITIONING

When we speak of air conditioning, we think of a cool room or space which is cooled by different-size air-conditioning units. Some are small window or wall units, while others are larger and look like convector cabinets.

For very large areas such as public buildings, hospitals, and factories, a central air-conditioning unit with a duct system is needed. Air-conditioning units, large or small, use the same cooling system as a refrigerator.

Room air conditioners are used in many homes, apartments, and small offices and are intended to cool just one room. Their Btu capacities range from 5000 to 18,000 Btu per hour.

Cabinet air conditioners look like cabinet-type heating convectors (Fig. 13-14) and are used in hospitals, offices, hotels, and motels. Cabinet units provide year-round air conditioning, that is, cooling in summer and heating in winter. They are capable of handling 11,700 to 14,000 Btu when cooling.

Central air conditioning is used in large stores, office buildings,

Figure 13-14 Year-round air-conditioning

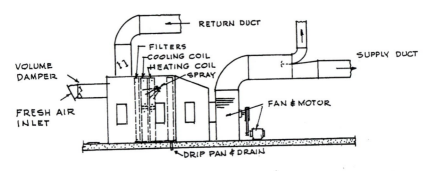

Figure 13-15 Air-conditioning system

and other large structures (Fig. 13-15). It is a boxlike unit called a
plenum. A motor-driven fan circulates the air into the rooms through
a duct system. The warmer room air is brought back in the return duct
to be recooled. A certain amount of outside air, about 20%, is mixed
with return air, about 80%.

The return air is first passed through filters for cleaning, then over
cooling coils for cooling the air. If the central system is also used for
winter heating, the air is passed over heating coils, making the system
a year-round air-conditioning system. It supplies cool air in summer
and warm air in winter, and can be used as a ventilating system between
seasons.

HEAT PUMP

The *heat pump,* a heating and cooling system, operates as an air-conditioning system. In the summer the heat from the room air is collected and then discharged to the outside. In winter, the process is
reversed. Heat is taken from the outside air, ground, or a nearby
stream, and brought into the house.

This may seem strange, for how can we take heat from the outside winter air? Suppose that an ice cube were placed on the outside
windowsill when the air temperature is 40°F. Obviously, the ice cube
melts. The ice cube absorbed or extracted heat from the 40°F outside
air. One of the laws of nature is that heat will move to a colder place
or substance.

REFRIGERATOR COOLING COILS

The refrigerator cooling coil carries a liquid coolant whose temperature
is far below 0°F. If this cooling coil were stuck into the ground whose
temperature, let us say, is 30°F, the cooling coil would extract heat

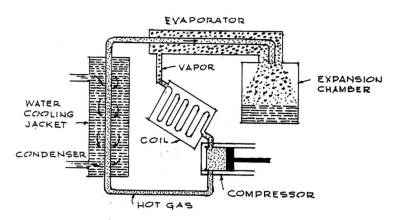

Figure 13-16 Refrigeration cycle: how a gas is liquified

from the ground. This is basically what a cooling coil does; it extracts heat from the cold air, the cold ground, or cold water and brings it to the inside to warm our rooms.

Imagine a coolant with a temperature of minus 190°F. With this temperature, heat can be extracted from extremely cold places or objects. The *refrigeration cycle* consists of four pieces of equipment that make it possible to cool our rooms in summer, and when used in a reverse manner, the same equipment is used in the heat pump (Fig. 13-16). The four pieces of equipment are:

Compressor
Condenser
Expansion valve
Evaporator

The *compressor* raises the temperature level of a refrigerant gas by compressing it. The hot gas flows through a pipe surrounded by a jacket of cold water called a *condensor*. As the cold water passes through the jacket, it draws the heat out of the gas and cools it off. Then the cool gas flows through an *expansion chamber* or *valve*, where it cools off more. From here it flows back to the compressor through a pipe *evaporator* that surrounds the pipe leading into the expansion chamber. The cool expanded gas helps to cool further the gas that is about to be expanded.

When the gas reaches the compressor, the process starts all over again. After the gas is cooled many times this way, its temperature becomes so low that the gas turns into a vapor and liquid. The vapor and liquid then pass through the cooling coil, making this the coldest part of the cycle. Warm air taken from the rooms and blown over

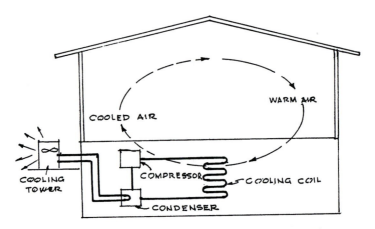

Figure 13-17 Heat transferred from room to outside

the cooling coils delivers the cooler air to the room (see Fig. 13-17). In a refrigerator, the cooling coil takes the heat from the food items within it, since a warmer object will always give up its heat to a colder receiver or object.

SELF-TESTING REVIEW QUESTIONS

1. The one-pipe hot water system pumps approximately how many gallons of hot water per minute?
2. What is the function of the flow control valve on the one-pipe hot water system?
3. Give the purpose of the expansion tank.
4. What is the essential difference between the two-pipe direct-return hot water system and the two-pipe reversed-return hot water system?
5. What type of heating system has become the most popular?
6. Describe the function of the heat pump.

14

HEAT-LOSS CALCULATIONS

The heat brought into a room by a heating system is constantly being lost through walls, windows, ceilings, and floors when there exists a temperature difference between the inside and outside of the walls, windows, ceilings, and floors.

The amount of heat that will be lost depends largely on (1) how much surface is exposed to the colder temperature, (2) how good a heat barrier (insulation) the surface is, and (3) how great the temperature difference is that is causing the heat flow.

A simple rule for computing heat loss is:

heat loss = area × wall effectiveness × degree temperature difference

Area in the equation above refers to the square feet of only those surfaces that are exposed to a temperature less than room temperature. By "surface" is meant walls, glass, door, ceiling, floor, and partition. It should be noted that no heat loss occurs between adjacent rooms when each room is heated to the same temperature.

Wall effectiveness expresses the ability of a material to resist the flow of heat. A heat-flow transmission coefficient has been assigned to every type of commercially used construction. Those constructions with low transmission coefficient factors indicate good insulators, while those with relatively high factors indicate poor insulators.

These factors are called *U-factors* and have been derived by the American Society of Heating, Refrigeration and Air-Conditioning

Engineers (ASHRAE). Heat transmission coefficients (U-factors) for residential construction vary from 0.07 for well-insulated walls to 1.13 for glass and thin wood doors.

The U-factor, or overall coefficient of heat transmission, represents the amount of heat in Btu that will pass through 1 square foot of a structural section per hour, per degree Fahrenheit of temperature difference between the outside and inside air temperatures. The U-factor is also the reciprocal of the sum of the thermal resistance values (R) of each element of the structural section.

The materials of a masonry cavity wall, with its elements of 4 in. face brick, an air space, 4 in. common brick, and gypsum lath with a $\frac{1}{2}$-in. plaster finish on the inside, have thermal resistance values (R) as shown in Table 14-1.

Table 14-2 gives the resistivity of building materials and their R-values.

Temperature difference is the arithmetical difference between the inside room temperature and the coldest outside temperature likely to occur in a given locality expressed in degrees Fahrenheit. The symbol for this temperature difference is the letter T. It is common practice to use 70°F for inside design temperature, with the outside temperature varying with geographical locations. The outside design temperature is not the coldest temperature ever recorded in a given locality, since extreme low temperatures exist for only short periods of time and it would not be economical to design for such a condition. Table 14-3 shows outside design temperatures in some parts of the country.

The basic rule for heat loss can now be stated as follows:

$$\text{heat loss} = A \times U \times T$$

TABLE 14-1 Construction Elements and Their R-Values

Elements	R-Value
Outside surface air (15-mph wind)	0.17
Face brick, 4 in.	0.44
Common brick, 4 in.	0.80
Air space	0.97
Gypsum lath, $\frac{3}{8}$ in.	0.32
Plaster, sand aggregate, $\frac{1}{2}$ in.	0.09
Inside surface (still air)	0.68
Total resistance	3.47

$$U = \frac{1}{R} = \frac{1}{3.47} = 0.29$$

TABLE 14-2 Resistivity of Building Materials, $U = 1/R$

Materials	Resistance, R	U-Value
Building boards		
Gypsum or plaster board		
$\frac{3}{8}$ in.	0.32	3.12
$\frac{1}{2}$ in.	0.45	0.5
Plywood		
$\frac{3}{4}$ in.	0.47	2.12
$\frac{1}{2}$ in.	0.63	1.58
Plywood or wood panels, $\frac{3}{4}$ in.	0.94	1.06
Plywood, fir or pine		
sheathing, $\frac{25}{32}$ in.	0.98	1.02
Wood, fir or pine, $1\frac{5}{8}$ in.	2.03	0.49
Plaster, sand, aggregate, $\frac{1}{2}$ in.	0.09	2.04
Air		
Space, $\frac{3}{4}$–4 in.	0.85–0.97	1.51–1.03
Outside surface (15 mph wind)	0.17	5.88
Inside surface (still air)	0.69	1.44
Building paper		
Vapor, permeable felt	0.06	16.66
Vapor, seal, two layers of mopped	0.12	8.33
15-lb felt		
Flooring materials		
Asphalt tile, $\frac{1}{2}$ in.	0.04	25.0
Carpet and fibrous pad	2.08	0.48
Carpet and rubber pad	1.23	0.81
Felt, for flooring	0.06	16.66
Floor tile or linoleum, $\frac{1}{8}$ in.	0.05	20.00
Plywood flooring, $\frac{5}{8}$ in.	0.78	1.28
Terrazzo, 1 in.	0.98	1.02
Wood subfloor, $\frac{25}{32}$ in.	0.98	1.02
Boards		
Acoustical tile		
$\frac{3}{4}$ in.	1.78	0.56
$\frac{1}{2}$ in.	1.19	0.84
Roof deck slab		
$1\frac{1}{2}$ in.	4.17	0.23
2 in.	5.56	0.17
3 in.	8.33	0.12
Sheathing		
$\frac{1}{2}$ in.	1.32	0.75
$\frac{25}{32}$ in.	2.06	0.48

TABLE 14-2 (Continued)

Materials	Resistance, R	U-Value
Roof insulation		
Preformed for use above deck		
$\frac{1}{2}$ in.	1.39	0.72
1 in.	2.78	0.36
$1\frac{1}{2}$ in.	4.17	0.24
2 in.	5.26	0.19
$2\frac{1}{2}$ in.	6.67	0.15
3 in.	8.33	0.12
Masonry units		
Face brick, 4 in.	0.44	2.27
Common brick 4 in.	0.80	1.25
Hollow clay tile		
3 in.	0.80	1.25
10 in.	2.22	0.45
Concrete block		
4 in.	0.71	1.40
8 in.	1.11	0.90
12 in.	1.28	0.78
Cinder concrete block		
3 in.	0.86	1.16
4 in.	1.11	0.90
8 in.	1.89	1.12
Roofing		
Asbestos cement shingles	0.21	4.76
Asphalt roll roofing	0.15	6.66
Built-up roofing, $\frac{3}{8}$ in.	0.33	3.03
Slate, $\frac{1}{2}$ in.	0.05	20.00
Wood shingles	0.94	1.06
Siding		
Asbestos cement, $\frac{1}{4}$ in. lapped	0.21	4.76
Wood drop, 1 × 8 in.	0.79	1.26
Wood bevel		
$\frac{1}{2}$ × 8 in. lapped	0.81	1.23
$\frac{3}{4}$ × 10 in. lapped	1.05	0.95
Wood-plywood, $\frac{3}{8}$ in. lapped	0.59	1.69
Structural glass	0.10	10.00

TABLE 14-3 Outside Design Temperature

Location	°F	Location	°F
ALASKA		NEW JERSEY	
Anchorage	-25	Newark	10
Juneau	-5	Trenton	10
ARKANSAS		NEW YORK	
Little Rock	15	Albany	5
Hot Springs	15	New York City	10
CALIFORNIA		Buffalo	0
Los Angeles	40	PENNSYLVANIA	
San Franciso	35	Philadelphia	10
Mission Viejo	40	Scranton	0
Sacramento	30	SOUTH DAKOTA	
CONNECTICUT		Aberdeen	-20
New Haven	5	Sioux Falls	-15
Bridgeport	10	TEXAS	
FLORIDA		Dallas	20
Miami	45	Amarillo	5
Tallahassee	25	VERMONT	
ILLINOIS		Burlington	-10
Chicago	-10	VIRGINIA	
Springfield	-5	Richmond	15
KANSAS		Norfolk	20
Dodge City	0	WASHINGTON	
Wichita	5	Seattle	20
MASSACHUSETTS		Tacoma	20
Boston	5	WISCONSIN	
Springfield	-5	Green Bay	-15
MINNESOTA		Madison	-10
Minneapolis	-15	WYOMING	
Alexandria	-20	Cheyenne	-10
NEW HAMPSHIRE		Laramie	-15
Concord	-10		
Manchester	-10		

INFILTRATION

In any room containing windows and doors, there is a certain amount of air leakage that seeps inward through window and door cracks when the wind blows. This leakage is called *infiltration*. Every cubic foot of cold outside air that leaks into the room imposes an additional load on the heating system. It is entirely correct to consider the heat required to warm the infiltrated air to room temperature as an additional heat loss inasmuch as the heating system has to supply it. The method

TABLE 14-4 Infiltration Factors

Note: Multiply the volume of the room by the appropriate U-factor.

Wind protection	Doors and Windows Weatherstripped	No Weatherstripping
	One Side Exposed	
	U	U
Without fireplace	0.012	0.02
With fireplace	0.032	0.04
	Two Sides Exposed	
	U	U
Without fireplace	0.018	0.03
With fireplace	0.038	0.05
	Three or Four Sides Exposed	
	U	U
Without fireplace	0.024	0.04
With fireplace	0.044	0.06

used in calculating the air infiltration is to find the cubic content of the room by multiplying the volume by the U-factor 0.018, by the design temperature difference. See Table 14-4.

Figure 14-1 and Table 14-5 illustrate a heat-loss calculation for a single corner room of a small building as recorded on a worksheet. Other rooms within the structure are similarly treated.

Construction of:	R-Value
Walls	
Outside surface air (wind 15 mph)	0.17
Face brick, 4 in.	0.44
Common brick, 4 in.	0.88
Air space (between brick)	0.97
Gypsum lath, $\frac{3}{8}$ in.	0.32
Plaster, sand aggregate, $\frac{1}{2}$ in.	0.09
Inside surface (still air)	0.68
Total resistance	3.55

$$U = \frac{1}{R} = \frac{1}{3.55} = 0.28$$

Construction of:	R-Value
Floor	
Carpet and fibrous pad	2.08
Plywood, $\frac{5}{8}$ in.	0.78
Vapor barrier, permeable felt	0.06
Wood subfloor, $\frac{25}{32}$ in.	0.98
Total resistance	3.90

$$U = \frac{1}{R} = \frac{1}{3.90} = 0.26$$

Ceiling	
Gypsum board, $\frac{3}{8}$ in.	0.32
Air space	0.97
Sheathing, $\frac{1}{2}$ in.	1.32
Vapor seal, two layers of	
mopped 15-lb felt	0.12
Roof insulation, $\frac{1}{2}$ in.	1.39
Total resistance	4.12

$$U = \frac{1}{R} = \frac{1}{4.12} = 0.24$$

SIZING THE WARM AIR HEATING SYSTEM

There are two considerations in sizing a warm air heating system. One is the amount of ductwork needed to carry the cubic feet of air per minute (cfm), and the other is the size (capacity) of the furnace. They are both related to heat loss.

Ductwork Needed

This depends only on the heat loss of the space, such as walls, doors, roof, floor, windows, outside walls, and infiltration allowance (usually 15% of the room heat loss), and on the final supply air temperature chosen (usually taken at about 110 to 120°F).

Thus air entering a room at 115°F will give up (115° - 70° room temperature) = 45° of its temperature in replacing the room heat loss to maintain the design room temperature of 70°F. This process requires a calculated amount of air as follows:

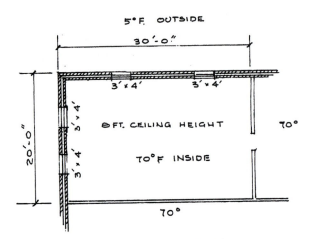

Figure 14-1 Heat-loss calculations

TABLE 14-5 Heat-Loss Calculations

Name: Corner Room
Location: Newark, N.J.

Design   Outside 5°F
Temperature: Inside 70°F

Room (Size) (cu ft)	Item	Area	U	Temp. Diff.	Heat Loss (Btu/hr)	Total Btu/hr
30 × 20 × 8 = 4800 cu ft	Exposed Wall 30 + 20 = 50 × 8	400				
	Windows 4 × 3 × 4 = 48 sq ft	48	1.12	65	3,494	
	Net wall	352	0.28	65	6,406	
	Ceiling 30 × 20 =	600	0.24	65	9,360	
	Floor 30 × 20 =	600	0.26	65	10,140	
					29,400	
	Infiltration = 4800 × 0.018 × 65 = 5616				5,616	
					35,016	35,016

$$\text{cfm} = \frac{\text{heat loss, Btu/hr}}{td \times 1.08}$$

where td represents the temperature difference between entering room air temperature and room temperature, and 1.08 is a constant derived from the specific heat of air (0.242 Btu/lb dry air), 60 (minutes in 1 hour), and 0.075 (density of air, lb/cu ft at sea level). Thus

$$0.241 \times 60 \times 0.075 = 1.08$$

Furnace Heating Capacity

This is the sum of the heat loss (Btu/hr) plus the heat required to warm the fresh air being introduced (not the same as infiltration), plus a pickup loss allowance for warming a building on a cold day after a shutdown period. This pickup factor is usually about 60%, or 1.6 multiplier. Therefore,

Furnace capacity = room heat loss + fresh-air loss + pickup factor

The fresh-air load can be found by cross-multiplying the cfm formula, and using td = (room temperature – outside-air design temperature) such as

$$cfm = \frac{\text{Heat Loss, Btu/hr}}{td \times 1.08}$$

Cross-multiply:

$$\text{heat loss} = \text{cfm} \times 1.08 \times td$$

where cfm = fresh air being used (usually 10% of supply CFM)
$td = 70° - 0°F$

The $0°F$ is the design outdoor temperature in Buffalo, New York, but this can change for other areas. The outside design temperature for Sacramento, California, is $30°F$.

SINGLE-LINE DUCT LAYOUT

Ductwork of an air-conditioning or ventilating system is often shown in single line. This is particularly true in large buildings, where the usual plans drawn to $\frac{1}{4}$ in. = 1 ft would be too large to show the entire plan on one sheet. A $\frac{1}{8}$ in. = 1 ft scale plan would then be used, provided that the duct layouts also permit space on the plans for plumbing, heating, and other pipe lines. A simple single-line air-conditioning duct system is shown in Fig. 14-2.

Every duct system consists of a main duct, branch ducts, and register outlets. The main duct starting at the unit is usually of the largest cross-sectional size and diminishes in size as air volume is given off into the branch lines.

Data on Designing a Duct System

Before the sizes of ducts in a duct system can be sized, it is necessary to know the cfm which are to be delivered into the various rooms. This was discussed in the early part of this unit. Once the quantities

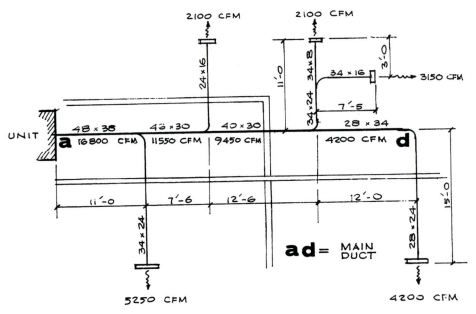

Figure 14-2 Single-line duct layout

of air are known for each room, it is a simple matter to size the ducts which are to deliver the air, provided that the velocity or feet per minute (fpm) at which the air is to travel in the duct is also known. When these two factors are known, the size of the duct can be determined by the formula

$$A = \frac{\text{cfm}}{\text{fpm}}$$

where A is the area of the duct in square feet, cfm is the quantity of air (cubic feet per minute), and fpm is the velocity of air (feet per minute). Standard air velocities through ducts and registers for residences are given in Table 14-6.

Sizing Ducts

From the formula $A = \text{cfm/fpm}$, the velocity used in a 28 in. X 24 in. duct carrying 4200 cfm can easily be found by transposing the formula, thus:

$$\text{fpm} = \frac{\text{cfm}}{A}$$

$$= \frac{4200}{4.7} = 894$$

TABLE 14-6 Standard Air Velocities Through Ducts

(a) In Residences

Description	Low-Velocity System (fpm)	Medium-Velocity System (fpm)	High-Velocity System (fpm)
Main ducts	500	750	1000
Branch ducts	450	600	750
Wall stacks	350	500	600
Baseboard registers	300	350	400
Wall registers above 5 ft	500	550	600

(b) For Public Buildings

Description	Velocity (fpm)
Outside air intakes	1000
Connections to and from heating unit	1000-1200
Through main discharge ducts	1200-1600
Branch ducts	600-1000
Vertical flues	400- 600
Registers or grilles	100- 400
For industrial buildings where noise is seldom a consideration	2800-3600

Example:

Find the area of a main duct in a building whose cfm is 16, 800 and whose velocity is 1325 fpm.

Solution; $A = \dfrac{cpm}{fpm} = \dfrac{16,800}{1325} = 12.67$ sq ft $\times$ 144 = 1826 sq in.

1826 square inches can be translated into a duct size of 48 in. $\times$ 38 in., approximately.

SELF-TESTING REVIEW QUESTIONS

1. The heat loss from a room depends largely on what three factors?
2. If a thermal resistance factor (R) is 4.02, what is the U-factor?
3. State the heat-loss formula.
4. State the formula for finding the cfm for a room.
5. What formula is used in finding the cross-sectional dimensions of a duct?

15

SHEET METAL STANDARDS AND CONVENTIONS

The past 20 years have changed yesterday's versatile, highly skilled sheet metal craftsman into the technically skilled sheet metal specialist of today. The craft has grown until it is now one of the most important trades in the construction and shipbuilding industries. With this growth and increased scope in an industry that is becoming more complex has come greater specialization within the trade and a need for competent, well-trained specialists.

The sheet metal draftsperson, known as the sketcher in the trade, was practically unknown 50 years ago. Today this person must understand the field and also have knowledge of piping for plumbing and heating as well as some of the engineering principles.

To understand the work of the sheet metal draftsperson it is necessary to know something of the sheet metal firm that employs this person. A firm will receive a contract from a heating and ventilating contractor to prepare, install, and otherwise be entirely responsible for the proper functioning of the duct system for conveying air, either cooling or heating.

The sheet metal contractor therefore is charged with three separate functions:

Preparation of the shop or field drawings
Fabrication of the joints and fittings that comprise the duct system
Installation of the joints and fittings that make up the duct system

Of these three functions, the preparation of the shop and field drawings is the key function of the sheet metal trade.

SHOP AND FIELD DRAWINGS

In preparing shop and field drawings, the sheet metal draftsperson works from engineered heating plans that show the designed layout of the duct work. Such plans, however, are not complete enough for the sheet metal contractor. Working drawings of the duct system must be prepared so that the shop can fabricate the system and those in the field can install the system.

Sheet Metal Shop Drawings

A shop drawing is a scale drawing of the duct system drawn larger than that shown on the engineered drawing and sectioned off into joints and fittings. Each joint and fitting is sized so that it can be conveniently fabricated from a standard stock sheet metal sheet. Each joint and fitting is also consecutively numbered to facilitate rapid assembly. Locations for registers, grilles, or openings for air diffusers are spotted by center line dimensions.

The entire system must include tie-in dimensions which permit the installation of the duct system in its exact location specified on the heating plans. The shop drawing also indicates the cubic feet of air per minute (cfm) supplied or returned at the registers, grilles, or other openings, so that the system can finally be balanced by adjustments made on volume control dampers.

BEVELS, DUCT TURNS, AND VANES

Bevels

Elbows direct air in a 90° angle, while bevels usually direct the air in 30°, 45°, or 60° angles (Fig. 15-1).

When air traveling through a duct system at a certain speed (velocity) is required to change its direction of flow, to turn a right angle, for example, it is made to do so by the use of the duct elbow. This sudden change of direction of flow of air causes additional resistance on the fan and motor. Since the sizes of the fan and motor are determined by all the resistance built up within the duct system, it is desirable to reduce this resistance as much as possible. This can be done by using large-sweep elbows, or square elbows with duct vanes or turning vanes.

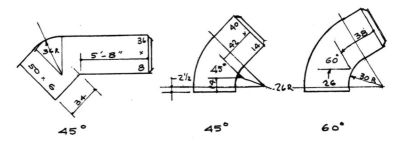

Figure 15-1 Bevels

Duct Turns

It has been found that a square elbow with duct turns offers no more resistance to the flow of air than a large-sweep radius elbow. The number and spacing of the duct turns depend entirely on the size of the elbow in which they are installed.

One rule is to allow a 3-in. minimum and a 5-in. maximum space between the blades (see Fig. 15-2). For example, a 28-in. duct, with duct turns spaced at 4 in. will have seven spaces or six duct turns. It follows, then, that a 24-in. duct, with duct turns spaced at 4 in., will have six spaces or five duct turns, and a 30-in. duct, with duct turns spaced 5 in., will have six spaces or five duct turns.

All that need be done is to divide the width of the duct by 3, 4, or 5, whichever will give the least number of duct turns.

Turning Vanes

The rule for the number of turning vanes within the elbow is the same as for duct turns, namely 3-in. minimum and 5-in. maximum spacing. The vane itself varies in size with the size of the duct—for example, for ducts up to 36 in., the radius $R = 3$ in., and for ducts 37 to 48 in., the radius $R = 4$ in. The vane has one short leg which is equal to one radius; the other leg is equal to twice the radius used.

Rigid Vanes

When rigid vanes are installed in a radius elbow, each vane has a progressive radius increase. The throat radius of the elbow is $\frac{1}{4}$ of the width of the elbow, or $\frac{1}{4}W$. If a duct is 16 in. wide, the throat radius is $\frac{1}{4}$ of 16, or 4 in. R.

The radius of the first vane will be 8 in., while the second and third vanes will have radii of 12 and 16 in., respectively. The heel radius is 20 in.

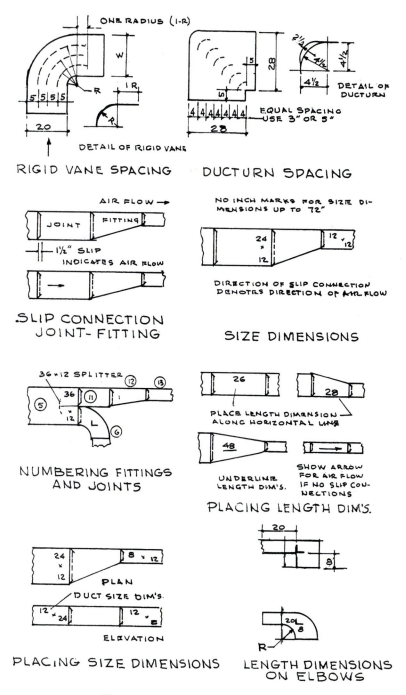

Figure 15-2 Standard duct conventions

JOINTS AND FITTINGS

There is a distinct difference in the accepted meaning of the words "joint" and "fitting" regarding an air-duct system. A *joint* is any straight section of duct which has no change in its cross-sectional dimensions. A *fitting* is a duct section with a change in its cross-sectional dimensions.

Size Dimensions

Size dimensions are those which indicate the width and depth of a joint or fitting, or if multiplied will give the cross-sectional area of the joint or fitting. Such dimensions are indicated directly on the duct. Since such dimensions are always in inches, it is not necessary to include the inch marks.

Numbering Fittings and Joints

Every fitting and joint must be numbered consecutively, when assembled to make a duct system, beginning at the first fitting, which is at the unit. The number of the fitting is enclosed in a circle. On small ductwork the circled number is shown outside the joint or fitting.

Length Dimensions

Length dimensions are placed in the center of the joint or fitting and to the top of the duct section. When a fitting reduces, the length dimension is placed on the line of the duct remaining horizontal.

PLACING SIZE DIMENSIONS

Size dimensions are those which give the width and depth of a duct. On small ductwork, these dimensions are lettered diagonally, so the numerals need not be reduced in size.

DIMENSIONING DUCT ELBOWS

Duct elbows are generally dimensioned by giving the throat radius, the size of the duct, and the intersection of the perpendicular distances measured from the end faces of the duct, or as indicated.

Flexible scoops, splitter dampers, duct obstructions, a combination rigid scoop and splitter damper, and adjustable scoop and regular dampers are shown in Fig. 15-3.

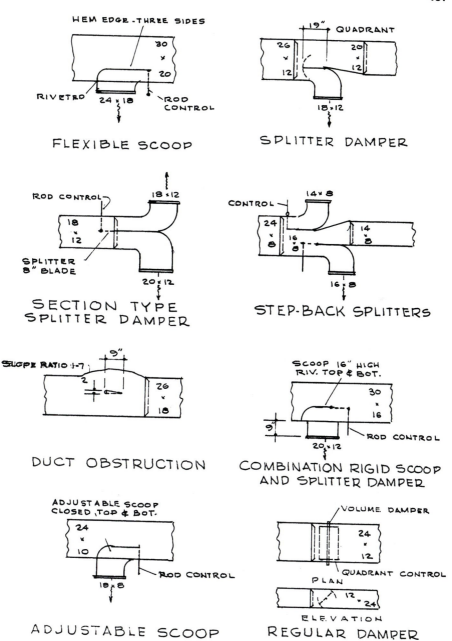

Figure 15-3 Scoops, splitters, dampers, and obstruction.

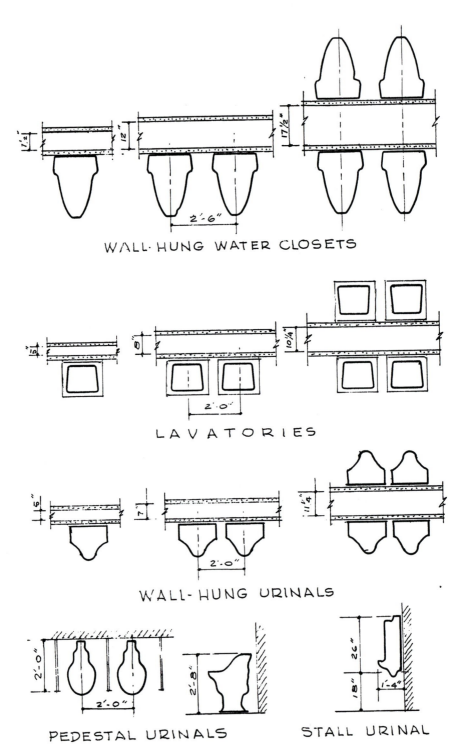

WALL·HUNG WATER CLOSETS

LAVATORIES

WALL·HUNG URINALS

PEDESTAL URINALS   STALL URINAL

Figure 15-4 Pipe space required for various fixtures

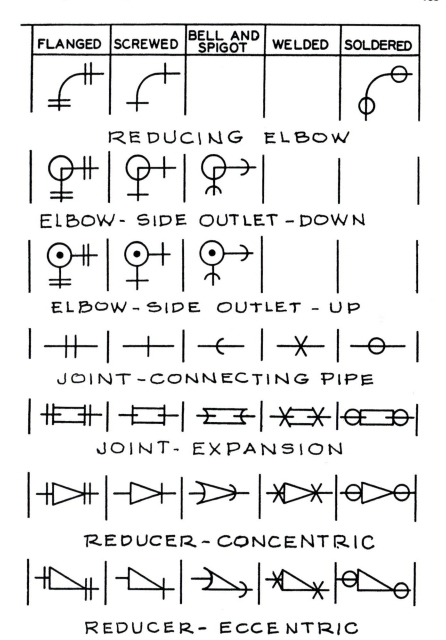

FLANGED	SCREWED	BELL AND SPIGOT	WELDED	SOLDERED

REDUCING ELBOW

ELBOW- SIDE OUTLET -DOWN

ELBOW - SIDE OUTLET - UP

JOINT -CONNECTING PIPE

JOINT- EXPANSION

REDUCER - CONCENTRIC

REDUCER- ECCENTRIC

Figure 15-5 Graphical symbols: pipe fittings and valves

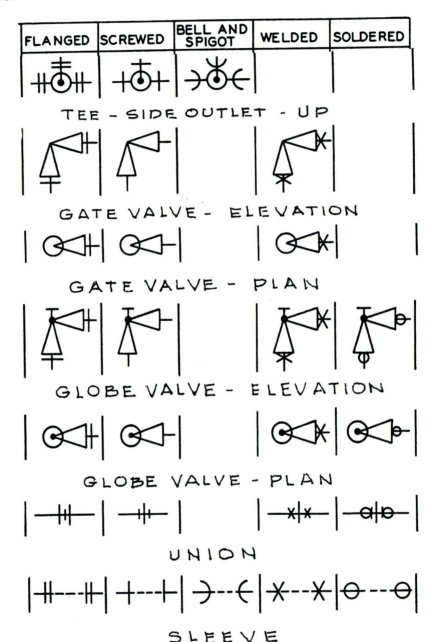

FLANGED	SCREWED	BELL AND SPIGOT	WELDED	SOLDERED

TEE - SIDE OUTLET - UP

GATE VALVE - ELEVATION

GATE VALVE - PLAN

GLOBE VALVE - ELEVATION

GLOBE VALVE - PLAN

UNION

SLEEVE

Figure 15-5 (Continued)

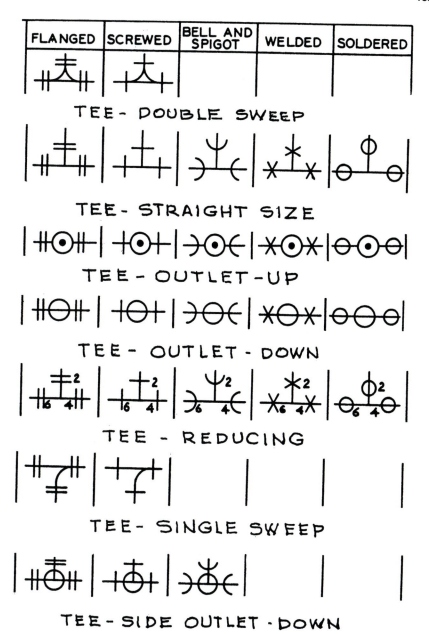

FLANGED	SCREWED	BELL AND SPIGOT	WELDED	SOLDERED

TEE - DOUBLE SWEEP

TEE - STRAIGHT SIZE

TEE - OUTLET - UP

TEE - OUTLET - DOWN

TEE - REDUCING

TEE - SINGLE SWEEP

TEE - SIDE OUTLET - DOWN

Figure 15-5 (Continued)

FLANGED	SCREWED	BELL AND SPIGOT	WELDED	SOLDERED

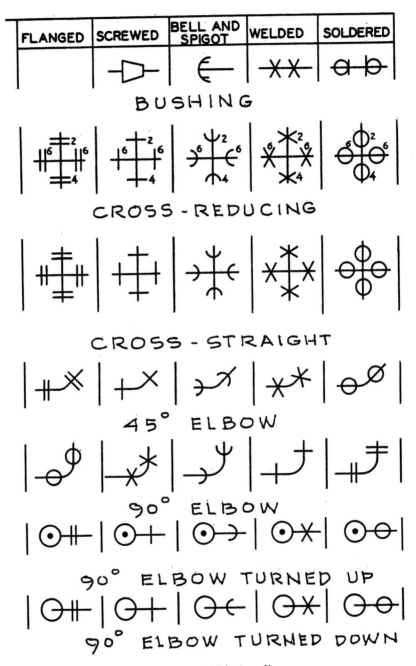

BUSHING

CROSS - REDUCING

CROSS - STRAIGHT

45° ELBOW

90° ELBOW

90° ELBOW TURNED UP

90° ELBOW TURNED DOWN

Figure 15-5 (Continued)

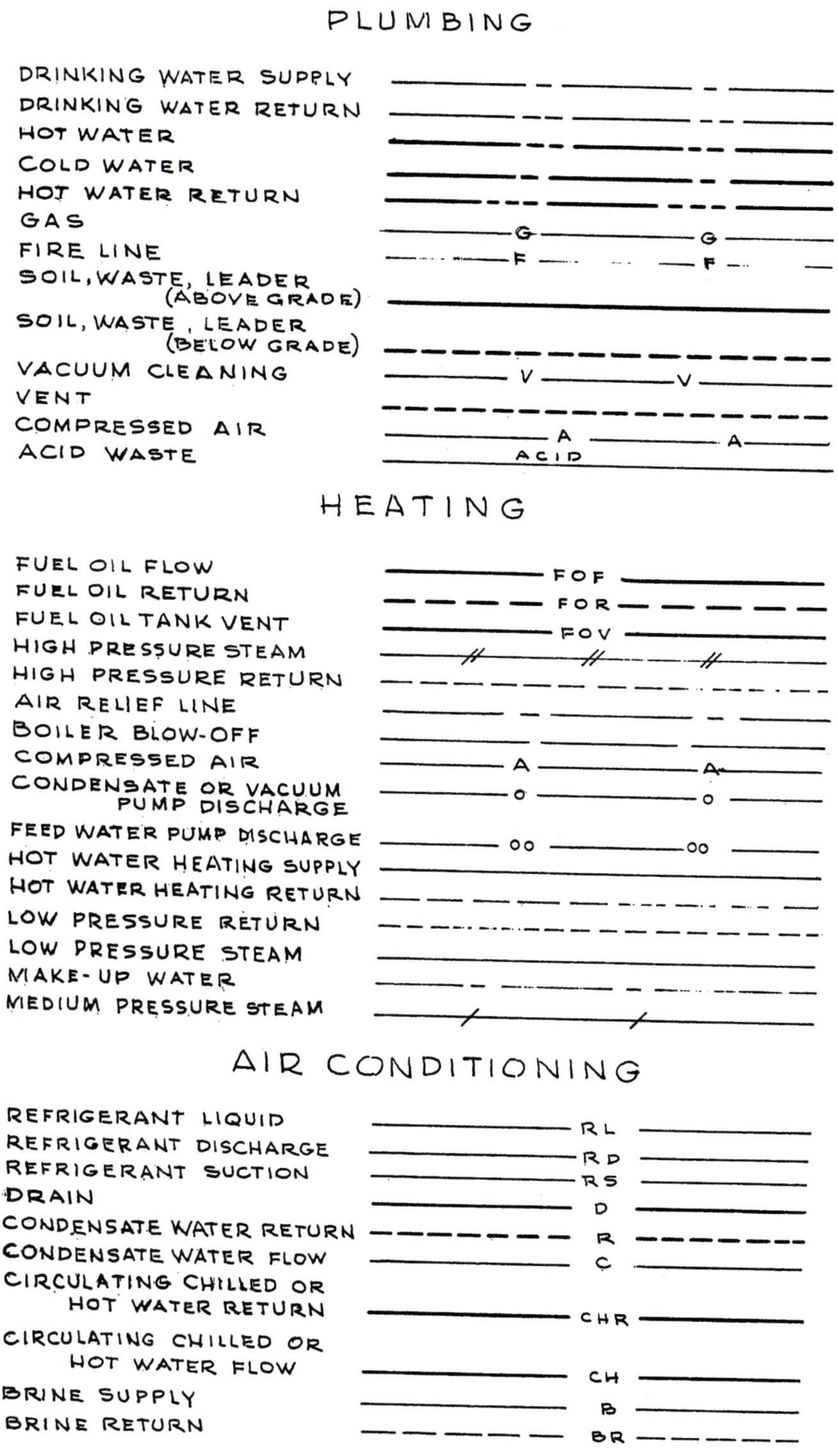
PLUMBING
DRINKING WATER SUPPLY
DRINKING WATER RETURN
HOT WATER
COLD WATER
HOT WATER RETURN
GAS
G
G
FIRE LINE
F
F
SOIL, WASTE, LEADER (ABOVE GRADE)
SOIL, WASTE, LEADER (BELOW GRADE)
VACUUM CLEANING
V
V
VENT
COMPRESSED AIR
A
A
ACID WASTE
ACID
HEATING
FUEL OIL FLOW
FOF
FUEL OIL RETURN
FOR
FUEL OIL TANK VENT
FOV
HIGH PRESSURE STEAM
HIGH PRESSURE RETURN
AIR RELIEF LINE
BOILER BLOW-OFF
COMPRESSED AIR
A
A
CONDENSATE OR VACUUM PUMP DISCHARGE
o
o
FEED WATER PUMP DISCHARGE
oo
oo
HOT WATER HEATING SUPPLY
HOT WATER HEATING RETURN
LOW PRESSURE RETURN
LOW PRESSURE STEAM
MAKE-UP WATER
MEDIUM PRESSURE STEAM
AIR CONDITIONING
REFRIGERANT LIQUID
RL
REFRIGERANT DISCHARGE
RD
REFRIGERANT SUCTION
RS
DRAIN
D
CONDENSATE WATER RETURN
R
CONDENSATE WATER FLOW
C
CIRCULATING CHILLED OR HOT WATER RETURN
CHR
CIRCULATING CHILLED OR HOT WATER FLOW
CH
BRINE SUPPLY
B
BRINE RETURN
BR

Figure 15-6 Pipe-line symbols

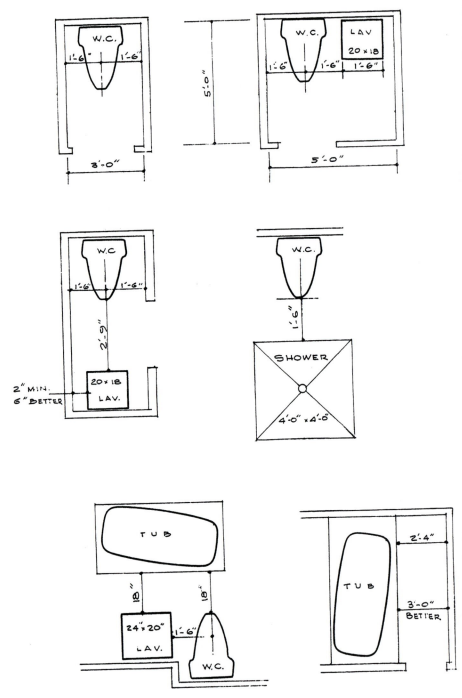

Figure 15-7 Bathroom fixtures and placement

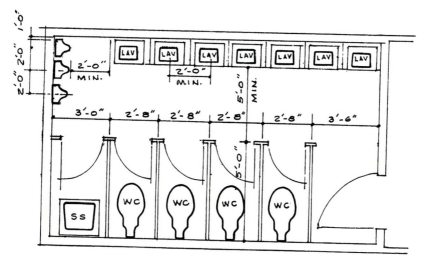

Figure 15-8 Minimum toilet clearances

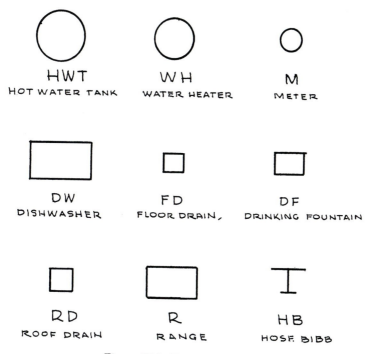

Figure 15-9 Plumbing symbols

In Fig. 15-4 are shown wall-hung water closets, lavatories, and wall-hung urinals with their wall thicknesses when single, double, or double back-to-back units are used. Pedestal urinals are shown with their mounting dimensions.

Figure 15-5 shows the standard graphical symbols for pipe, fittings, and valves, and Figure 15-6 shows standard pipe-line symbols for plumbing, heating, and air conditioning.

Figure 15-7 illustrates bathroom fixtures and their minimum spacings and placement. A bank of water closets and lavatories are shown with their minimum clearances in Fig. 15-8.

Additional plumbing symbols are indicated in Fig. 15-9.

SELF-TESTING REVIEW QUESTIONS

1. In the trade, the sheet metal draftsperson is known by what name?
2. Briefly explain a shop drawing.
3. Give the function of a duct turn.
4. Where are length dimensions placed on a joint?
5. How are duct elbows dimensioned?

16

TOOLS FOR PLUMBING

BASIN WRENCH

The basin wrench (Fig. 16-1) is used for the removal of nuts and small piping pieces from the underside of sinks and lavatories or for the removal of these same nuts from inaccessible spaces.

The basin wrench consists of a solid metal shaft with a sliding pin handle at its heel. At the back of the shaft is an adjustable semicircular grooved vise that may be rotated either to tighten or to loosen nuts and small pipe.

OPEN-END WRENCHES

Open-end wrenches (Fig. 16-2) should be part of the plumber's tool-chest. These wrenches are most useful when removing small lock nuts, bolts, and so on, from areas that are easily accessible. A good set of wrenches, in sizes from $\frac{1}{4}$ to $\frac{3}{4}$ in., are sufficient for most plumbing work.

COMMON PLIERS

Pliers (Fig. 16-3) are useful for removing and installing small nuts, fittings, and so on. When working in confined areas where the use of wrenches is not practical, pliers are indispensable.

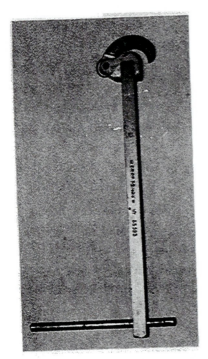

Figure 16-1 Basin wrench

Figure 16-2 Open-end wrenches

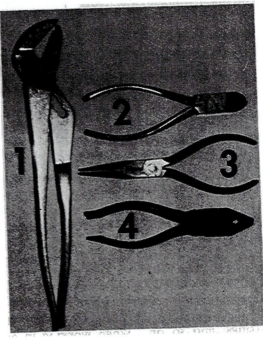

Figure 16-3 Common pliers

TIN SNIPS

For cutting light sheet metal up to $\frac{1}{16}$ in. thick, the hand snip or tin snip (Fig. 16-4) is indispensable. The straight hand snip has straight blades and cutting edges sharpened to an 85° angle. This type of snip is available in various sizes ranging from 6 to 14 in. in length.

When using tin snips it is good practice to cut somewhat outside the layout line, allowing the opportunity to dress the cutting edge while keeping the material within required dimensions.

Many snips have small serrations on the blades to prevent back-slipping while cutting. There are special types of hand snips used for special jobs, such as the circle snip used for cutting out circles and elliptical and curved shapes.

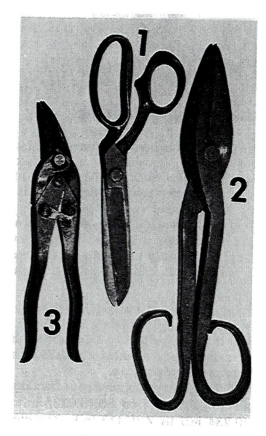

Figure 16-4 Tin snips

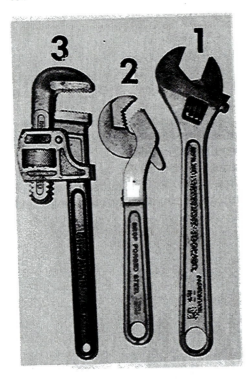

Figure 16-5 Pipe and adjustable
open-end wrenches

PIPE AND ADJUSTABLE OPEN-END WRENCHES

The pipe wrench (Fig. 16-5) is used for connecting and disconnecting
threaded pipe and fittings. Convenient plumbing work sizes of the
pipe wrench range from 6 in. to 2 ft. When using pipe wrenches to
install or remove pipes, they should always be used in pairs of the
same size or nearly the same size.

Adjustable open-end wrenches differ from pipe wrenches in that
their jaws have a smooth finish, as opposed to the grooved jaws of pipe
wrenches. They are used mostly on stainless steel or chrome-finished
nuts. The smooth jaws will not mar the finish of the material.

HAND DRILLS

The hand brace and the hand drill (Fig. 16-6) are essential tools of the
plumber. There are two kinds of drills, the drill for making holes in
metal and the drill for boring wood.

Drills for metal drilling come in numerous fractional sizes, number
sizes ranging from 1 (0.288 in.) to 80 (0.0135 in.) and letter sizes
ranging from A (0.234 in.) to Z (0.413 in.). The dimensions are the
diameter of the hole produced.

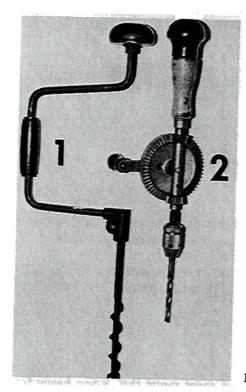

Figure 16-6 Hand drills

SPUD WRENCH

The spud wrench (Fig. 16-7) is used to tighten or loosen the lock nut under a sink or lavatory. The lock nut screws onto the strainer body of the sink or lavatory.

Figure 16-7 Spud wrench

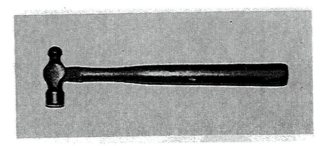

Figure 16-8 Ball-peen hammer

BALL-PEEN HAMMER

The ball-peen hammer (Fig. 16-8) has a dual purpose. The flat face is used to drive nails or hammer surfaces, while its head or ball is useful for striking areas that are too small for the face to enter.

Ball-peen hammers are made of different weights, usually 4, 6, 8, and 12 oz and 1, 1½, and 2 lb. For most work a 1½-lb hammer is ideal.

HACKSAWS

Hacksaws (Fig. 16-9) are used to cut sheet metal that is too heavy for snips and metal bar stock, as well as many types of pipe. Hacksaws may have an adjustable or rigid frame and blade. Adjustable frames can hold blades that are from 8 to 10 in. long, while rigid frames take only saws of one size. The blades are made of high-grade tool steel and are tempered and hardened. The blades come in different numbers of teeth per inch. Use a blade of 14 teeth per inch when cutting large sections of mill material. For large sections of tough steel use a blade with 18

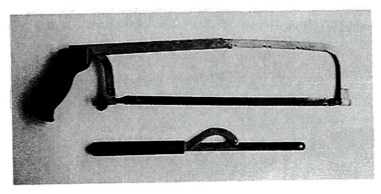

Figure 16-9 Hacksaws

teeth per inch. Use 24 teeth per inch for angle iron, heavy pipe, brass, copper, and 32 teeth per inch for thin tubing.

CHISELS

Chisels (Fig. 16-10) are used for chipping or cutting metal and wood. They are made from a good grade of tool steel. Cold chisels are classified according to the shape of their points; the width of the cutting edge indicates their size. The common shapes of chisels are flat, round nose, diamond point, and cape.

The flat cold chisel cuts rivets, splits nuts, chips castings, and cuts cast iron pipe and thin metal sheets. The cape chisel is used for cutting keyways or narrow grooves. Round-nose chisels cut circular grooves while the diamond-point chisel is used for cutting V-grooves.

FILES

Files (Fig. 16-11) are made with single-cut or double-cut teeth. Single-cut files have rows of teeth cut parallel to each other, and are used for finish filing, sharpening tools, and are good for taking off rough edges from sheet metal and burrs from pipe.

Figure 16-10 Chisels

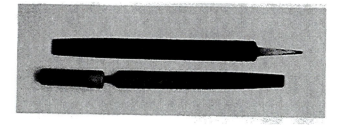

Figure 16-11 Files

Double-cut files have crisscrossed rows of teeth, forming teeth that are diamond shaped. They are used for rough work and fast cutting.

Files are graded according to the fineness or roughness of their teeth. This is largely influenced by the length of the file, which typically ranges from 3 to 18 in.

SCREWDRIVERS

The screwdriver (Fig. 16-12) is perhaps the most incorrectly used tool, often being used as a chisel or punch or scraper. Its only true purpose, however, is to drive and remove screws. When using the screwdriver, the most important thing is to select the proper size so that the blade fits the screw slot. There are two major types of screwdrivers, the flat shank and the Phillips. The Phillips screw has a cross-shaped slot into which the Phillips screwdriver fits. There are many sizes of screwdrivers. Some screwdrivers are very short and can be used in very narrow spaces.

PIPE AND TUBING CUTTER

The pipe and tube cutter (Fig. 16-13) is made to cut pipe made of steel, iron, brass, copper, and aluminum. The hand pipe cutter, known as a No. 1 cutter, has a capacity of $\frac{1}{8}$ to 2 in., while a No. 2 cutter has a

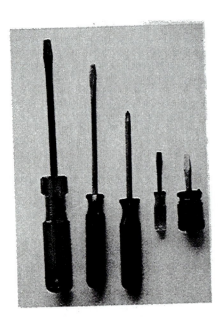

Figure 16-12 Screwdrivers

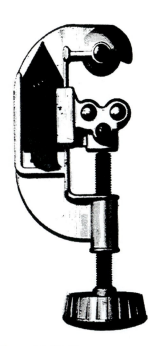

Figure 16-13 Pipe and tubing
cutter

Figure 16-14 Propane torch

range of 2 to 4 in. in diameter. Most tube cutters resemble pipe cutters
except that they are of lighter construction.

PROPANE TORCH

The propane torch (Fig. 16-14) is a bottled gas unit containing a
specially controlled air–fuel mixture which produces a high-speed
swirling flame. It is used for sweating copper or brass tubing joints
and soldering work. It is also used for repairing gutters, thawing pipes,
and has many other uses around the house, shop, and farm.

VISE

The vise (Fig. 16-15) is used for holding down pipe when it is sawed,
drilled, or threaded. It consists of a fixed lower jaw upon which the
pipe rests. The upper jaw is brought down by turning the handle. By
raising the locking lever, the work can quickly be removed.

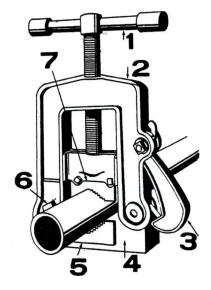

Figure 16-15 Vise

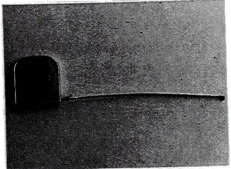
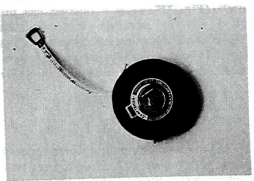

Figure 16-16 Plumber's measuring rules

PLUMBER'S MEASURING RULES

There are a number of measuring rules (Fig. 16-16) that are essential to the plumber. Some of the more important ones are the 6-ft zigzag rule, the flexible push-pull rule, the steel or fiber tape, and the straight steel rule.

LEVEL

This useful tool (Fig. 16-17) is used to level a plane in either a true horizontal or vertical position. It consists of a wood, aluminum, or steel frame into which a partially filled glass vial containing alcohol is fitted. Leveling is accomplished when the air bubble is centered between the lines.

PLUMB BOB

The plumb bob (Fig. 16-18) is used to determine true verticality. It is made of brass or bronze, pointed and tapered, and is suspended from a cord. Common weights are from 6 to 24 oz in increments of 2 oz.

POWER DRILL

The power drill (Fig. 16-19) is another useful tool for the plumber. The work to be drilled is usually held in a vise, if possible, or if the object is large enough, held tightly so that it will not spin around. The

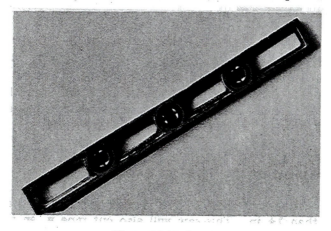

Figure 16-17 Level

Figure 16-18 Plumb bob

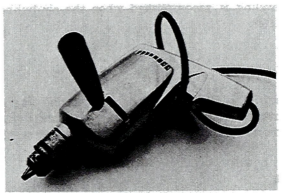

Figure 16-19 Power drill

exact location of the hole to be drilled must first be center-punched, which forms a starting point or seat for the drillpoint.

POWER SAW

The power saw (Fig. 16-20) with a circular blade is another useful and often used tool. It is used for cutting wooden members such as through floors, walls, and partitions to create pipe space.

RECIPROCATING SAW AND COMPASS SAW

The reciprocating saw (Fig. 16-21) is used primarily where material is thicker than $1\frac{1}{2}$ in. This saw will also cut pipe when the proper blade is inserted.

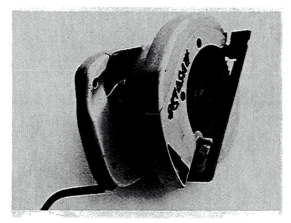

Figure 16-20 Power saw

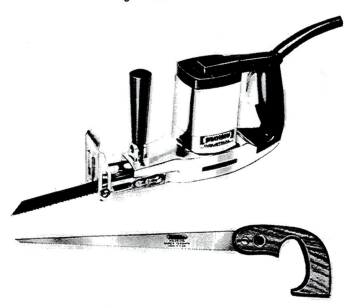

Figure 16-21 Reciprocating saw and compass saw

For holes that must be cut larger than 1 in. in diameter, the compass saw is most likely to be used. It also cuts large curves and circles.

DRILL BITS AND HOLE SAW

The multisaw bit (Fig. 16-22) cuts holes from $\frac{1}{2}$ to 2 in. in diameter, while a spade bit will produce holes from $\frac{3}{8}$ to $1\frac{1}{2}$ in. in diameter.

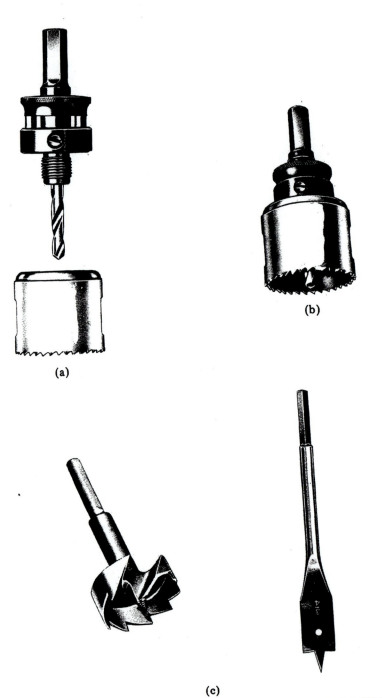

(a)

(b)

(c)

Figure 16-22 (a) Hole saw, (b) cylindrical saw blade, and (c) drill bits.

The hole saw (Fig. 16-22) combines a drill bit and cylindrical saw blade. The bits and hole saw can be attached to a portable electric drill.

SELF-TESTING REVIEW QUESTIONS

1. Explain the purpose of the basin wrench.
2. A good set of open-end wrenches comes in what range of sizes?
3. Drills for drilling holes in metal come in what range of number sizes?
4. What is a spud wrench? Where is it used?
5. What hacksaw blade is used for cutting large sections of mill material?
6. For what type of work are double-cut files used?

APPENDIX

SI UNITS, SYMBOLS, AND DEFINITIONS

Quantity	SI Unit	Symbol
Length	metre	m
	millimetre	mm
Area	square metre	m^2
Volume	cubic metre	m^3
Frequency	hertz	Hz
Density	kilogram per cubic metre	kg/m^3
Mass	kilogram	kg
Force	newton[a]	N
Pressure, stress	newton per square metre	N/m^2
Temperature interval	degree Celsius	deg C: C
Coefficient of heat transfer	watt per square metre per degree Celsius	W/m^2 deg C
Power	watt	W
Energy	joule	J
Quantity of electricity	coulomb	C

[a] A newton is a unit of force which, applied to a mass of 1 kilogram, gives it an acceleration of 1 metre per second per second (i.e., $N = kgm/s^2$).

Pressure (force).   There are a number of ways in which pressure is indicated in building services. The basic unit is the pascal (Pa), equal to 1 newton per square metre (N/m^2), but it is not always used. The following will help to clarify the condition:

Imperial Units[a]				SI Units[a]			
Unit WG	Feet Head	psi	mmWG	m Head	mbars	N/m^2 or Pa	kN/m^2
1	0.08	0.056	25	0.025	2.5	250	0.25
12	1	0.434	500	0.30	30.0	3 000	3.0
27.6	2.3	1.0	690	0.69	69.0	6 900	6.9
39.38	3.26	1.414	1 000	1.0	100.0	10 000	10.0

[a]WG, inches water gauge (column of water);
mmWG, millimetres water gauge (column of water);
ft head, feet head of water;
m head, metres head of water;
mbars, millibars;
N/m^2, newtons per square metre;
kN/m^2, kilonewtons per square metre;
psi, pounds per square inch;
1 bar pressure, 100 000 N/m^2 (100 kN/m^2) or 1000 millibars.

The relationship to atmospheric pressure at sea level can be stated as follows:

IMPERIAL

Unit	psi	feet Head	in. Mercury	kN/m^2 (Pa)	m Head	mm Mercury
1 atmosphere	14.7	34	30	101	10.33	760

Vacuum conditions may also be expressed in several ways and are related to the ability of the atmosphere to hold up to a column of mercury. Any pressure below normal atmospheric becomes a vacuum, such as:

Condition	Imperial Units		SI Units		
Atmospheric pressure	0.01 in. Hg[a]	760 Torr[b]	0.0 mm Hg	0.0 kN/m^2
Absolute vacuum	30.0 in. Hg	0.0 Torr	760 mm Hg	101 kN/m^2

[a]Hg, mercury.
[b]Torr is named after the Italian physicist Torricelli, who experimented with columns of mercury.

Energy.   Work or quantity of heat, measured in joules (J):

$$1 \text{ J} = 1 \text{ N/m}$$

$$1 \text{ Btu} = 1055 \text{ J}$$

The joule is also used to calculate the amount of heat energy required to raise 1 kg of air through 1°C (1.3 J) or 1 kg of water through 1°C (4.2 J).

Power.   The final total of heat losses required for a building is converted from heat energy (joules) to power in watts. This is done by dividing the number of joules by time (seconds). Thus, if we need the heat losses in terms of kilowatt-hours, then

$$\frac{\text{kilojoules}}{3600 \text{ seconds}} = \text{kW}$$

$$1 \text{ kilowatt} = 3420 \text{ Btu (approx.)}$$

$$1 \text{ horsepower} = 746 \text{ W}$$

Mass and Density.   The use of mass (kg) and density (kg/m^3) plays a large part in the design of building services. The flow of water in some instances can be expressed in kilograms per second, which is also the same as expressing the flow of litres per second, as 1 litre of water weighs 1 kilogram at approximately 4°C.

$$1 \text{ litre per second} = 15 \text{ gallons per minute}$$

Nominal Metric Pipe Sizes With Imperial Dimensions

Imperial Diameter (in.)	Nominal Metric Diameter (mm)	Material Diameter (mm)				
		Cast Iron	Clay Pipe	PVC (Drain)	Copper (O.D.)	Mild Steel
$\frac{1}{2}$	15	—	—	—	15	13
$\frac{3}{4}$	19	—	—	—	22	19
1	25	—	—	—	28	25
$1\frac{1}{4}$	32	—	—	32	35	32
$1\frac{1}{2}$	38	—	—	38	42	38
2	51	50	50	51	54	50
3	76	75	75	76	76	75
4	102	100	100	100	108	100
6	152	150	150	152	159	150

Velocity or Speed. Speed is measured in metres per second (m/s), or kilometres per hour (km/h) = 1 km/h = 0.2778 m/s

Temperature. The SI unit for temperature is the kelvin (K). However, the degree Celsius (formerly called centigrade) is used for most commercial and everyday applications. A temperature interval of 1 degree Celsius is equal to the unit kelvin, but their reference points are different. Water freezes at 0°C, which is 273.15 K.

Area. Small areas are usually measured in square centimetres (cm^2). In building and construction the square metre (m^2) is used. Farmland is measured in hectares (ha) and very large areas in square kilometres (km^2).

1 are (pronounced ah-ree) = 0.0247 acre

1 hectare (ha) = 2.471 acres

USEFUL FORMULAS

Areas of Plane Figures

Square:

$$A = L \times L$$
$$= L^2$$

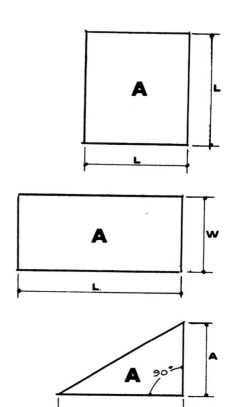

Rectangle:

$$A = L \times W$$

Right-Angle Triangle:

$$A = \text{altitude} \times \text{base} \div 2$$
$$= \tfrac{1}{2}(B \times A)$$

Circle:

$$A = 3.14(R \times R)$$
$$= 3.14 \times R^2$$
$$= \pi \cdot R^2$$

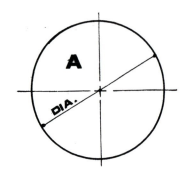

Ellipse:

A = multiply minor axis by major axis by 0.7854

$$= D \times d \times 0.7854$$
$$= 0.7854\,Dd$$

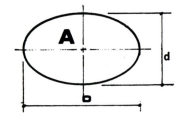

Hexagon:

A = square the short diameter and multiply by 0.866, *or*

= square the long diameter and multiply by 0.6495

$$= 0.866d^2$$
$$= 0.6495D^2$$

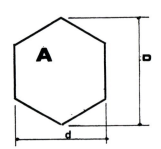

Octagon:

A = square the short diameter and multiply by 0.828, *or* square the long diameter and multiply by 0.707

$$= 0.828d^2$$
$$= 0.707D^2$$

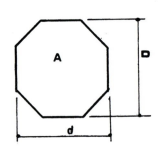

Sector of a Circle:

$$A = \frac{3.14 \times R \times R \times A}{360}$$

$$L = 0.01745 \times R \times a$$

$$A = \frac{L}{0.01745 \times R}$$

$$R = \frac{L}{0.01745 \times a}$$

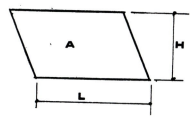

Parallelogram:

A = multiply length by
   perpendicular height

$= L \times H$

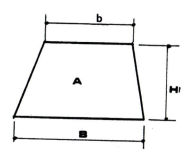

Trapezoid:

A = multiply height by
   half the sum of the
   top and bottom bases

$$= \frac{H(b + B)}{2}$$

Volumes of Typical Solids

Any prism or cylinder, right or oblique, rectangular or not:

volume = area of base × altitude

altitude = distance between parallel bases, measured
   perpendicular to the bases

When bases are not parallel:

altitude = perpendicular distance from one base to the center of
   the other

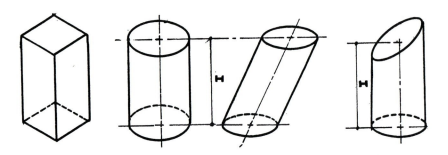

Any pyramid, or cylinder, or cone, right or oblique, regular or not:

volume = area of base $\times \frac{1}{3}$ altitude

altitude = distance from base to apex, measured perpendicular to base

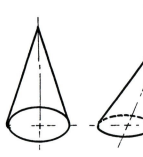

FACTORS AND STATEMENTS

Unit of Refrigeration.

Capacity: 1 ton = 200 Btu/min = 12,000 Btu/hr

$$\frac{2000 \text{ lb} \times 144 \text{ Btu/lb}}{24 \text{ hr}} = 12,000 \text{ Btu/hr}$$

Ton. The word "ton" (in refrigeration) is used as follows: A "75-ton plant" produces 75 tons of ice in 24 hr.

Rate of Cooling. The rate of cooling required to freeze 1 ton of water at 32°F into ice at 32°F in 1 day is

$$\frac{(1\text{-ton}) \, 2000 \text{ lb/ton} \, (144 \text{ Btu/lb, heat of fusion})}{24 \text{ hr}} = 12,000 \text{ Btu/hr}$$

Btu.

$$1 \text{ Btu} = 778 \text{ ft lb}$$

$$= 0.293 \text{ watt-hr}$$

$$= \tfrac{1}{180} \text{ of heat required to change temperature}$$
of 1 lb of water from $32°F$ to $212°F$

Temperature.

$$°C = (°F - 32) \times \tfrac{5}{9}$$

Weight of Water.

1 cu ft at $50°F$ weighs   62.41 lb

1 gal at $50°F$ weighs   8.34 lb

1 cu ft of ice weighs   57.2 lb

Water is at its greatest density at $39.2°F$:
1 cu ft at $39.2°F$ weighs 62.43 lb

ABBREVIATIONS

ABS	Acrylonitrile butadiene styrene
AGA	American Gas Association
AHAM	Association of Home Appliance Manufacturers
AISI	American Iron and Steel Institute
ANSI	American National Standards Institute
API	American Petroleum Institute
ASA	American Standards Association
ASME	American Society of Mechanical Engineers
ASTM	American Society for Testing and Materials
AWWA	American Water Works Association
CISPI	Cast Iron Soil Pipe Institute
CS	Commodity Standards Division of U.S. Department of Commerce
CS&PS	Commercial Standards and Product Standards
EDR	Effective direct radiation
Fed	Federal Specifications, U.S. Government Department of Commerce
IAPMO	International Association of Plumbing and Mechanical Officials
IBR	Institute of Boiler and Radiator Manufacturers
I.P.S.	Iron pipe size
JAN	Joint Army-Navy Specifications, U.S. Government, Department of Defense

MIL   Military Specifications, U.S. Government
MSS   Manufacturers Standardization Society of the Valve and Fittings
             Industry
NSF   National Sanitation Foundation
PB   Polybutylene
PDI   Plumbing and Drainage Institute
PS   *Material and Property Standard*, published by IAPMO
PVC   Polyvinyl chloride
SBI   Steel Boiler Institute
SWP   Solvent Welded Pipe
UL   Underwriters' Laboratories
UPC   *Uniform Plumbing Code*, published by IAPMO
WQA   Water Quality Association

DEFINITIONS

Angle Valve: Similar to a globe valve, but pipe connections are at right angles.

Area Drain: A device designed to collect rainwater from an open area.

Areaway: A wall surrounding a window below grade allowing light to enter.

Backflow: When potable water supply in a water supply system tends to flow in an opposite direction to the intended flow.

Back Siphonage: The flow of water which is opposite to the intended direction of flow due to negative pressure in the pipe.

Boiler Blow-Off: An outlet on a boiler to allow for the entering or discharging of water or sediment in the boiler.

Branch: A part of the plumbing piping system other than the main stack.

Branch Vent: A vent that connects with one or more vents from fixtures and leading to a vent stack.

Building Drain: The horizontal sewer pipe inside the house that receives the sewage soil stacks. It extends 3 to 5 ft outside the house.

Building Sewer: The horizontal sewer line that connects from the building drain and is connected to the public sewer.

Building Storm Drain: A draining system used to receive rainwater, surface water, and groundwater connecting to the house sewer 5 ft outside the building.

Building Storm Sewer: The piping that connects to the end of a building storm drain to receive and convey the contents to a public storm sewer or combined sewer.

Bushing: A tapped fitting which is used to reduce the size of an end opening of a fitting or a valve.

Catch Basin: A cast iron, concrete, or wooden receptacle into which the water from a roof, floor, and so on, will drain. It is connected with a sewer or drain tile.

Check Valve: A valve that closes automatically when the flow in a pipe is reversed.

Combined Building Sewer: A building sewer that receives storm water, sewage, and other liquid waste.

Common Vent: The vertical vent piping portion that serves two fixture drains installed at the same level in a vertical stack.

Conductor Pipe: A round, square, or rectangular metal pipe used to lead water from the roof to the sewer.

Convector: A heat transfer surface designed to transfer its heat to surrounding air largely by convection currents.

Corrosion: The deterioration of piping material due to a chemical action or galvanic action.

Deep Seal Trap: A trap with a seal of 4 in. or more.

Drain: A pipe that carries a liquid flow.

Drainage System: The piping that conveys sewage, rainwater, or other liquid wastes to a place of disposal.

Drum Trap: A trap consisting of a cylinder with its axis vertical. The cylinder is larger in diameter than its inlet and outlet diameters.

Drywell: A pit located on porous ground walled up with rocks which allows water to seep through the pit. Used for disposal of rainwater or the effluent from a septic tank.

Effluent: The liquid waste that flows from a septic tank into a leaching field.

Elbow: A pipe fitting made to allow a turn in direction of a pipe line.

Expansion Bends: A loop in a pipe line which permits the expansion and contraction of the pipe.

Female Thread: Internal threads.

Fixture: A receptacle attached to a plumbing system in which water or other waste may be collected for ultimate discharge into the plumbing system.

Fixture Branch: The drain from the fixture trap to the junction of the drain with a vent.

Fixture Drain: The drain from the fixture branch to the junction of any other drain pipe.

Fixture Unit: A unit flow rate from a fixture. The unit flow rate is determined to be 1 cu ft or 7.5 gal of water per minute. A design factor to determine the drain pipe size for a fixture.

Flange: A rim-like end on a valve, or pipe fitting for bolting another flanged fitting. Usually for large diameter or pressurized pipe.

Flood Level Rim: The top edge of a plumbing fixture from which water will overflow.

Floor Drain: An opening at floor level connected to a trap to receive the floor drainage.

Flushometer: A device that allows a predetermined quantity of flushing water, actuated by water pressure.

Gate Valve: A valve that regulates flow within a pipe. It is known as the on-off valve.

Globe Valve: This allows for throttling the flow of water.

Grade: Slope, pitch, or fall of a drain pipe, usually $\frac{1}{4}$ in. per foot.

Gutter: A trough for carrying off water.

Hanger: Supports specially designed to support pipe lines.

Horizontal Branch: A drain pipe extending laterally from a soil or waste stack or building drain.

Horizontal Pipe: Any fitting or pipe that makes $45°$ or more with the vertical.

House Drain: That part of the horizontal sewer piping inside the building receiving waste from the soil stacks.

Hub End: Pipe end connections that are leaded and caulked, such as on cast iron sewer piping.

Increaser: A short pipe fitting with one end of a larger diameter.

Joint: Where two pipes are connected either by bolting, welding, or by a screwed connection.

Lavatory: A basin for washing hands and face.

Leader: The vertical rainwater pipe leading from a roof gutter or roof drain to a storm sewer, or a combination storm and sanitary sewer system, to a point of disposal.

Liquid Waste: The discharge from any fixture other than that from body wastes.

Louvres: A series of shutters used for the circulation of air.

Main: The principal pipe of a plumbing system.

Main Vent: The principal pipe of a plumbing venting system.

Male Thread: An external pipe thread.

Manhole: An opening constructed in a sewer to allow access for a person.

Nipple: A short length of pipe threaded at both ends to allow for joining pipe elements.

Nonrising Stem Valve: A valve where the stem does not rise when opening the valve.

Packing: Material used in stuffing box of a valve to keep a leakproof seal around the stem.

Plug: A cap used for shutting off a tapped opening.

Potable Water System: Supplies drinking water to fixtures, hot water for domestic purposes.

Pressure Regulator: A valve used to reduce and maintain pressure automatically.

Reducer: A pipe fitting with a smaller opening at one end.

Relief Valve: A valve that will automatically open when the pressure inside a vessel or container exceeds a specific amount.

Rising Stem Valve: A valve whose stem rises when the valve is opened.

Roof Drain: A roof outlet designed to receive rainwater, leading it into a leader or downspout.

Sanitary Plumbing System: Consists of fixtures, traps, branches, vent branches, vent drain, cleanouts, and building sewer.

Septic Tank: A watertight box (usually concrete) which receives the discharge of a drainage system; designed to separate the solid matter from the liquid part, allow for digestion of organic matter for a period of detention, and permit the liquids to discharge into the soil through a piping or "leaching" system.

Soft Jaws: Covers of lead or copper placed over vise jaws to prevent damage to materials held in the vise.

Soil Pipe: A pipe that receives the discharge of a water closet.

Soil Stack: The vertical pipe in the house plumbing system into which sewage from fixtures and branches discharge.

Solder Joint: A connection of piping made by soldering. Generally used with copper tubing.

Storm Sewer: A piping system used to convey storm water.

Storm Water System: Complete piping system that collects rainwater from roofs, yards, areaways, and conducts it to a public sewer, private sewer, or drywell.

Subsurface Drain: A drain that receives only subsurface water and conveys it into an underground basin.

Tap: A tool for forming internal or female threads.

Tee: A three-way fitting shaped like the letter "T."

Temperature: Heat and cold recorded in degrees on a thermometer.

Thermostat: An automatic device for controlling the supply of heat.

Threader: A device or tool used to cut thread on a piece of pipe.

Trap: A U-shaped pipe filled with water and located beneath plumbing fixtures to form a seal against the passage of foul odors or gases.

Tubing: Lightweight pipe such as copper, brass, or plastic.

Union: A type of fitting used to join lengths of pipe for easy opening of a pipe line.

Valve: A device designed to regulate flow of fluids or gases.

Vent Pipe: A vertical pipe used to ventilate plumbing systems and to provide a release for pressure caused by flushing.

Vent Stack: The upper portion of a waste or soil stack extending through the roof of the building, installed primarily for the purpose of providing circulation of air.

Vitreous: Pertaining to a composition of materials that resemble glass, such as lavatories or drain pipe.

Waste Pipe: Any pipe that receives the discharge of any fixture except the water closet.

Water Main: The principal water supply pipe.

Water Service Pipe: The water pipe leading from the street main to the building.

Conversion to Metric
International System of Units (SI)

To Convert:	to:	Multiply by:
Btu	joules	1.055
Btu/hr	watts	0.2931
Btu/min	kilowatts	0.01757
Btu/min	watts	17.57
circumference	radians	6.283
cubic centimetres	cubic inches	0.06102
cubic feet	cubic metres	0.02832
cubic feet	litres	28.32
cubic feet/min	cubic centimetres/sec	472.0
cubic inches	cubic centimetres	16.39
cubic metres	gallons (U.S.)	264.2
degrees Celsius ($^\circ$C)	degrees Fahrenheit ($^\circ$F)	(C - 32) $\times \frac{9}{5}$
feet	centimetres	30.48
feet	metres	0.3048
feet	millimetres	304.8
gallons	litres	3.785
horsepower	watts	745.7
horsepower-hr	kilowatt-hr	0.7457
kilograms	pounds	2.205
kilometres	miles	0.6214
kilometres/hr	miles/hr	0.6214
kilowatt-hr	Btu	3.413
litres	cubic feet	0.3531
litres	gallons (U.S.)	0.2142
metres	feet	3.281
metres	inches	39.37
metres	yards	1.094
ounces (fluid)	litres	0.02957
pounds	kilograms	0.4536
psi	pascal	6.895
quarts (liquid)	litres	0.9463
radians	degrees	57.30
square inches	square millimetres	645.2
watts	Btu/hr	3.4129
watts	Btu/min	0.05688

USEFUL TABLES

Decimal Equivalents of Fractions

Inch	Decimal of an Inch	Inch	Decimal of an Inch	Inch	Decimal of an Inch
$\frac{1}{64}$	0.0156	$\frac{11}{32}$	0.3437	$\frac{43}{64}$	0.6718
$\frac{1}{32}$	0.0312	$\frac{23}{64}$	0.3593	$\frac{11}{16}$	0.6875
$\frac{3}{64}$	0.468	$\frac{3}{8}$	0.375	$\frac{45}{64}$	0.7031
$\frac{1}{16}$	0.0625	$\frac{25}{64}$	0.3986	$\frac{23}{32}$	0.7187
$\frac{5}{64}$	0.0781	$\frac{13}{32}$	0.4062	$\frac{47}{64}$	0.7343
$\frac{3}{32}$	0.0937	$\frac{27}{64}$	0.4218	$\frac{3}{4}$	0.75
$\frac{7}{64}$	0.1093	$\frac{7}{16}$	0.4375	$\frac{49}{64}$	0.7656
$\frac{1}{8}$	0.125	$\frac{29}{64}$	0.4531	$\frac{25}{32}$	0.7612
$\frac{9}{64}$	0.1406	$\frac{15}{32}$	0.4687	$\frac{51}{64}$	0.7968
$\frac{5}{32}$	0.1562	$\frac{31}{64}$	0.4843	$\frac{13}{16}$	0.8125
$\frac{11}{64}$	0.1718	$\frac{1}{2}$	0.5	$\frac{53}{64}$	0.8281
$\frac{3}{16}$	0.1875	$\frac{23}{64}$	0.5156	$\frac{27}{32}$	0.8437
$\frac{13}{64}$	0.2031	$\frac{17}{32}$	0.5312	$\frac{55}{64}$	0.8593
$\frac{7}{32}$	0.2187	$\frac{15}{64}$	0.5468	$\frac{7}{8}$	0.875
$\frac{15}{64}$	0.2343	$\frac{9}{16}$	0.5625	$\frac{57}{64}$	0.8906
$\frac{1}{4}$	0.25	$\frac{37}{64}$	0.5781	$\frac{29}{32}$	0.9062
$\frac{17}{64}$	0.2656	$\frac{19}{32}$	0.5937	$\frac{59}{64}$	0.9218
$\frac{9}{32}$	0.2812	$\frac{39}{64}$	0.6093	$\frac{15}{16}$	0.9375
$\frac{19}{64}$	0.2968	$\frac{5}{8}$	0.625	$\frac{61}{64}$	0.9591
$\frac{5}{16}$	0.3125	$\frac{41}{64}$	0.6406	$\frac{31}{32}$	0.9687
$\frac{21}{64}$	0.3281	$\frac{21}{32}$	0.6562	$\frac{63}{64}$	0.9843

Inches Into Decimal Parts of a Foot

Inches

Inch	0	1	2	3	4	5	6	7	8	9	10	11
↕		0.083	0.167	0.250	0.333	0.417	0.500	0.583	0.667	0.750	0.833	0.916
1/16	0.005	0.088	0.171	0.255	0.338	0.421	0.505	0.588	0.671	0.755	0.838	0.921
1/8	0.010	0.093	0.177	0.260	0.343	0.427	0.510	0.593	0.677	0.760	0.843	0.927
3/16	0.015	0.099	0.182	0.265	0.349	0.432	0.515	0.599	0.682	0.765	0.849	0.932
1/4	0.020	0.104	0.187	0.270	0.354	0.437	0.520	0.604	0.687	0.770	0.854	0.937
5/16	0.026	0.109	0.192	0.276	0.359	0.442	0.526	0.609	0.692	0.776	0.859	0.942
3/8	0.031	0.114	0.197	0.281	0.364	0.447	0.531	0.614	0.697	0.781	0.864	0.947
7/16	0.036	0.119	0.203	0.286	0.369	0.453	0.536	0.619	0.703	0.786	0.869	0.953
1/2	0.041	0.125	0.208	0.291	0.375	0.458	0.541	0.625	0.708	0.791	0.875	0.958
9/16	0.046	0.130	0.213	0.296	0.380	0.463	0.546	0.630	0.713	0.796	0.880	0.963
5/8	0.052	0.135	0.218	0.302	0.385	0.468	0.552	0.635	0.718	0.802	0.885	0.968
11/16	0.057	0.140	0.224	0.307	0.390	0.474	0.557	0.640	0.724	0.807	0.890	0.974
3/4	0.062	0.145	0.229	0.312	0.395	0.479	0.562	0.645	0.729	0.812	0.895	0.979
13/16	0.067	0.151	0.234	0.317	0.401	0.484	0.567	0.651	0.734	0.817	0.901	0.984
7/8	0.072	0.156	0.239	0.322	0.406	0.489	0.572	0.656	0.739	0.822	0.906	0.989
29/32	0.075	0.158	0.242	0.325	0.408	0.492	0.575	0.658	0.742	0.825	0.918	0.992
15/16	0.078	0.161	0.244	0.328	0.411	0.494	0.578	0.661	0.744	0.828	0.911	0.994
31/32	0.080	0.164	0.247	0.330	0.414	0.497	0.580	0.664	0.747	0.830	0.914	0.997

Decimals of an Inch to Millimetres

Fractions of an Inch	Decimal Equivalent	Millimetres
9/32	0.28	7.14
5/16	0.31	7.94
11/32	0.34	8.73
3/8	0.375	9.53
13/32	0.41	10.32
7/16	0.44	11.11
15/32	0.47	11.91
1/2	0.5	12.7
17/32	0.53	13.49
9/16	0.5625	14.29
19/32	0.59	15.08
5/8	0.625	15.88
21/32	0.66	16.67
11/16	0.69	17.46
23/32	0.72	18.26
3/4	0.75	19.05
25/32	0.78	19.8
13/16	0.81	20.6
27/32	0.84	21.4
7/8	0.875	22.2
29/32	0.91	23.0
15/16	0.94	23.8
31/32	0.97	24.6
1	1	25.4

Imperial Conversions

To Convert:	to:	Multiply by:
inches	feet	0.083
inches	millimetres	25.4
feet	inches	12
feet	yards	0.33
yards	feet	3
square inches	square feet	0.00694
square feet	square inches	0.111
square yards	square feet	9
cubic inches	cubic feet	0.00058
cubic feet	cubic inches	1728
cubic feet	cubic yards	0.03703
cubic yards	cubic feet	27
cubic inches	gallons	0.00433
cubic feet	gallons	7.48
gallons	cubic inches	231
gallons	cubic feet	0.1337
gallons	pounds of water	8.33
pounds of water	gallons	0.12004
ounces	pounds	0.0625
pounds	ounces	16

INDEX